MOTIVE POWER CHIEF
Introduction

The period during which I worked on the railway - 1932 to 1976 - must have been one of the most interesting since the turn of the century. The pre-war phase including as it did the era of the Streamliners reached what was virtually the zenith of steam operation. Then came the war years when the load on the railways was tremendous and services had to be operated under the difficult conditions of blackout and enemy action.

Finally came the period of post-war recovery when we had to recover peace-time standards of operation with war-like volumes of traffic as well as plan for the phasing out of steam in favour of alternatives which in many cases were untried and of suspect reliability.

Almost from its inception the steam locomotive engendered immense interest in its design and performance and was more than fondly regarded both by the public generally and by those who worked with them. I was one of the latter and enjoyed more than my share of the dirt of hard work which is associated with their maintenance and operation.

I remember standing on the footbridge which led to New England depot, Peterborough, watching a filthy J6 0-6-0 arriving on the shed and wondering to myself why it was that I was so fond of these rather dirty and thermally inefficient machines?"

I came to the conclusion, so far as there was one, that the very fact that steam locomotives are so comparatively mechanically primitive and thermally inefficient meant that we who operated them could, by minor alteration to details or methods of maintenance, effect a marked improvement in the performance and reliability of the locomotives under our care: a very satisfying thing to be able to do and the very basis of complete job satisfaction.

Electric and diesel locomotives offer very little scope in this direction and if a locomotive design does not function well there is very little a depot can do to improve matters, something that leads to a sense of frustration rather than the challenge presented by steam.

Sir Nigel Gresley once said that the steam engine was the most human machine ever designed by man; I agree with him and that is why the following history is devoted in the main to the steam locomotive.

ACKNOWLEDGEMENTS

The author and Publisher would like to express their thanks and appreciation to the following for their contributions to the book.

P.N. Townend,
Mr and Mrs H. Creamer,
P. Hay, T. Greaves,
G. Tee, P. Abt,
A Lambert,
Mrs G. Hatherill,
BR Derby, W. S. Becket,
Society of Model & Experimental Engineers.

The Great Western more than any other part of BR went to great lengths to ensure that their engines were clean and smart and it was uncommon to see a begrimed locomotive at Paddington. For all that, in 1959 King 4-6-0 6000 was booked for an important special from Paddington and to give the finish required, the Kings Cross cleaning gang was sent over to Old Oak to do the job. Quite a compliment from a system not known for the dirtiest of engines and one that prompted me to make a visit and see how things were progressing.

At the peak of my career I was closely involved with the fitting of Kylchap blastpipes to the Gresley Pacifics. A number of A4, A3 and V2 locomotives were dealt with but the greatest return was given by the A3 Pacifics which in their final years more than gave the 2000hp diesel-electrics a run for their money. Equipped with its double-chimney but awaiting the German smoke deflectors with which these engines finished their careers, A3 Pacific 60108 'Gay Crusader' slows to 20mph at Peterborough North with a Leeds (Central) - Kings Cross express on 19th April 1960.

There was very little information on locomotive performance passed from bottom to top, running sheds were given locomotives with which to run the service and they had to be made to work irrespective of any design faults. Acting collectively footplatemen could sometimes make representations about classes of locomotives which were deficient but the instances of remedial attention were rare. Senior staff had no such voice and it was demanded of them that they produce first class work from engines that were sometimes of doubtful ability. To add to the woes of the running shed there was very little in the way of standardisation and local managers were required to exhibit a high degree of expertise with the widest range of locomotives imaginable. The list to the right illustrates the classes of engine with which the author had not only to be familiar but had to keep running whatever the circumstances. Excuses were not accepted.

TYPE	CLASS
4-6-2	A1.A2.A3 Britannia
4-6-0	B1,B7,B9,B12
4-4-2	C1
4-4-0	D6,D9,D10,D16
2-4-0	E4
2-4-2T	F4,F5,F6.F7
0-4-4t	G5
0-6-0	J3,J6,J10,J11,J15,J17,J19,J20,J39. LMS 2F,3F,4F
0-6-0T	J50,J52,J65,J66,J67,J68,J69,J70
2-6-0	K2,K3, LMS 4MT
2-6-2	V2,V4
2-6-2T	V1. LMS 3MT
2-6-4T	L1,L3. BR 4MT
0-6-2T	N2,N5,N7
2-8-0	O2,03,04
4-6-4	W1
0-4-0	Y4
2-10-0	9F

PUBLISHER'S NOTE

The world is sometimes a small place but never so much as in the case of this book. Years ago I was a very junior railwayman at Kings Cross with the enviable task of allocating engines to trains and being paid for it. My Chief - who I only saw between nine o'clock and half past each morning - was a man who had not only rubbed shoulders with God-like names such as Gresley, Thompson and Peppercorn but who had been brought up in the L.P. Parker tradition of managing things and who, consciously or otherwise, passed on the rather austere but essential disciplines of that school to such miserable creatures as myself so that when the time came for us to go off and run our piece of railway we not only had a fair idea of the goals we should set ourselves but an idea of fair play, so essential when dealing with subordinates.

My chief of course was Jack Somers (or, as I called him then, sir) and it has been an extraordinary piece of luck that many miles and years later our paths should cross, he as a retired railwayman and me as his publisher after a lifetime with the railway.

The kindest - and most accurate - tribute paid to the LNER was that it bequeathed to BR a wealth of intellectual talent that was lacking elsewhere. How very true this was and it was the great unwritten rule of the company - there is no such word as can't - that Jack Somers instilled in me and those of my generation and made us better railwaymen than we might otherwise have been. Like most LNER men he seemed to have little interest in matters outside the railway and the thought of this rather unassuming and slightly amiable figure indignantly picking up incendiary bombs and extinguishing them as they fell on Stratford MPD as an alternative to their exploding and delaying the departure of engines from the shed was something that inspired me throughout my career. Neither did - does - his intellect take second place to physical courage: witness the episode when ingenuity got a bad engine to steam when all traditional methods had failed.

'AJ' retired from mainline work some years ago - he is amongst the last people to have done three figures on a Gresley Pacific - but that is not to say he is inactive and one suspects that for some years to come the disciplines of L.P. Parker et al will reverberate around at least one narrow gauge railway in Wales.

EARLY BEGINNINGS

The seeds of a career are sown. A youthful Jack Somers peers over the boiler of a model LNER Pacific whilst H.N. (Late Sir Nigel) Gresley 'winds 'er back a bit...'.

My interest in steam locomotives started at an early age, my parents often relating how, at a few months old, the only time I could be kept quiet was when I was on a train. At four and a half I was invited onto the footplate of a North Eastern 0-4-4 tank at Alnwick station and eighteen months later was presented with a Bassett-Lowke George V 4-4-0 in 0 gauge. Costing the princely sum of 2 guineas - a small fortune in those days - it gave value for money in that it exists - rather battered through many years of use - to this day.

Our family holidays usually involved long journeys by the LNER or its constituent companies - the grouping was going through parliament during my earlier years - to a variety of haunts in the North East and, as a result I acquired an early predilection for the Great Northern in spite of being brought up in GE territory in East London. Little did I think as I sped by places such as New England and Retford that one day this youthful enthusiast would be the man in charge.....

Perhaps my opinion of the Great Eastern was soured a little by journeys to Enfield Town in gas-lit four wheeled stock with barred windows.

Occasional trips to Kew Gardens from Dalston Junction in the original LNWR Oerlikon electric stock enabled me to see the North London 4-4-0 tanks on trains to Poplar and to and from the GNR, as well as a wonderful high level view of Kings Cross top shed crowded with Atlantics, 4-4-0s, 2-6-0s, 0-6-2 tanks and the occasional Pacific. The last, then only starting to appear, made a curious contrast with the Stirling saddle tanks with their half cabs which acted as shed shunters. Further west there were fleeting glimpses of the Midland, LNWR and GWR; a great delight to

a small boy with a developing interest in locomotives.

My father was a civil servant with no more than a passing interest in railways but he used to tell of trips to Bristol on the broad gauge where his maternal grandfather had been a boiler inspector with the Great Western. In spite of two generations being skipped, it appeared that I had railways in the blood.

During the early twenties holiday journeys took me to the Yorkshire coast over the precipitous branch line from Scarborough to

Whitby. Delays on this line were appalling, trains being frequently more than an hour late. The departure from Scarborough was usually from one of the short platforms on the up side of the station, whence the train was hauled to Londesboro' Road blocking all roads in and out of Scarborough in the process. The locomotive would then run round and eventually we would depart for Whitby. Motive power was provided by either an A6 4-6-2T and a G5 0-4-4T. Hauled by one of the Pacific tanks we were reasonably certain to reach Ravenscar in

Running into Stratford from the east, F4 2-4-2 'Gobbler' 7215 arrives with an Ilford - Fenchurch Street local. Although this particular engine was withdrawn in May 1935 after 28 years service, many of the class survived until the 1950's. The F4's were also well travelled engines, a number of the class being moved from East London to the far north of Scotland where the last survivor - an Aberdeen (Kittybrewster) engine - was withdrawn in June 1956. The sidings behind the engine were known as the Colchester yard and it was said that it took wagons three days to get there from Stratford Market, a ten minute walk away.

The antiquity of some Great Eastern stock can be judged from this photograph of Bury St Edmunds, taken at about the time of the grouping.

During my very early days - before joining the railway - a 'big' engine was something like a GN mogul which, whilst it may have lacked the grace of a Single or an Atlantic, had the attraction of outside motion which enabled one to see more of what made a locomotive tick and sowed the seeds of an interest in mechanics. K2 1703 approaches Wood Green with an outer suburban service shortly after being built in June 1925. By the time the engine was withdrawn in 1959 I was in charge of half the locomotives allocated to the Kings Cross district.

The kindness of driver Sparshatt in allowing me to mount the footplate of 4476 'Royal Lancer' during a trip from Edinburgh did nothing to dim my enthusiasm for a career in the locomotive world. The engine was still hard at work on the east coast when the one-time schoolboy enthusiast progressed to introducing diesels at Kings Cross and was not withdrawn until 1963.

one go but with an overloaded 0-4-4T it was a terrible struggle and stops to blow up because of steam shortage were frequent and added to the delay.

The late 1920s and early 30s saw me a frequent observer at the end of No.10 platform at Kings Cross - known for years as 'Cranks Corner' - where I made the acquaintance of many well known top-link drivers of the day such as Bill Sparshatt, Tommy Topliss, 'Slasher' Payne and others.

Probably the highlight of my schoolboy days was to be allowed through the corridor tender and onto the footplate of 4476 Royal Lancer when returning from a holiday in Scotland on the 'Non-Stop' - it was never the Flying Scotsman to those in the service - thanks to Driver Sparshatt recognising me as I was boarding the train at the Waverley.

A useful and popular observation point on the GN in those early days was the footpath which then existed alongside the line just south of Harringay station on the down side close to where the Tottenham and Hampstead line was to make a connection with the Great Northern. I also made occasional sorties onto the station footbridge to observe the shunting in Ferme Park marshalling sidings and it was from this vantage point that I saw one of the two surviving domeless saddle tanks in the London area, 3149A. Its mate, 3144A, I never managed to see.

In those days it was possible to get home from School, have tea and cycle from my home in Clapton to Harringay in time to watch the evening peak which reached its height shortly after 6pm. It was always a thrill to observe two trains depart northwards simultaneously, racing as far as Hornsey, especially if one of the workings was hauled by an N1 0-6-2T instead of the usual N2. The North London trains were still worked from Broad Street to Potters Bar and Gordon Hill with four-wheeled stock although the NLR 4-4-0 tanks had given way to the LMS 3F 0-6-0Ts. Not only did these foreign shunting engines seem strange working down the GN mainline but they always seemed to lose two beats when trying to run fast. Another peculiarity about the North London trains was that the wheels of the stock appeared to be uniformly spaced, producing a perfectly even 'dum-dum-dum-dum' over the rail-joints.

Hornsey locomotive depot, in addition to supplying power for local shunting and a proportion of local passenger trains, had some workings to the London docks via Victoria Park for which Ivatt saddle tanks with clerestory roofs were provided. One of these was 4251 which was allocated to regular crews and was kept in spotless condition. The cab fittings looked like a jeweller's shop and the interior was kept smart with paint bought by the footplatemen. 4251 earned a special place in my affections as it became the first engine I ever drove. During one of my infrequent shed visits I was permitted to take the engine off the ash pit and into one of the shed roads.

The only other memorable shed visit was one to Stratford where a colleague and I stared wide-eyed at the Graf Zeppelin airship through the cab windows of the shed shunting engine. Little did I guess how intimately I was to get to know this huge depot in the years to come.

APPRENTICESHIP

The staff of the Millwrights shop, Stratford, pose for a group photograph in August 1937. The man holding his pipe, centre left, took part in the erection of J15 0-6-0 930 when it was built and steamed in 9 hours 47 minutes during a successful attempt at the record in 1891.

In 1932 I left school and because of lack of opportunity elsewhere - in spite of my obvious interest in the subject, my father was not entirely in favour of my having a railway career - I became a premium apprentice at the Stratford works of the LNER at the rate of twelve shillings and eightpence (63np) per week - slightly less than the cash equivalent of a cheap return from London to Peterborough. My weekends were spared, however, since the depression had resulted in short time for the works with no work being done on a Saturday and after five years of Saturday work at School this effect of the depression was something I greeted with relief.

With the benefit of hindsight I might have taken the trouble to remember the interview I attended before Starting at Stratford. The Officer into whose presence I was ushered was none other than Edward Thompson but all that I can recall of the interview was the impression of a few questions of a general nature being fired at me by an austere but not unfriendly man. Although a *force majeur* at Stratford, Thompson had yet to become a household name and to me at the time he was simply a senior and very remote manager.

I started work on a Monday morning in October 1932 to be greeted by a shop chargeman - " 'ang yer coat up, Matey" - who promptly set me to work centring forgings by hand ready for the lathes, a bruising time for the hands until you got used to it. I then progressed to my first machine, an ancient shaper, where I squared the heads of slide bar bolts for what I fondly imagined where the rebuilt

Claud Hamilton 4-4-0s, which were just starting to go through the shops as I arrived. Alas for dreams of being involved at such an early stage in top-link management. The bolts I so proudly turned out were of the ordinary Great Eastern pattern and not for the glamorous Clauds at all - which had J39 type four bar crossheads - but for rather more humble locomotives of Great Eastern origin.

The next step was to the 'bolt' lathes installed during the Great War for armament work. Young apprentices like myself turned out thousands of brake and spring pins on these lathes which by 1932 were quite worn out and required no little ingenuity on the part of the operator to get them to turn parallel. Since these pins were all made on piecework - so much for each pin - much depended on ones skill at setting the lathe at the commencement of work if one's basic rate of pay was to be improved upon.

Like all workshops in those days, the machine shop at Stratford had its share of characters. One I remember in particular because of his disregard for the foreman; his name was 'Teddy' Woodhouse and he worked a vertical slotting machine which cut the slots for the lubrication pads in coupling rod bushes. Should a bowler hat - as the foremen were known - appear to urge him to greater effort, Teddy would promptly leave his machine going up and down cutting air and depart to the toilet.

Fred Wills, the machine shop chargehand, stands out in my mind for quite a different reason. He rolled his own cigarettes but to such a

small diameter that they burst into flames as soon as he drew on them. All in the name of tobacco economy.

There was a turner who worked a terrifying lathe which turned the bearings on weighbar shafts and whose face seemed to depict the danger of being struck down by the flailing weighbar shaft arms.

There was, in those days, no such thing as a works canteen and those who did not walk, cycle or catch the Pudding train - 12.34 ex Stratford - home ate their sandwiches beside their machines.

The pudding train consisted of 5 six-wheelers and ran to and from Snaresbrook and suffered a low priority under the operators who frequently cancelled it during foggy weather. Late running of this train was the one valid reason for being late back from lunch and not having a quarter-hour knocked off your pay.

Discipline was strict but not as brutal as it had been in earlier days. Dismissal for trivial matters such as eating a sandwich whilst at work had not been uncommon prior to 1918 and it was probably the broadened horizons and changed attitudes of men returning to work from the front that ameliorated matters. (Some of the earlier strictures had their amusing side - one man was assigned a temporary post in the works at about the turn of the century and retired, doing the same job, several decades later).

Several of the premium apprentices, myself included, found a very congenial way of spending the lunch break by passing the time on the footplate of the works shunting engine,

The condition of B12 4-6-0 8569 shows the class as it appeared when I started my career at Stratford in 1932. I never established whether their nickname - Hikers - arose from the ACFI equipment behind the chimney or whether it was because firemen had to 'walk' the length of the long cab when firing.

a Y4 class 0-4-0, 7210. In contrast to its contemporaries (i.e. Industrial locomotives) it had a powerful chunky appearance due to its large side tanks, Belpaire firebox and short chimney. An friend of mine described the Y4 as being a proper locomotive on four wheels. (They had the same tractive effort as a GN Atlantic and one only realised how small they actually were when seen standing alongside main-line engines).

On other occasions I would walk across to Stratford station with my sandwiches and now and again I would find myself in the company of a very senior officer who would chat away almost as though I was an equal. Later on I discovered my companion was none other than Arthur Peppercorn, destined for the highest motive power office on the LNER.

Had I known then what I now know, naturally I would have done my best to influence his design policies - he was enough of a gentleman to have listened - which might have resulted in a post-war batch of A4's instead of the engines we actually got. An opportunity missed for want of a bit of clairvoyance although I was rather too junior for such outspokenness and in any event the A4's had yet to be built!

Each working day there was what must have been one of the most extraordinary trains to run on the LNER if not on British railways. This was a return transfer trip from the stripping shop on the west side of the main line to Cambridge to the old works on the east. The whole cavalcade made a most incongruous sight as it trundled along the main line from the

Polygon signalbox to Hall Farm Junction. In the formation were engine frames stripped for general repair, boiler trolleys, inwards ones with boilers on them and ancient open wagons, some of which had dumb buffers. The whole ensemble was hauled by one of the local 0-6-0 crane engines.

The boiler trolleys were interesting as they were the frames of locomotives long defunct and amongst them I recognised the remains of what had been Worsdell 2-4-0s and Massey Bromley 0-6-0s together with the remnants of some slightly more modern classes.

Another unusual sight was that of tender engines, usually Claud 4-4-0s, running across from the old works to the paint shop under their own steam but without a tender. These movements seemed to pass without incident but there was nothing to prevent either the fireman or driver from falling from the back of the cab if they misjudged their step or lost their balance.

It should not be imagined that the life of an apprentice consisted wholly of bashing rusty bolts and nipping out of the works, when the opportunity arose, to watch trains. They were the interesting aspects and the other side of the coin concerned the endless nights of study, at college and at home, in order to acquire the required degree of proficiency in theoretic engineering matters. An ounce of theory may be worth a ton of practice but the LNER considered, probably rightly, that we needed more than a wagon load of each.

Nowadays we would have spent three years at a university with a smattering of practical work after receiving a degree but the philosophy was quite different before the war and - since it gave me an instinct for sniffing out the problems that steam engines were prone to - it was probably a very good way of doing things.

Progress through my training took me from the machine shop on to the fitting shop and finally to the erecting shop, during the course

Most Great Eastern main line passenger work was performed by 4-4-0 locomotives such as D13 8036 which is seen near Kings Lynn with a train of clerestory stock.

F4 2-4-2T 7233 showing the results of my handiwork at Stratford at the outbreak of war. In addition to the glare-sheets, the engine along with 36 others of the type had its chimney cut down to conform to the London Transport Underground loading gauge in order to work trains over the electrified system in the event of enemy action effecting the electric supply. As it happened the eventuality did not arise and the engines drifted back to their normal duties. 7233 survived until April 1951.

of which progression was arranged so that the quality of work expected from an apprentice gradually increased. For instance, in the fitting shop one started on items such as sanding gear but finished on the more skilled area of motion details and regulator valves.

One of the tasks I found to be particularly unpleasant was having to chip clearance grooves at the extremities of expansion links prior to regrinding the slot for the die block. The links had previously been case hardened but although having been put through an annealing process they were still extremely tough and difficult to chip with a cross-cut chisel. Unless you got the depth of cut exactly right, the chisel would either dig in or fly off, in the case of the latter causing your hand to come into painful contact with the link and become uncomfortably bruised.

The fitting shop also had its characters. The chargehand of the motion bench, for instance, used to be immaculately attired in the fashion of a City broker when coming to work or heading for home. He was complemented by a fitter, named Notman, who spoke in precise Oxford tones. Notman's father was a driver who had spent many years in charge of the Liverpool Street main line pilot which at that time was one of the two Johnson 4-4-0s.

Henry Greenly, of model railway fame, was very friendly with Driver Notman in his younger days and gave him some of his early freehand drawings. These came into his son's possession and, to my great delight, were passed on to me. The wheel turned full circle some years later when attending the pre-war Model Engineer Exhibition I returned them - to his obvious joy - to Greenly at his stand. The best of the drawings was one of Johnson 4-4-0 No. 306.

From the general fitting shop I progressed to the Westinghouse shop where all the brake fittings, both Westinghouse and vacuum, were overhauled. The great attraction of this shop was the task of accompanying a fitter to conduct brake tests on locomotives having their first steaming after overhaul.

Normally the apprentice did the menial tasks such as carrying the tools and packing various glands but I was fortunate in that, having learnt the job pretty thoroughly, my fitter was changed for one who had never done the job before. This meant that I had to do the testing whilst the fitter packed glands, etc. I still had to carry the tools.

Westinghouse pumps were repaired on a piecework basis, so much being paid for each pump overhauled, tested and found to be satisfactory and if you selected, from the heap of pumps in for repair, one that was in fair condition, you stood a good chance of earning a worthwhile bonus, whereas a pump requiring a new cylinder meant a great deal of extra work and less money.

One day I was sent to select a pump for overhaul and, bearing the bonus in mind, spotted one which had obviously come off an F7 2-4-2T. These engines had two pumps because of their push and pull apparatus although normally the enginemen used the same pump all the time. Thus one of the pumps received very little wear although it would still come into the works when the other was due.

The pump I selected was one of these, virtually unused and in mint condition. Having stripped it down, my fitter decided a bush required renewing; a decision that was our undoing since when it came to being tested the reversing piston stuck in the new bush and we had to half-strip the pump again to put matters right. Goodbye bonus and leave well alone in future!

Some of the F7 tanks were fitted with a primitive form of ATC (Automatic Train Control) which was activated by a shoe, not unlike

A B12 4-6-0 comes off the Channelsea curve at Stratford with a train of stock. More examples of antique Great Eastern rolling stock are visible behind the engine.

Two of the Running Foremen at Stratford in 1939 beside their 'office'. There were two grades of Foreman, the senior of the two dealing with traincrews whilst his assistant had charge of the locomotives. Both jobs required an encyclopaedic knowledge of engine diagrams and mens workings since it was an everyday matter to rearrange engines and crews at a moments notice to suit traffic conditions. The carriage body behind the two men served as their office and doubled as their air-raid shelter during the war.

the gear used by the Great Western Railway although a much heavier piece of apparatus. Alas, I took little interest at the time and cannot remember how the gear worked or what the fittings were in the cab.

By this time our friend on the works engine, 7210, had retired so we were forced to go further afield during the lunch breaks, over to the west side shops and the running shed where, against all regulations, we used to help the enginemen who moved engines from the

coal stage into the shed. These engines were often low in steam and if the leading engine in the rake was unable to haul the rest, we gave a helping hand from one of the others. One misty day I was moving a J39 0-6-0 from the coal road, the foggy ambience and steam from other engines reducing visibility to a few yards. The driver in charge of the move, who was hanging out of the cab to see where we were going, suddenly shouted "Whoa....mind the bump" but there was no bump. I had slammed on the

brake but being low in steam - the vacuum only registering about 15 inches - the engine came to a smooth halt instead of the usual sudden stop. When I walked to the front I found that we had stopped about 18 inches from the shed shunting engine which had been coming towards us until its driver saw us approaching. My friend and I however quickly returned to our places in the works.

Engines varied considerably with regard to the minimum steam pressure with which they could be moved and I once saw a J20 0-6-0 being moved with the pressure almost on the zero mark.

From the comfortable distance of the machine and fitting shops, the erecting shops looked glamorous but to me, when I got there, it was a disappointment. Apprentices were given much of the heavy and relatively uninteresting jobs such as grinding horn cheeks or hanging up brake gear whilst specialists erected the motion and set valves. There were, however, two jobs that I enjoyed, one being the insertion of cold rivets in a frame patch and peening them over, the other dealing with an axlebox during wheeling operations when two of us climbed onto the edge of the pit, leaning back until we supported each other, leaving our hands free to guide the axlebox into position between the horn cheeks.

The best of times.....A4 4492 'Commonwealth of Australia' heads through Harringay with a down streamliner at the time I had been 'denied' access to such workings - the utility of apprentices did not extend to assisting with High Speed trains . It is clear from the exhaust that the fireman is 'putting a bit round the edges' in preparation for the climb from Wood Green to Potters Bar.

During this operation men with pinch bars were on hand to make any necessary adjustments to the positioning of the wheels if they did not at first align with the horn cheeks. Even a slight incorrect positioning of the wheelset as the frame was lowered would cause the

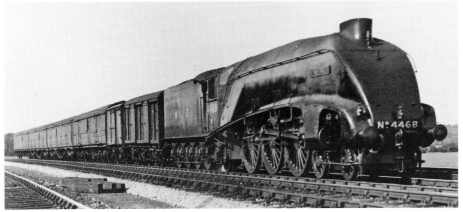

...and the worst. The record breaking Mallard approaches Greenwood, relegated to a down wartime parcels train.

TRAIN WORKING : THAMES WHARF (1923)				
TRAIN	ARR	Co.	DEP	DESTINATION
23.05 Temple Mills	00.10	LNER		
		LNER	00.20	Whitemoor
		LNER	00.35	Stratford Market
00.10 Goodmayes	01.00	LNER		
		LNER	02.00	Temple Mills
02.30 Woolwich	02.45	LNER		
02.45 Victoria Park	03.05	LMS		
22.15 Temple Mills	03.20	LNER		
		LNER	04.00	Temple Mills
		LMS	04.15	Cricklewood
03.20 Cricklewood	04.26	LMS		
04.55 Silvertown	05.05	LNER		
04.30 Cricklewood	05.35	LMS		
		LNER	06.05	Woolwich
		LMS	06.30	EBV Cricklewood
		LNER	06.58	London Docks
06.30 Cricklewood	08.00	LMS		
07.55 Beckton	08.12	LNER		
07.50 Temple Mills	08.20	LNER		
08.12 Woolwich	08.25	LNER		
		LMS	08.45	LE Cricklewood
06.55 Goodmayes	08.53	LNER		
		LNER	08.55	Beckton
		LNER	09.00	Temple Mills
		LNER	09.00	Silvertown
07.30 Cricklewood	09.03	LMS		
03.30 Cricklewood	09.18	LMS		
		LMS	09.20	Upper Holloway
		LNER	09.35	Whitemoor
09.15 Temple Mills	09.38	LNER		
09.30 Silvertown	09.40	LNER		
		LMS	10.10	Cricklewood
		LNER	10.15	Temple Mills
		LMS	10.15	Silvertown
10.00 Temple Mills	10.25	LNER		
09.45 London Docks	10.25	LMS		
07.00 Cricklewood	10.38	LMS		
09.30 Cricklewood	10.58	LMS		
		LNER	11.00	London Docks
10.45 Plaistow	11.00	LMS		
		LMS	11.15	Canning Town
10.00 Cricklewood	11.25	LMS		
11.23 Silvertown	11.35	LNER		
10.20 Cricklewood	11.38	LMS		
11.25 Beckton	11.40	LNER		
		LNER	11.55	Temple Mills

The meat and drink of the railway was in goods rather than passenger traffic, something that is demonstrated by the number of trains arriving and departing from Thames Wharf (London Docks) in LNER days. The volume of traffic remained high until the late 1950's when road transport made serious inroads.

axlebox to tip and jam bringing an immediate cry of alarm (Whoa…a!) from the person guiding the axlebox. When this happened the crane driver would have to raise the engine for another attempt.

Having wheeled the engine, the motion was then set up and valve setting started, the unfortunate apprentice having to turn the wheels with a ratchet device known as a jigger whilst not being able to see what was going on at the valve spindle although sometimes we saw the results scribed on the valve setting plate. Stratford set valves to equal port openings rather than equal leads.

I often wondered why a mechanical means of turning the wheels during valve setting could not have been adopted since jigging round a 7-foot wheel was an unnecessarily laborious and time-consuming task which had to be done four times or more if adjustments had to be made to the rods. The time saved alone would have paid for a compressed air machine.

Occasionally one of the Great Eastern Tram engines would come in for repair. These machines, because they were used alongside the public highway, were covered over with a structure which made them resemble some sort of brake van and when this was removed the impression was given of a very early type of locomotive without a cab.

They were fitted with a very primitive type of speedometer reading up to 12 mph at which point steam was supposed to have been automatically cut off. This form of governor was worked by a belt which I never once saw connected up.

Rebuilding of the Claud Hamilton 4-4-0s was in progress during my time in the erecting shop although the first rebuilds, which had been fitted with 8" piston valves, had shown such little advantage over the balanced slide valve engines that the provision of piston valves was suspended with rebuilding being confined to fitting the Gresley type round topped boiler and smokebox. However an extremely capable draughtsman, A.E.English, designed a new valve gear which incorporated 9" diameter long-travel piston valves.

The engines to which this modification was fitted gave quite remarkable results and, in my opinion, were fully the equal of the rebuilt SECR 4-4-0s. Claud 8791 which was rebuilt in the English style was the only one of the class in my experience to take a Cambridge Buffet - normally seven coaches - on the 1/200 from Wood Green to Potters Bar at over 50 mph. It has to be said that the increased power resulted in undue strain to the frames and axleboxes and it is a fact that these quite re-markable engines were amongst the first of the rebuilt Clauds to be withdrawn.

There were no especially memorable characters amongst the fitting staff I worked with in the erecting shop except, perhaps, for the Assistant Foreman who was the one called for in the event of difficulties. His no-nonsense approach to trouble shooting is something that sticks in the mind.

From the erecting shop I moved to the axlebox shop where wheel sets were prepared to be put under engines in the erecting shop. Here I did meet a character - a remarkable fitter by the name of Russell who was related to the celebrated F.W.Russell, the chief draughtsman at the time the B12 4-6-0s were being designed. He was a small dark man who could work like lightning when he wasn't gossiping. He knew his job thoroughly and taught me how to fit axlebox bearings and GE pattern eccentric sheave cotters, a skill which stood me in good stead when, later, I was in the running shed at Stratford.

An amusing incident involving eccentric sheaves occurred at this time, just after Stratford had taken over the repairs of the GN N1 0-6-2Ts based in the Kings Cross district. One of these engines was being steamed outside the Polygon - the original Stratford running

Shortly before being superseded by the new A4 Pacifics, A3 4-6-2 2596 'Manna' leaves Grantham with the 10.0 Edinburgh - Kings Cross on 17th May 1937. This run took place during the winter schedules and the engine worked only between Newcastle and London as opposed to the summer diagrams when the locomotive worked the train throughout. The high standards of discipline required by the LNER can be gauged from the fact that the train is climbing at 1/200 yet there is very little exhaust smoke coming from the engine.

J65 0-6-0T 8214 of the type used at Stratford for shunting the wagons into which stacked coal had been loaded. It is seen here in wartime guise during 1940.

shed - yet when the regulator was opened it would only move for half a turn of the wheels in the wrong direction. I forget how I happened to be there but I dropped into the pit and saw immediately, thanks to my period in the axlebox shop, what was wrong. The right hand eccentrics had been mounted on the axle so that the sheaves followed the crank instead of leading it. The left hand side had been mounted correctly so that the two sides of the engine opposed one another.

Great Eastern engines had both sheaves in one casting and therefore could not be keyed on the axle incorrectly. GN engines - or at least the N1 0-6-2s - had independent sheaves and someone, not spotting the difference, had fallen into the trap.

Before leaving the works for the running shed where I was to spend the last few months of my apprenticeship, I worked in the wheel shop proper - as opposed to the axlebox fitting shop - where tyres were turned up and wheels forced onto or off their axles. Wheels which were very tight on their axles came away with an almighty bang when the load reached about 300 tons. Tungsten carbide tipped tools had recently been introduced for tyre turning which allowed a much higher cutting speed although as a result the swarf, instead of coming off in small chips which would fall into a conveniently placed tray, came off in continuous coils blue with heat which promptly wrapped themselves around the machine and tool holders. If this wasn't problem enough the coil was both very hard and rough at the edges which caused great difficulties in clearing it away for scrap.

At last I was transferred to the running shed and again suffered a disappointment. I was put into the machine shop amongst the most decrepit machinery imaginable, heated by coke stoves which filled the place with such dense fumes that it is surprising the inmates didn't perish from carbon monoxide poisoning. For-

tunately for both my respiration and career prospects I was not detained long in the machine shop and once outside matters brightened up somewhat.

In the main works, premium apprentices were not trained on boiler work and it was with some pleasure, in spite of rather uncongenial surroundings, that I found I could work with boilersmiths and tubers. The variety of jobs seemed to be endless with firebox seams to caulk (where one had to learn to work left-handed), tubes to expand and bead over, and stays to re-rivet. Occasionally boilermakers or tubers had to undertake firebox work when an engine was still in steam, the blower being used to create a cool draught whilst the men were inside the firebox. The water softeners at Stratford and elsewhere had not been put into use and this resulted in a considerable amount of tube work to be done. They had to be withdrawn from the boiler and the barrel cleared of scale - a process known as sifting - at fairly frequent intervals.

In comparison with what was done in the works, repairs in the running shed were largely carried out as a matter of expediency in order to keep locomotives at work rather than to effect a thorough long-lasting job. For instance leaking regulator valves were only touched up sufficiently to remove cuts in the faces, whereas in the works they were meticulously scraped from surface to surface.

Great Eastern locomotives were not regarded as being particularly free steamers, although it has to be said that steam production was adequate for normal requirements, thus it was important to ensure that steam leaks - especially those in the smokebox - which could impede steaming were discovered and dealt with. To do this the boiler was connected up to the water washout plant which delivered hot water under pressure. When the boiler was full with the pressure registering on the gauge,

the regulator was opened to fill the main steam pipes with water under pressure, the idea being that any leaks would be instantly revealed. The effectiveness of this process was rather doubtful since trying to discover a defective joint amongst a puree of wet soot and smokebox char was difficult to say the least.

There were a few GN N2 0-6-2 tanks at Stratford in those days which incurred an inordinate amount of smokebox work because of the Gresley pattern superheaters. These had top and bottom headers into which the elements were bolted, steam tightness depending on copper jointing washers which were continually being disturbed by the slight movements of the boiler during expansion and contraction. This trouble persisted for many years and was only eradicated by the substitution of Robinson type superheaters.

In common with all locomotive depots, Stratford had to deal with numbers of overheated axleboxes, a trouble which exists amongst preserved engines to this day even though they receive far more attention than we were able to give our charges. To deal with this particular defect there was a tall corrugated iron structure known as the Ark which housed a wheel drop and a heavy pair of sheer legs, the latter only being used at times when an excessive number of hot boxes needed attention. During my time in the Ark I remember a Claud under the sheer legs which had its driving wheels removed for journal turning and was propped up on two baulks of timber, one under each buffer. Apart from the safety aspect it occurred to me that such visits to the Ark must have imposed severe strains on the frame and indeed may have contributed to the frame fractures to which this class was prone during its declining years. In general the reconditioning of axleboxes in the running shed was a very rough and ready operation compared with the careful filing, scraping and bedding I

A4 4-6-2 4490 'Empire of India' takes water before leaving Kings Cross top shed. This engine held the record for haulage of the London - Edinburgh Coronation streamliner, working 12% of the workings between 1937 and 1939.

had seen in the works. The very minimum of finishing work was done to obtain a reasonable fit, after which the bearing was allowed to season itself by running the locomotive on slow speed work for a few days. Failures, however, were comparatively rare.

As mentioned earlier my contacts with the axlebox shop came in very useful during my period in the running shed as was demonstrated one day when I found myself working with a running shed fitter who had taken down all the motion on the left hand side of a B12 4-6-0 to deal with some loose eccentrics. This was not a common trouble on Great Eastern engines and when the sheaves were dismantled on this particular locomotive it became obvious that new cotters were required. The new cotters were obtained from the running shed store but were rough forgings requiring so much fettling up and fitting that it was obvious that the engine could not be dealt with in the time allowed.

I therefore slipped across to my friends in the works axlebox shop and obtained (scrounged) a pair of part-machined cotters which needed far less work to make them fit. In spite of this assistance we only just managed to complete the job as the footplate crew arrived to oil up and take the engine out for its booked working.

The climax of my period in the running shed was, of course, my six weeks on the footplate, which started with local shunting and ended with a week on the GN main line.

The shunting turns took me to all sorts of peculiar places such as Thames Wharf, Silvertown, Stratford Market and Temple Mills hump marshalling yard.

Thames Wharf was interesting, partly because it was situated close to the old Thames Ironworks where Brunel's giant ship the Great Eastern had been built and partly because our J67 and J69 shunters shared the yard with LMS 3F 0-6-0s - on our railway the LMS was always referred to as the 'Derby'. Visits beyond Thames Wharf to Silvertown were made worth while, quite apart from the interest, because shunting Keillers sweet factory sidings gave the opportunity to buy quantities of sugared almonds at a very reduced rate.

The local goods turns took me a little further afield, sometimes to places I had scarcely heard of such as Tufnell Park which was a GE goods depot situated just East of Kentish Town

on the Tottenham & Hampstead Joint (GE & MR).

It was the practice to use such local turns to run in the larger freight engines - J17, J19 and J20s - after general repairs in the works and allowed me to get some experience in main line firing without having to break my back.

The most interesting local trip I made was from Spitalfields low level yard to Hither Green on the Southern. These trains were worked by trip-gear fitted J69 0-6-0 tanks, the wagons having been lowered down from the top yard at Spitalfields by means of the hydraulic wagon hoist which was later destroyed during the war.

The descent into the tunnel from Wapping was very steep and after lurching round the curve at the end of Wapping station platform, away you went hell for leather until the pace was slowed by the rising gradient on the south side of the Thames. After picking up the slack in the couplings you gave the engine all the steam it would stand in order to struggle out into the fresh air at Rotherhithe.

Colour light signals were few and far between on the LNER but had been installed in many locations on the Southern, one of these being between St Johns and Hither Green on the South Eastern main line. It was at a particular signal on this stretch of line where I first had my attention drawn to the difficulty in observing colour-light signals from a reasonable distance against bright sunlight, particularly when the sun was low on the horizon.

Gravitating towards the mainline, I was introduced to the delights of night runs on goods trains and lodging turns where train crews slept away from home. This was a familiar aspect of train working in those days and our lodging turns were to Lowestoft, Kings Lynn, Norwich and Bury St Edmunds. Most of the lodges were spotless although the one at Bury did not quite come up to scratch.

My long distance firing trip was on the express freight which left Spitalfields at 21.03 for March with traffic for Doncaster and the north. The load taken was 50 vans, all fitted with the vacuum brake which - given that the Great Eastern was a Westinghouse railway - conferred on the train the nickname the 'Vacuum'. Hauled by a Great Northern K2 2-6-0, it was hard graft for the fireman but I was pleased to have succeeded in firing for the entire round trip which was one of the longest on the system.

The driving trip was altogether more comfortable; the train being one of the stream of empty wagon services which ran from Temple Mills to Whitemoor hauled by a March 02 2-8-0, steam brake fitted. I only needed to open the second valve of the regulator for the ascent to Elsenham - the steepest climb on the run - and managed not to wrap the guard around the stove pipe either in starting or stopping. It is however possible that my timekeeping would have been suspect under close inspection but I survived.

After a run round on the Great Eastern suburban services I took the opportunity of observing Mr L.P. Parkers' insistence on full regulator working, even on saturated slide valve engines where the results were less than satisfactory. L.P. was the Locomotive Superintendent for the Stratford area and something of a legend in his time. Highly autocratic but widely respected for his intellect and the results he obtained. In any event I had the temerity to tell him that I thought the small amount of superheat produced by wiredrawing through the first port of the regulator on saturated engines was of more value than the extra pressure available with the regulator wide open. With superheated engines the position was, of course, quite different and a fully opened regulator gave good results. L.P. at any rate seemed to accept my suggestion.

My footplating on the Great Eastern was completed with some express runs although, curiously, I remember very little about them other than an instance with a rebuilt B12 4-6-0 where a late start from Colchester provided the incentive to make a dash for Shenfield, producing 75 mph at Witham - rather a good effort for those days - and a trip on a B17 4-6-0 on an up express from Cambridge when I attempted to do a share of the firing but was jumped off my feet as the engine tore down the Stort valley towards Broxbourne.

The very last week of my apprenticeship provided the climax of my footplate training and was spent on Great Northern main line

TRAIN WORKING : THAMES WHARF (1923)				
TRAIN	ARR	Co.	DEP	DESTINATION
11.50 Temple Mills	12.12	LNER		
		LNER	12.15	Silvertown
11.45 London Docks	12.32	LMS		
11.30 Cricklewood	12.50	LMS		
		LMS	13.00	Cricklewood
		LNER	13.10	London Docks
13.23 Silvertown	13.35	LNER		
		LMS	13.35	Victoria Park
12.15 EBV Cricklewood	13.35	LMS		
		LNER	13.42	Beckton
		LMS	13.50	Cricklewood
13.55 Canning Town	14.00	LMS		
		LNER	14.06	Temple Mills
13.48 Temple Mills	14.10	LNER		
13.15 Cricklewood	14.38	LMS		
13.25 Cricklewood	14.57	LMS		
		LNER	15.10	Silbvertown
14.30 Cricklewood	15.30	LMS		
15.20 Temple Mills	15.45	LNER		
13.45 Brent	15.52	LMS		
15.15 London Docks	16.00	LNER		
		LNER	16.30	Beckton
16.47 Canning Town	16.52	LMS		
15.45 Cricklewood	17.10	LMS		
16.00 EBV Cricklewood	17.28	LMS		
17.25 Stratford Market	17.32	LNER		
18.00 EBV Cricklewood	19.20	LMS		
19.10 Temple Mills	19.30	LNER		
18.15 Cricklewood	19.35	LMS		
18.30 LE Cricklewood	20.00	LMS		
18.30 Brent	20.08	LMS		
		LNER	20.20	Silverton
20.10 Temple Mills	20.50	LNER		
19.30 Cricklewood	21.08	LMS		
21.05 Temple Mills	21.30	LNER		

Y4 0-4-0 7210 was the works shunter at Stratford from January 1921 until December 1963 and provided apprentices with a diversion during lunch breaks. Acting driver A.J.Somers strikes a pose on the footplate in 1934.

expresses between Kings Cross and Grantham or Leeds. Unfortunately I was restricted to ordinary trains, my pass being specifically endorsed 'Not available on Streamlined Trains', although this was not too much of a drawback since the performance on conventional trains was, at that time, of a very high standard which demanded high power outputs from the locomotives and hard work by the footplatemen.

A typical trip was that of the 10.00 Flying Scotsman in which I had one of the older A1 Pacifics pressed to 180lbs but with left hand drive. Weighing about 600 tons - the tare weight was 537 - the seventeen bogies meant really opening the engine out on the climb from Kings Cross and I was all but asphyxiated by the smoke in Gasworks tunnel. At the north end of Copenhagen tunnel the engine began to prime on the recently introduced softened water and it took until Finsbury Park before the engine settled down, by which time we had lost five minutes running time. At this point, to my horror, I was handed the shovel and commenced firing. I shovelled absolutely non-stop until we had passed Hitchin and were well on the falling gradient to the Ouse Valley at which point the regular fireman took over.

Regardless of my efforts I could not get the boiler pressure to exceed 165 lbs and whilst peeved at the time thought afterwards that perhaps it wasn't such a bad effort and in any event no doubt the driver enjoyed see me work hard.

A run to Leeds Central on the Queen of Scots Pullman was a real whirlwind effort, touching 94 mph at Arlesey and passing Peterborough in sixty-seven and a half minutes - 68 mph average. Alas, our hurricane progress ceased halfway up Stoke bank when we came to a stand at Little Bytham with the signals hard on. The fireman walked across to the box to carry out rule 55 only to be told that the train hadn't been expected so soon. Small

wonder since by that time we were about ten minutes ahead of time. After restarting we still had so much time in hand that things were taken easily to Stoke whilst the fireman took the opportunity to have something to eat.

The up run from Leeds was something of an anticlimax in that time was kept so far as I can remember with a maximum speed of only 74 mph down Stoke bank. I rather fancied that the driver underestimated the effect of the very strong south-west wind and therefore drove the engine rather too easily from Stoke downhill. Both trips, incidentally, were made on Pacific engines which had recently taken over from Ivatt Atlantics on the Pullman trains.

The A4s were at that time still something of a novelty but I did manage one trip on an example although to my shame I cannot recall

with accuracy which engine it was. I thought for many years that it had been 4487 Sea Eagle but discovered later that it could not have been since 4487 was not delivered until after my run. It is possible that I may have confused it with 4482 Golden Eagle which, like my engine, was in green livery at the time and had been in traffic for a couple of months at the time. The trip must have been uneventful since nothing about it sticks in my mind except that I recollect how superbly the engine rode at 90 mph on the descent of Stoke. A glass of water placed on the fireman's seat would not have spilt a drop.

In spite of the glamour surrounding the Gresley Pacifics, I still think that the most thrilling of my footplate trips was on a GN Atlantic whilst working the 12.10 from Cromer

Following the grouping the LNER decided that engines would be cleaned at fixed intervals - once per day for express locomotives - and whilst the policy saved expenditure it was reflected in standards which generally fell below those of Edwardian days. Stratford could however turn the clock back when the occasion demanded, an instance being the condition of B12 4-6-0 8507 for the visit of King George V.

Although carriage repairs were a familiar feature of life at Stratford, I was surprised to discover that coaches were maintained and repaired at Top Shed, Kings Cross. The facilities were transferred to Bounds Green in 1931.

(Beach) between Peterborough North (15.04) and Kings Cross. The train consisted of a moderate load, seven coaches and a fish van, but had a fast timing of 76 minutes for as many miles. On the instance of my trip neither the regular engine, 4406, or its New England driver were available and we had to take 4460 instead with a driver who normally worked goods trains.

The fireman, however, was an old hand and when we reached the bottom of Abbots Ripton bank he must have thought we were not running hard enough, so he crossed the footplate and pushed the regulator wide open, leaving the cut-off unchanged at about 35 or 40%. As far as I remember the controls remained unchanged until we were brought to a stand at Cambridge Junction, Hitchin, for signals. Getting away on 50% and full regulator - the driver opened it wide this time - produced 70 over Langley troughs, after which we sighted adverse signals at Knebworth, thereby spoiling what promised to be a lively run into London.

The engine, 4460, performed magnificently. The boiler pressure gauge seemed glued on the 170lb mark and, in spite of the late cut-off, the steam chest pressure gauge (Yes, the Atlantics had such things in those days) showed a drop of only about 10lb/square inch. The firing, although continuous, was quite easy; each shovelful being flicked into the back corners with a quick twist of the wrist which would produce a puff of light grey smoke at the chimney top, otherwise combustion was smokeless.

GN Atlantics running fast were always a thrill to work on or watch and when working hard at high speed the exhaust was almost as sharp as that of a motorcycle. Gresley was, of course, very fond of them and when the success of the high superheat on the French compounds was being discussed at the Institute of Locomotive Engineers, he drew attention to the fact that the temperatures quoted had been closely approached by pyrometer readings taken from Atlantics many years before.

My apprenticeship and footplate exploits came to an end with a trip on a Cambridge Buffet Express - with another Atlantic - when the seven coach train was worked over the 11.6 miles from Welwyn Garden City to Hitchin in 12 minutes 28 seconds with a top speed of 86 mph at Wymondley. Happy days!

I was not the only railwayman to take an outside interest in his industry but one of a small army of professional enthusiasts whose number included LNER Driver Bill Irvine who, when not driving the full-scale article, could be found at the regulator of his three and a half inch model of Atlantic No.1459. When working hard at exhibitions in the Horticultural Hall the exhaust of this rather remarkable model was audible in the street outside.

IN CHARGE.....AT TIMES

The J39 0-6-0 of 1926 handled a great deal of the goods and mineral traffic on the Great Eastern except for a handful of fitted express goods for which K3 2-6-0's were provided. At Stratford the J39's were referred to as 'Standards'.

By 1937 the country was beginning to recover from the severe trade recession of the early 1930s and instead of being dismissed at the end of my apprenticeship, as had been the lot of many who preceded me during those unfortunate times, I was offered a job as a fitter in the main works at Stratford, a post I was only too pleased to accept.

However instead of returning to locomotive work, the post I was offered was in the millwrights shop which involved the disadvantage of having to work on Saturday mornings. The extra few shillings increase in pay was hardly adequate compensation but I was, at least, still working on the railway.

Much of the work involved climbing ladders and working high above floor level for which I gained a head for heights. On one occasion we had to give attention to one of the electric motors in the blacksmiths shop which was right up near the roof amongst all the heat, smoke and dust. My colleagues had some other job to do with the ladder and took it away, leaving me perched aloft on the motor bracket where, to say the least, I felt distinctly uncomfortable.

Some of our activities in those days would make a modern factory managers hair turn grey and In think particularly of having to drill 1200 holes in lengths of angle iron with a fixed spindle drill and no jig of any kind.

Day to day maintenance of the stationary boilers supplying steam to the works was the responsibility of the millwrights and because if this I became involved in a project to install mechanical stokers on some of these boilers to effect a saving in manpower. However, as has happened many times in the past, the steam output of a hand-fired locomotive boiler was hopelessly underestimated and the mechanical stokers completely failed to achieve the steam output required.

There was an interesting sideline to this experiment; A representative of the firm who supplied the stokers said that he was surprised that there had been no question raised about 'slush' money and that it was the first contract

he had had for some time in which no-one requested a back-hander. I felt rather proud of the LNER over that.

Occasionally we were required to work during the lunch hour which allowed us to go home an hour earlier than usual. By this time I had moved from Clapton to Knebworth and the early finishes use to enable me to catch the 17.10 semi-fast from Kings Cross; the train used by Sir Nigel Gresley en route to his home at Watton-at-Stone. Several times I followed the great man down the steps to the station entrance feeling somewhat overawed.

After I had spent about eighteen months in the millwrights, the LNER launched a scheme involving special training for your men in order to groom them for supervisory positions in the running department. I was not selected but instead was given six months special training locally at Stratford depot under that most remarkable of District Superintendents, Mr L.P. Parker which, in the event, was probably of greater benefit, certainly in terms of both intellectual growth and practical experience, than having gone on the other scheme.

Mr Parker's ideas on how your men should be trained were exemplary and such was his confidence in his powers of administration that he sent us - I was not the only young man in his care - on all sorts of missions which, had we not been up to the mark, could have rebounded on him and caused considerable embarrassment.

An example of this concerned the stream of complaints that L.P.P. received from the operating people blaming delays on the shortcomings of the motive power organisation. (If an engine was late arriving at its starting point, the tendency was to shout 'engine late off shed' rather than to enquire if it had been delayed en route by traffic congestion. There was an equal tendency for such snap judgements to be taken without question which was a source of some annoyance to L.P.P.).

He therefore decided to see if the operating department were in fact covering up some of their own sins and sent his trainees to points

all over the London suburban area to watch for an report on operating errors which caused delays. Great was the surprise of the Operating Superintendent when he received the results of our survey and for a time the letter-writing roles were reversed.

One ought to add that whatever obstacles were placed in our way, the timetable not only had to operate but trains - goods and passenger - had to be run punctually. There was simply no question of compromise on this point and an individual who caused a service to be delayed had very good reason to worry. The

ENGINE DIAGRAMS (SX) : BRENTWOOD DEPOT				
PLAT	ARR	STATION	DEP	PLAT
		BRENTWOOD MPD	04.00 LE	
		BRENTWOOD	04.19	
8	05.15	LIVERPOOL ST	06.58	12
	07.45	ROMFORD	08.03	
17	08.55	LIVERPOOL ST	09.21 ECS	18
	09.33	STRATFORD	18.06 ECS	
6	18.21	LIVERPOOL ST	18.55	6
	19.22	WOODFORD	19.23	
	19.50	ILFORD	19.52	
14	20.17	LIVERPOOL ST	21.54	13
	22.50	BRENTWOOD		
		BRENTWOOD MPD		
		BRENTWOOD MPD	04.30 LE	
		BRENTWOOD	05.36	
12	06.31	LIVERPOOL ST	07.57	15
	08.36	ROMFORD	08.57	
15	09.43	LIVERPOOL ST	10.50	15
	11.47	BRENTWOOD	13.12	
18	14.08	LIVERPOOL ST	16.02	14
	17.20	CHELMSFORD	18.15	
18	19.39	LIVERPOOL ST	20.06	15
	20.47	ROMFORD	21.27	
16	22.23	LIVERPOOL ST	00.12	17
	01.05	BRENTWOOD		
		BRENTWOOD MPD		
		BRENTWOOD MPD	06.20 LE	
		BRENTWOOD	06.36	
15	07.30	LIVERPOOL ST	08.35	13
	09.22	ROMFORD	10.32	
15	11.38	LIVERPOOL ST	12.42	17
	13.55	INGATESTONE	14.40	
17	15.50	LIVERPOOL ST	16.51	17
	17.35	ROMFORD	18.30	
8	19.18	LIVERPOOL ST	19.48	17
	20.43	BRENTWOOD		
		BRENTWOOD MPD		

LE : LIGHT ENGINE. ECS : EMPTY CARRIAGE STOCK

Neither the war or the blitz prevented men such as Driver Kinsey of Wood Street from keeping his engine in a presentable condition and even in the gloom of 1940 he polished his N7 0-6-2T until the brasswork shone.

Whilst the Great Eastern boasted the largest motive power depot in the country it also possessed a large number of very small sheds where aspiring running managers could cut their teeth before being promoted to more prominent locations. One such was Yarmouth (Vauxhall), a two-road shed with an allocation of about ten engines for services between the coast and Norwich. The shed is seen on 29th April 1934 with a D13 4-4-0 (7766) and a J15 0-6-0 (7566) being prepared for their next turn of duty.

In spite of attempts at modernisation during the 1950's, the substance of Stratford station has not changed a great deal and the view above, familiar to me in the 1930's, exists to this day. Gone, of course, is the B17 4-6-0 and the Great Eastern signalling whilst London Transport services share part of the station with BR workings. I often walked to the station during lunch-breaks in the company of A.H. Peppercorn.

current trend of cancelling trains for shortage of resources was beyond contemplation. We were paid to run a railway and not to make excuses.

At about this time the first of the V1 2-6-2 tanks began to arrive and replaced the highly unpopular N2 0-6-2s on workings from Brentwood depot. These engines are often associated with Scotland and the North East and it seems to have been forgotten that there were 15 of the class at work on the Great Eastern between 1938 and 1948 when they were displaced by the rather inferior L1 2-6-4Ts. The 2-6-2's were the first tank engines which were the masters of the Great Eastern outer-suburban services and it was a great shame that we lost them.

Nominally these engines carried 2000 gallons of water but L.P.P. - as Mr Parker was forever known - had doubts about the accuracy of this and arranged for one of his trainees to check the amount actually available to the injectors. It was found that in actual fact only about 1880 gallons could be fed to the boiler which was particularly unfortunate as there was an urgent need for a tank engine which could

D49 4-4-0 297 'The Cottesmore'. 6:290/195 tons. June 1937						
m.ch	point	Grade	WTT	Actual	mph	dbhp
0.00	SELBY	0.00	0.00		-	-
2.64	Hemingborough	-3820		5.40	50.0	459
8.52	North Howden	-7354		11.32	60.0	393
11.56	Eastrington	level		14.30	63.5	379
14.03	Staddlethorpe	15823		17.02	35.0	pwc
16.46	Broomfleet	-3059		19.57	65.5	1004
20.41	BROUGH	2765	24.00	24.20	-	-

An interest in performance and locomotive efficiency on the road was an integral part of the authors professional activities which occasionally strayed beyond the boundaries of his district as in the case of the above run made by a rotary geared D49 4-4-0 on the NER.

work to Southend without taking water en route. The V1s were perfectly capable of timing these expresses and could achieve 80 mph with ease but unfortunately their water capacity was insufficient. It has always mystified me as to why some were not modified to 2-6-4s in order to provide the extra reserve of water.

Fog was the bane of the Great Eastern suburban working during pre-war winters although L.P.P. ensured that the best possible was done in those difficult circumstances. By sending his inspectors and people like myself to strategic points all over the suburban area, he ensured that engines and enginemen were restored to their correct workings as soon as possible after the disruption caused by the fog. Other districts in which I later worked did not adopt this practice and as a result fog disruption lasted much longer than it need have done.

Just before my period of special training ended, I assisted with some brake trials for freight trains on the Epping branch as a prelude to resignalling for Underground electric trains; the new signals having to be spaced to suit the loose coupled goods trains that were to continue on the line, interspersed with LTE electrics. The trial was also to test the effect of the operation of the trip gear which had to be fitted to all steam engines working over London Transport electrified lines. The operation of the trip arm produced a full application of the automatic brake on the locomotive (a Westinghouse-fitted J15 0-6-0 in the case of the trial) and there was some concern that it might be so sudden as to cause injury to the guard. With a full load - 18 wagons of coal - the operation of the trip gear was simulated by making a sudden full application of the brake but no untoward buffering-up occurred and the 0-6-0 brought its train to a stand on a steep falling gradient in a reasonable distance. In the light of subsequent experience I wonder what results we would have had with a longer

but lighter train and with the engine still pulling as the brake was applied.

Sometimes the most irritating difficulties could have ridiculously simple solutions as I discovered in a curious incident at Stratford station one day. A train ran in from the Shenfield direction, came to a stand and, so far as I recall, there was a change of enginemen. The right-away was given but for some reason the engine refused to move. Bad as the situation was, it was made worse by the fact that L.P.P. used the train to travel to Liverpool Street for his lunch.

I mounted the footplate, looked at the brake pressure gauges and everything seemed to be in order. The brake could be applied and released correctly on the coaches, so what could be the matter? Suddenly it occurred to me that I had eliminated everything but one possibility - the handbrake must be on. Sure enough the incoming fireman had applied the handbrake and, until it dawned on me, no-one had thought of releasing it. (It was the normal practise for firemen to apply the hand brake when coming to a station stop, especially at Liverpool Street).

After conducting the brake trials my special training came to an end and I had to return to the millwrights shop although not for very long, as it happened, as I was very soon sent for by L.P.P. who wanted me to return to the running shed, nominally as a fitter but in fact to assist in the preparations for the war that appeared to be looming.

The immediate task was to fit all the district's locomotives with hooks and rails to enable anti-glare sheets to be hung in order to prevent light from the firebox door being seen from the air. It will be appreciated that as Stratford was the largest on the LNER - and probably in the country - this was a considerable task involving so far as my memory serves 568 locomotives. To accelerate matters, L.P.P. decreed that oxy-acetylene burning be used in

On all railway systems one class of engine is always held in higher esteem than the rest and on the Great Eastern it was the Claud Hamilton D16 4-4-0 that was usually the motive power favourite. My respect - and affectionate memories - of the class is such that my house continues to exhibit a mural-sized picture of an example in the hall. The D16's had a long reign on passenger work and even as late as 1957 could be found in large numbers north of Cambridge.

preference to the more conventional drilling for the rods and eyes upon which the sheets were to be hung. It was not such a neat job but it allowed the job to be completed in much less time.

V2 2-6-2 4771 'Green Arrow'. 14:425/450 tons. September 1937						
m.ch	point	1/in	WTT	Actual	mph	dbhp
0.00	KINGS CROSS	-	0.00	0.00	-	-
2.41	Finsbury Park	195		8.08	36.0	656
4.78	Wood Green	2261		11.50	47.5	684
				pwc		
12.57	Potters Bar	258		28.31	27.2	-
17.54	HATFIELD	-335	27.00	34.38	60.0	625
23.44	Woolmer Green	377		41.02	45.0	607
25.03	Knebworth	-755		43.05	53.0	597
28.46	Stevenage	-2346		47.00	55.5	476
31.74	HITCHIN	-209	44.00	50.15	66.2	154
35.56	Three Counties	-231		53.22	75.0	336
37.03	Arlesey	-501		54.28	75.0	338
41.12	Biggleswade	-750		57.56	68.5	-
44.10	Sandy	-834		60.26	70.5	660
47.41	Tempsford	-627		63.23	69.5	295
51.58	St Neots	901		67.12	63.2	716
55.76	Offord	-480		70.52	72.5	766
58.70	HUNTINGDON	1129	68.00	73.24	68.7	678
63.42	Abbots Ripton	448		78.09	63.5	811
67.32	Connington	-203		81.26	72.5	137
69.23	Holme	level		83.04	73.0	828
72.48	Yaxley	606		86.03	58.5	132
74.78	Fletton Jcn	-1807		88.41	53.5	-
76.29	PETERBOROUGH	1385	87.00	90.45	20.0	-
79.40	Werrington Jcn	-8201		96.10	53.0	811
84.67	Tallington	1471		101.44	60.0	1273
88.51	Essendine	422		105.33	60.0	1060
92.18	Little Bytham	360		109.21	53.5	770
97.07	Corby Glen	276		115.22	46.7	828
100.08	Stoke	187		119.18	43.2	1099
105.36	GRANTHAM	-214	121.00	124.42	67.2	-

The ability of the V2 2-6-2's to work heavy express passenger trains came as something of a surprise given that the class had been intended to replace the K3 2-6-0's on fast goods services and the eponymous 4771 was recorded on a 14 coach east coast train in September 1937. It was not the most spirited of runs but the time lost at Greenwood had been recovered by Retford with Doncaster being reached two minutes ahead of time.

Although most of the engines were based at Stratford or other depots where mechanical staff were available, there were quite a number of out-stations which only had a driver in (nominal) charge who had to be shown how to fit the anti-glare sheets in the event of war being declared. So, with the help of a fitter's assistant, I had to visit such places as Kelvedon, Buntingford, etc, which presented quite a contrast to the parent depot Stratford. Not only was 1939 an exceptionally good summer but the Strawberry season was in full swing which, in the case of Kelvedon, made the task a very pleasant one.

After all our engines had been fitted with rails for anti-glare screens I was sent round the district to locate all the open braziers for frost fires which had to be replaced by the close stove type because they were not vsible from the air. This exercise took me to all sorts of out of the way places such as Millwall and Blackwall; locations at which I had had no idea there were any water columns.

On my way back I met L.P.P. in front of the new shed at Stratford and he asked me what I had been doing. I gave him a full description to which his response was "I suppose they will be paying you something like 2d a day expenses."

"Oh no, sir." I responded, "I was living in hopes of a shilling…." And we went off laughing. L.P.P. was not often given to laughter!

Soon after the exercise was complete, the war clouds grew darker and - after a temporary period in charge at Wood Street - I was summoned to fit the anti-glare sheets on the engines I had prepared. Such

was the urgency of the job that two of us had to work non-stop twelve hour shifts for about a fortnight - myself on nights and my opposite number on days.

Then the war began.

The first big event which heralded the coming storm was the evacuation of school children from London and, whilst I had little to do with it myself, it was a gigantic exercise which worked extremely well. The suburban service was severely pruned and its locomotives pressed into evacuation service together with the rolling stock. The N7 0-6-2Ts worked trains to places all over East Anglia, for longer distances than they had ever worked before, yet I understand only one example failed and that was when it had all but reached its destination.

Almost immediately after war had been declared, the peace time summer service was replaced by a special wartime emergency timetable which resulted in a drastic reduction in the number of passenger trains and the speeds at which they operated. This in turn reduced the number of enginemen required and produced considerable consternation amongst the staff representatives. However L.P.P. , with his usual foresight, reassured them by telling them that it would not be long before they were busier than ever and, of course, subsequent events proved him right.

Whilst passenger services had been severely pruned, the freight traffic remained at its normal level. As a result it tended to be the passenger classes which became surplus to requirements and some were placed in store. A number of these, mainly Claud 4-4-0s which served little use in a goods environment, were despatched to outstations to be placed over pits and sand-bagged up to provide some sort of rudimentary bomb shelter. One of these D16s served thus at Wood Street.

At about the same time a number of F4 2-4-2 tanks were taken into the works to be overhauled and have their chimneys cut down in

In the years between the grouping and the war the fifty F3 2-4-2 tanks played a major part in the working of rural passenger services, the class - known at Stratford as the 'ten hundred tanks' - being widely distributed over the system. 8066 waits at Thorpe-le-Soken with a branch train on 26 July 1938

order to provide power for the London Underground lines in the event of enemy action causing the electricity supply to fail. These engines were stored on a road at the side of the running shed known as 'The Bank' and an instruction issued that in no circumstances were they to be used for normal suburban work.

After some months, during which there had been practically no enemy action, it was realised that the war curtailment of passenger services was unnecessarily severe and increases were therefore authorised which introduced the general pattern of services which were to last for most of the war. Consequently the stored engines were gradually returned to traffic, except for the F4s.

Until the end of 1939 I was employed as outstation relief chargeman covering Palace Gates, Epping and Wood Street, the latter de-

pot still retaining a curious overlapping shift pattern of 11.00 - 19.00 and 06.00 - 14.00, alternating each week between myself and the sub shed chargeman whose surname I have forgotten, probably due to the fact that as an ex-Royal Navy man he was known to all as sundry by the nickname 'Sailor'.

1940 was ushered in with some exceptionally severe winter weather which kept me busy trying to thaw out frozen injector feed pipes; an exercise which saw the blackout regulations well and truly flouted by my torches of flaming rags on the end of a shunting pole.

Although Stratford did not suffer too badly from the snow, the cold was so intense that at least one Claud 4-4-0 was put out of action through having the boiler feed delivery pipe on the driver's side frozen up. It has to be said that these engines in their original condition had a long unlagged copper delivery pipe which was exposed to the icy wind and I suspect this one suffered because of infrequent use of the driver's side injector. Even so for something to freeze solid only inches away from a boiler full of boiling water suggests an abnormally cold winter.

The worst of the weather hit the north of England and hurt us indirectly through the interruption of our loco coal supplies. Our response was to lift coal from the stacks where it had been husbanded over the years for some eventuality or other; the stuff in 1940 having been stacked in 1926 as a precaution against the coal strike of that year. Curiously the quality of the coal had not deteriorated significantly.

At first the coal was lifted by hand from the stack but it soon proved to be too slow and expensive a method and so a

Ruston mechanical digger was hired, the digger having a diesel engine which was started from a compressed air bottle. Of course the inevitable happened - the air bottle not having sufficient air in it to start the diesel - and our powers of improvisation resolved the difficulty by harnessing a Westinghouse-fitted J65 0-6-0T - used to shunt the wagons for the coal - and rigging up an air line between it and the digger. The 0-6-0, pumping like mad, just managed to supply enough air to start the diesel.

Both the weather and my career prospects started to improve in the Spring when I received my first management appointment, being given (temporary) charge of Hertford (GE) shed in 1940. Not only did I have a depot of my own but I also had the sub-shed of Buntingford which sported two F6 2-4-2 tanks, one of which worked the St Margarets service whilst the other stood spare. Two engines under such circumstances may seem a luxury but in fact any repairs that were needed by the engine in work had to be completed within the forty minute turn-round at Buntingford otherwise you found yourself marooned with the option of performing unpaid overtime when you even-

C1 4-4-2 4402. 10:291/305 tons. October 1936						
m.ch	point	1/in	WTT	Actual	mph	dbhp	pc
0.00	KINGS CROSS	-	0.00	0.00	-	-	
2.41	Finsbury Park	195		6.17	41.5	710	2
4.04	Hornsey	5271		8.25	50.0	580	2
6.34	New Southgate	200		11.00	54.0	1188	6
8.29	Oakleigh Park	200		13.17	52.0	817	4
9.12	New Barnet	200		14.10	50.0	718	4
10.46	Hadley Wood	200		15.55	50.0	862	4
12.57	Potters Bar	208		18.55	45.5	653	3
14.37	Brookmans Park	-304		20.35	60.0	654	3
17.54	Hatfield	-354		23.30	71.0	525	3
20.25	WELWYN G.C.	421	25.00	26.15	-	-	-
0.00	WELWYN G.C.	-	0.00	0.00	-	-	-
3.19	Woolmer Green	309		6.00	48.0	920	3
4.58	Knebworth	-755		7.50	58.0	644	3
					Signals		
11.49	HITCHIN	-382	14.00	17.15	-	-	-

By the mid-thirties the Atlantics had lost their hold in the express links and had been relegated to secondary duties by the large number of Pacifics that the LNER was producing. They retained a niche in the Cambridge Buffet workings until ousted by the B1 4-6-0's during the late 1940's where they continued to produce work of an outstanding nature as the author's observations confirm.

A3 4-6-2 2744 'Grand Parade'. 16:530/565 tons. August 1936						
m.ch	point	1/in	WTT	Actual	mph	dbhp	pc
0.00	PETERBOROUGH	-	0.00	0.00	20.0	-	-
3.11	Werrington Jcn	-8201		5.14	54.0	1571	6
8.38	Tallington	1471		10.29	64.0	1318	8
12.22	Essendine	422		14.11	60.0	1128	7
15.69	Little Bytham	360		17.49	58.5	1300	8
20.58	Corby Glen	276		23.34	50.0	1017	5
23.59	Stoke	187		27.24	44.0	1248	6
					Signals		
29.07	GRANTHAM	-214	34.00	33.49	57.7	-	-

No better illustration can be given of the power latent in the older Gresley Pacifics than the record made in 1937 by Grand Parade as it stormed Stoke bank with no less than 16 vehicles behind the tender. The pc of 8 - quite exceptional for a steam engine - is the equivalent of 1000 dbhp at 80 mph.

Ask any Kings Cross driver to nominate an engine more outstanding than the rest and the odds were that he would opt for a large boilered Atlantic. Driver Hagland, peering at the camera from the cab of 279 whilst being indicated by the CMEE's staff from Doncaster was no exception and whilst he later graduated to Pacific 60061 'Pretty Polly', his affection for the Atlantics remained undimmed - he was almost proud of the way their cab sides would bash the tunnel lining as they rocketed their way at high speed on the descent from Potters Bar into London.

tually got back to Hertford. Consequently the procedure I developed was to make an examination of the repair sheet at the start of each day and delegate what I could to my assistant, leaving me free to attend to more important work at Buntingford when, for forty minutes, the highest rates of piecework were probably exceeded.

During this period, with the threat of invasion looming and the prospect of more evacuation trains, my drivers found themselves ferreting out foreign parts when it was proposed that some of the possible specials would be routed from the GE to the GN via Hertford. I therefore had to see that route learning from Hertford (East) to Hatfield was undertaken as

a matter of urgency. As it happened neither the invasion and the additional trains materialised and my charges remained rooted to their familiar paths.

I soon discovered that the man in charge had to take blame from a wide range of sources although none so unusual as that I suffered during the Dunkirk evacuation when a deputation of angry housewives besieged me, complaining that my engines had covered their washing with smuts. I was somewhat mystified as there had been no trains in either direction for some time but promised to investigate. Eventually it turned out that the offending smuts had travelled all the way from the blazing oil tanks at Dunkirk, floating freely until being caught in the washing. War can be very hard at times but I think that Hitler went just a little too far when he provoked the housewives of Hertford!

Amongst the Hertford drivers was a remarkable character named Bill Brown who was a model engineer and, as a result, was not averse to trying his hand on the full scale object. He often adjusted his own brakes, for instance. One day he and I decided to see how fast we could get an N7 0-6-2T to go and, being safely out of the way, we chose the Buntingford branch for our experiment. With a train of only two coaches Bill opened out 2647 down the 1/50 from Hadham and reached no less than 68 mph before shutting off steam for the stop at Standon. The brake was applied but to no avail since our speed was too great and as a last resort Bill reversed the engine which perversely came to a halt short in the platform. Looking back on things I think we were fortunate that the engine didn't shed its motion - in spite of the speed attained 2647 was very rough and nearly due for shopping.

L.P.P. , who was not generally given credit for his sense of humour, used to visit the outstations periodically and one day came down to see me at Hertford. His attention turned

to the state of the turntable pit and he commenced to give me a right dressing down which rather astonished me as it had an earth bottom and there was nothing much which could be done to tidy it up. He told me that he had a good mind to remove me from Hertford - at which the Somers heart sank to the Somers boots - and to send me to Bishops Stortford instead, a coda which restored the Somers spirits to the skies since I knew that a permanent vacancy for a mechanical chargeman existed there. My career was beginning to move.

Bishops Stortford was a very small depot with six engines; four V1 2-6-2Ts, a J20 0-6-0 and a J15 0-6-0 which was used as the yard pilot. There was no shed building - the engines were parked on a siding to the east of the station - and all repair work had to be carried out in the open. (It was my good fortune that the 1940 summer was as fine as the preceding winter had been bitter).

Apart from the one in for washout, the V1 tanks were out all day and any minor repairs needed had to be done after the engines had returned from their day's work which meant me returning to the shed at about 22.00 and sometimes working into the small hours - without any overtime!

The V1's were excellent engines for the work undertaken from Stortford with good acceleration and the ability to hit high speeds if given a good run. The enginemen liked them and would complain bitterly when one disappeared into Stratford to be replaced by an N7.

One particular driver by the name of Thatcher proved himself a master at handling a V1. He would run into stations at quite a high speed, make one application of the vacuum brake and invariably come to a stand with the cab door just at the top of the platform ramp. His colleagues waited with expectation for him to misjudge matters and overrun but he never did, at least whilst I was in charge of the depot.

He did, however, cause excessive wear on the engine brake blocks which consequently had to be renewed every three weeks and with three engines being effected, that meant one renewal per week. It was one job I detested since being a little short in the leg, it was only by standing on tip-toe on top of the rail that I was able to lift the blocks high enough on my knee to insert the pin through the block and hanger.

Although there was no shed we did wash out boilers, the fitters mate and I doing it between us. Coaling was carried out in two stages. The day shift coalman would empty the loco coal wagons on the coal stage whilst his opposite number on nights would transfer the coal from the stage to the engines as they presented themselves after the days work.

Thanks to the paucity of staff at Bishops Stortford my practical experience was taking a stage further than management and maintenance. There was no engineman rostered for shed duties during the day shift and so it was left to me to man an 0-6-0 to clear the emptied coal wagons from the coal stage and to replace them with loaded ones from a nearby siding. It was whilst performing this shunt that I nearly met with disaster.

I had selected the big J20 on one particular occasion and, whilst preparing to set off, noted rather casually that the gauge glass was completely full. This put me on my guard and upon gently opening the regulator was alarmed by the horrible roaring noise which indicated

C1 4-4-2 4406. 7:222/235 tons. 9 October 1936						
m.ch	point	1/in	WTT	actual	mph	dbhp	pc
0.00	PETERBOROUGH	-	0.00	0.00	-	-	-
3.61	Yaxley	11037		6.26	54	622	2
7.06	Holme	-606		9.33	67	576	4
12.67	Abbots Ripton	301		15.11	56	523	3
17.39	HUNTINGDON	-448	20.00	19.52	72	365	2
20.33	Offord	-1129		22.20	75	442	3
24.51	St Neots	480		26.01	66	228	1
28.68	Tempsford	-901		29.37	75	442	3
32.19	Sandy	627		32.26	72	542	4
35.17	Biggleswade	834		35.00	70	481	3
39.26	Arlesey	750		38.58	34	pwc	-
44.35	HITCHIN	310	44.00	45.26	55	767	4
47.63	Stevenage	209		49.08	55	778	4
51.26	Knebworth	2346		52.39	62	558	3
56.04	Welwyn G.City	-554		56.53	80	612	4
58.55	HATFIELD	-421	58.00	59.00	74	-	-
63.52	Potters Bar	335		63.33	62	-	-
67.17	New Barnet	-202		66.32	73	151	1
69.75	New Southgate	-200		68.40	82	264	2
71.31	Wood Green	-200		69.46	83	-	-
72.25	Hornsey	-1160		70.30	73	-	-
73.68	Finsbury Park	-8700		71.48	72	-	-
76.29	KINGS CROSS	-195	76.00	75.06	-	-	-

It is not difficult to see why the Atlantics were held in such high regard on the Great Northern. The 15.04 from Peterborough was not a heavy train but it conveyed through coaches from the M&GN (Cromer 12.10) and Grimsby (12.45) and was of sufficient importance to be given a mile-a-minute schedule between Peterborough and Kings Cross. 4406 succeeded in achieving even time by Sandy, regaining it at Potters Bar after a pwc at Langford. Sustained speeds in the eighties were still a novelty in the 1930's.

water spewing out of the boiler into every part of the engine normally reserved for steam. I slammed on the steam brake in an instant and closed the regulator realising that water from the overfull boiler had entered the superheater and flashed into steam. The result of course was to give the engine far more steam than was needed and had I not put the steam brake on, there would have been no holding the engine which would have careered to the end of the sidings to crash through the buffers at the end of the line.

I was not the only one to misuse an engine at that time. Holland and Denmark had just been invaded by Germany and this caused a sudden shortage of eggs in London. This shortage communicated itself via the jungle telegraph to Bishops Stortford whose motive power staff - for reasons of either sympathy or profit, who knows - occasionally took off in the J15 for a private trip down the Braintree branch to collect eggs. The practice didn't last long although I am not sure of the reason for its cancellation - either the eggs gave out or someone in higher authority got to hear of it.

My phoney war - and everyone else's - finished in midsummer when a stick of delayed action bombs closed the London - Norwich main line at Brentwood with everything being diverted via Bishops Stortford, Braintree and Witham. This meant that we had to provide crews to conduct the diversions over the branch and, since trains had to reverse at Witham where they came off the branch facing London, additional engines as well. Somehow we managed to keep everything moving but for some reason the service was completely unbalanced due to a dearth of London-bound services which meant that eventually the branch signalmen ran out of single line tokens and had to suspend operations until the imbalance had been corrected. I felt very sorry for the staff at Witham - which had no loco depot - who not only had to bear the brunt of the diversions but had to turn every locomotive which arrived there.

The Brentwood bombing proved to be no more than a prelude and next came the air raid on the docks and East London which paralysed the Cambridge line service and had me on duty for a continuous twenty four hours. One of my V1 2-6-2Ts gained some kudos by being the first engine bigger than an N7 to reach Liverpool Street the next morning. Because of the raids and the disruption they caused there was nothing available for the 08.20 Cambridge express so the Liverpool Street Foreman hurriedly arranged for my V1 to stand in which, perhaps to the surprise of some (but not me), it did with ease.

With the bombs came my next promotion which seemed a mixed blessing since my posting was to Stratford shed as assistant to the night running foreman; being moved from the comparative safety of Hertfordshire to a location where the Luftwaffe arrived on my turn of duty night after night. The risks we took in order to gain experience.

Looking back I do not know how Stratford functioned as well as it did during that time, especially as we took duty each night not knowing whether our homes (or families) would be in one piece when we got back. Perhaps the Nazi intelligence network was not quite up to the mark and some Reichsmarshall in Berlin was under the impression that Stratford's B17's were of the Boeing variety and represented a direct threat to the Fatherland which had to be wiped out at all costs. It certainly seemed like it at times.

Because of the blackout restrictions engines were (somehow) disposed of and prepared under the cover of the shed whilst ad hoc arrangements were made to stable as many of the suburban engines as possible at places such as Woodford, Ilford and Loughton in an attempt to ensure that in the event of Stratford being crippled, there would at least be some locomotives available to run the morning trains.

Lists were drawn up showing the outbased engines -

known as sleeping engines - and these had to be verified each night with exchanges being made to deal with any engines which had developed a defect or were of the wrong type.

Although I never knew what the Germans were going to attack next during the blitz, in fact both Stratford and I were very fortunate since the shed area only received one direct hit. It was a pitch dark night, pouring with rain which makes me doubt whether the raider actually picked his target. It is probable that he let his load go, hoping for the best before turning tail for the Fatherland and better weather. At any rate the bomb was a big one and landed on the extension pits at the back of the shed just beyond the shed roof. It smashed its way through the concrete of the pits and exploded in the ground below, muffling the sound of the explosion. (A recent publication states that the bomb landed on the shed buildings. This was not the case and the damage was caused by the blast rather than the bomb itself).

Hearing the sound of objects flying through the air. I took refuge under the tender of a K2 2-6-0 until things quietened down and then went to the site of the explosion to see what exactly had happened and to see if anyone had been injured. As it turned out the only casualty was a driver who had been superficially cut by flying glass when the cab window of his V1 2-6-2T was blown in. He was extraordinarily fortunate since his engine just missed being hit by a huge lump of concrete which flew over the V1 and scored a hit on the adjacent coal stage.

In the company of the air raid warden I went to survey the scene and stood amazed at the size of the crater. No less that seven roads of metals had been engulfed and it was fortunate that we had had the foresight to have pulled nearly all the engines on the depot into the shed about half an hour before the raid. At first I thought the engines had sustained some damage since there was a roaring of steam from inside the shed but on investigation it turned out that a J17 had received a blow from a piece of displaced rail which had crashed through the wooden cab roof and knocked open the right hand injector steam cock.

Although my engines escaped generally unscathed, part of the shed roof had been brought down together with about sixty years accumulation of soot which spread itself over the surface to a depth of about 4 inches, giving the impression of walking upon a thick pile carpet.

Catching bombs as they fall from an aircraft is a topic imagined to be the province of the comic-book writer but at Stratford we could have given these imaginative scribes considerable food for thought when a stick of incendiaries fell in a row along the brick walkway in front of the shed. Instead of running for cover our reaction was pounce on each one as it fell and to smother them with ashes before they were able to ignite.

After the blitz had died away I found myself promoted twice in succession, going first to Brentwood where I had had the job of introducing the V1s before the war and then after only a few weeks, to the rather larger depot at Wood Street (Walthamstow) where I enjoyed about eighteen months of relative peace whilst Hitler turned his attentions towards Russia.

Wood Street depot had the responsibility for providing power for the Chingford - Liverpool Street services and had all the 7990 se-

A4 4-6-2 4498 'Sir Nigel Gresley'. 12:337/355 tons. May 1940							
m.ch	Point	1/in	WTT	Actual	mph	dbhp	pc
0.00	KINGS CROSS	-	0.00	0.00	-	-	-
2.41	Finsbury Park	195		6.45	39.2	774	2
4.78	Wood Green	2261		10.32	53.0	618	2
9.12	New Barnet	200		15.33	47.2	938	5
12.57	Poters Bar	202		20.32	39.7	725	3
14.37	Brookmans Park	-304		22.47	55.5	642	3
17.54	HATFIELD	-354	28.00	26.19	62.5	167	1
20.25	Welwyn GC	421		28.55	48.5	-	-
23.44	Woolmer Green	223		32.49	45.0	813	4
25.03	Knebworth	-755		34.48	65.2	1263	6
28.46	Stevenage	-2346		38.47	66.2	314	2
31.57	HITCHIN	-209	45.00	42.06	64.2	-	-
35.56	Three Counties	-231		45.45	60.7	-	-
37.03	Arlesey	-501		47.07	53.7	-	-
41.12	Biggleswade	-750		51.08	65.2	665	4
44.10	Sandy	-834		53.54	65.2	278	2
47.47	Tempsford	-627		57.06	65.2	-	-
51.58	St Neots	901		61.25	53.0	194	1
55.76	Offord	-480		65.47	60.0	281	2
58.70	HUNTINGDON	1129	72.00	68.41	59.2	580	3
63.42	Abbots Ripton	448		74.43	47.7	357	2
67.32	Connington	-203		78.35	66.2	273	2
69.23	Holme	level		80.27	57.7	-	-
72.48	Yaxley	606		84.07	46.5	-	-
74.78	Fletton Jcn	-1807		87.09	46.0	-	-
76.29	PETERBOROUGH	1385	93.00	89.41	-	-	-
3.11	Werrington Jcn	-8201		6.45	52.2	662	2
5.42	Helpston	2401		9.22	57.7	740	4
8.38	Tallington	1471		12.24	62.5	783	5
12.22	Essendine	422		16.06	61.7	895	5
15.69	Little Bytham	360		19.38	55.5	708	4
20.58	Corby Glen	276		25.28	49.0	729	4
23.59	Stoke	187		29.24	42.0	816	4
			Signals				
29.07	GRANTHAM	214	40.00	37.35	-	-	-

Surprise has often been expressed at the feats performed by the A4 Pacifics during the war when hauling loads in excess of twenty coaches out of Kings Cross. However moving 25 vehicles over Stoke bank at the speeds in force at the time called for only 1415dbhp which was quite within the limits of engines such as the A4. As the run above demonstrates the capabilities of the A4's were quite wasted on most ordinary wartime services.

One of the delights of the Great Eastern was its changelessness and right up to the arrival of diesels in the late 1950's many parts of the system seemed to make no concessions to the passage of time. The above scene could have been taken at almost any time in the company's history as E4 2-4-0 62785 pulls away from Mildenhall with a Cambridge train on 3 May 1958.

ries of right hand drive N7 0-6-2Ts plus a handful of the short valve travel left hand drive type. The former included a well travelled group of suburban engines which, although built at Stratford, had been sent to the far-off West Riding of Yorkshire where they worked from Bradford and Ardsley for a few months before being returned to the Great Eastern. Altogether I had nineteen engines under my care.

Firing techniques differed at Wood Street from other depots in the area, the latter employing the well known method of little and often. At Wood Street, on the other hand, most crews worked on the 'big fire' principle whereby a large amount of coal was put into the firebox before setting off with a train; a practice which often allowed engines to run the ten and a half miles between Liverpool Street and Chingford without having the fire touched. Interestingly this 'big fire' method rarely produced any cases of shortage of steam whereas the general method was much more uncertain.

Having survived unscathed the wrath of the Luftwaffe over Stratford, it was at Wood Street that I suffered my first blow from the enemy, albeit indirectly. The blackout was still in operation and every night operation had to carried out without any visual assistance whatsoever. Everything that was done was done by feeling ones way about.

In these conditions I needed to move an engine but in the blackness failed to notice the setting of the gear. Opening the regulator and expecting the engine to move off in reverse, it rolled the wrong way for about eighteen inches and clouted the engine ahead with enough force to bowl me over and I landed on the footplate, legs in the air. Fortunately the brakes of the engine in front had been firmly applied and so there was no reaction. Equally fortunately no-one was in the vicinity to pass the word on

about what had happened. I doubt if L.P.P. would have accepted the blackout as an excuse.

The period at Wood Street ended with my recall to Stratford, this time to take my place amongst the Running Foremen on shifts although on an acting basis. The war was at its height and the strain on the railways was terrific. Airfields were being built by the score in East Anglia and train after train of rubble from the London bombings had to be run in addition to a highly inflated freight service. Thus until the British and American 2-8-0s arrived on the scene the shortage of power was acute, engines coming onto the shed after finishing a days diagram being sent straight out to start another. The arrival of the big 2-8-0s was treated with great relief whilst the shortage of suburban power was eased as the F4 2-4-2Ts were released from the LTE contingency store and allowed back into normal service.

Whilst the engine position improved a little with the new arrivals, the manpower situation deteriorated and shed duties such as firelighting and steam raising became very difficult to cover and the Running Foremen frequently had to step in and do the tasks themselves in addition to the arduous job of keeping the shed running. Our own ranks were not unaffected and spells of twelve hour duty were quite frequent. Personally I found the most trying situation to be on the 15.00 - 23.00 shift and then receive a message at midday telling me to report for a twelve hour stint at 19.00. It was impossible to get adequate rest before taking duty and once at the depot there was no let up until 07.00 when one went home absolutely exhausted.

Being a railwayman of unlimited commitment, I never consciously shirked any responsibility and would rather give the company a free hour or two rather than see a job go un-

done but I have to say there came a time when this devotion - for such it was - deserted me for a while. I was leaving the shed one night after a twelve hour stretch when I saw my relief searching the ground with a very dim handlamp looking for all the world like some sort of glow-worm. He said something in great consternation about someone having gone and pulled a water column down but I am afraid I was so passed it I carried straight on for home. At any other time, of course, I would have helped him find the stop cock and shut off the flow of water.

The 'little blitz' we experienced in 1943 was of course nothing to what we had undergone during 1940/1 but I received a terrible fright one night when a bomb went off near Chobham Farm signalbox at Stratford whilst immediately afterwards a train went rattling by bound for Loughton. I had visions of an awful pile up but nothing happened and I presume the bomb must have failed to damage the railway. It showed how one's nerves were being effected though.

The American 2-8-0s whilst providing welcome relief in the power situation caused us problems in another direction. During lighting up after a washout the wire mesh in the self cleaning smokebox tended to become sooted up and the engines simply would not make steam. Arriving on duty one afternoon after a weekend off I noticed one of these engines standing smoking outside the shed and I asked what was being done with it. The foreman I was relieving told me that it would not raise steam and had been standing there for the entire weekend.

The sight of a good, usable engine sitting idle was not something I was prepared to countenance so I decided to try an old dodge to get the blower working in order to liven up the fire. To do this I coupled a yard pilot to the 2-

8-0 and told the driver to shunt it up and down the siding. I put a man on the 2-8-0 and told him to put the gear into the reverse of whichever way the engine was moving. This resulted in air being pumped into the boiler which in turn got the blower working and within half an hour I had the satisfaction of seeing the engine blowing off steam as though there had never been a problem.

This was not the only adventure I had with these engines and I recall an incident in which one of the 2-8-0s came into convergence with the shed shunting engine, a J66 0-6-0T. The shunter and the tender of the 2-8-0 both lifted into the air and remained stuck, leaning at a precarious angle, with their wheels about a foot above the rails. In addition the footplating of the J66 had cut into the tender tank of the American by slitting it from end to end. The great fear was that any attempt to rectify matters would cause the J66 to fall over on its side but I knew that if I pulled both engines away from each other, the likelihood was that they would fall back upright. I took charge and gave the necessary instructions, telling the spectators to stand well out of the way. I mounted the cab of the 2-8-0, put it into forward gear and, holding my breath, gently opened the regulator and had the satisfaction of seeing both tender and 0-6-0T sink back onto the rails without further damage. (A curious feature of the American 2-8-0's was that they had a lever reversing gear, which was unusual for a modern engine).

With the end of the 1940/1 blitz it no longer remained necessary to stable engines at outstations during the night and so, with Ilford sub-shed closed, the level of activity at Stratford grew to such an extent that it was having to despatch daily a greater number of engines that it had ever done in its history.

Monday mornings were especially heavy as the normal traffic engine requirements were swollen by the shunting engines that had to be sent out to the various goods yards in the area - Spitalfields, Canning Town and Temple Mills,

etc - where they remained for about a week at a time. Departures (of all engines) rose to a peak in the hour from 05.10 when no less that 46 locomotives - an average of one every minute and a half - were booked off shed. Had they travelled separately to their destinations the resulting congestion would have overwhelmed - and probably paralysed - the block signalling system on the main lines and therefore engines travelling to common destinations were sent off in convoys of up to five coupled together.

Whilst this eased the situation on the running lines, it caused considerable problems for the running foremen since the engines had to be in a particular order before setting off so that they could be placed on their trains at, for example, Liverpool Street without undue shunting. If they arrived out of order the confusion and movements called for to get them onto the right trains was such that the delay reacted onto the passenger service; a sin that would be visited upon the head of the Running Foreman concerned in no uncertain terms later in the day.

With so many engines using the depot, space was at a premium and eventually we had to resort to the New Shed - normally used for stopped engines - as a means for storing engines on nights until they went out in the morning. Every afternoon therefore we had to shunt the stopped engines out of the New Shed, place them 'down the hole' - the tender shops siding - and fill the shed with engines booked out for jobs the next morning.

Sorting good engines from bad was a full time job on Sundays and a Foreman had to be booked on duty especially for the task, starting at 20.00 and making a list of every engine on the depot. He would then decide which engines were serviceable and which were stopped and arrange the necessary shunting. It estimated that he walked something like four miles in the performance of this task.

This intensive working put a tremendous strain of the Running Foreman who, in spite of having their numbers increased by one man

per shift, must have been the hardest worked men in the grade in the whole of Britain. Tiredness would not be accepted as an excuse and much as I felt the strain, I was a young man whilst many of my colleagues were twice my age or more. Quite apart from being castigated by L.P.P. , mistakes tended to react in such a way as to land you with twice as much work as you would have had in the first place.

A routine example concerned the need to keep separate 'stopped' engines - those requiring repairs - from those being lined up ready to be allocated work. One had to keep a constant watch on this since a stopped engine in the middle of a row of 'running' engines meant having to perform a complex shunting movement which was almost certain to delay engines going off shed to work trains. On top of this any delays which could not be recouped in the ten minutes allowed from the shed front to the outlet - the point at which they entered the world of the operator - had to be reported - war or no war!

Expediency required ingenuity in unorthodox ways and one such was the use made of the diamond crossing which was situated outside the Running Foreman's office (an old carriage body). This made a different noise every time a different class of engine ran over it and before long one was able to tell what sort of engine was coming off the ash-pit simply by the sound of it passing over the crossing. This was especially helpful as it saved having to leave the office to see for oneself what sort of engines were coming on shed. One heard the noise of the engine, knew from the sound which one it was and was able to shout any necessary instructions to the driver as he went by.

In 1943 L.P.P. found himself elevated to the post of Locomotive Running Superintendent of the Eastern Section (i.e. Great Eastern) of the LNER and his place at Stratford was taken by E.H.Ker - the gentle giant - whom I served under for about nine months before being sent to pastures new, never to return to the depot at Stratford.

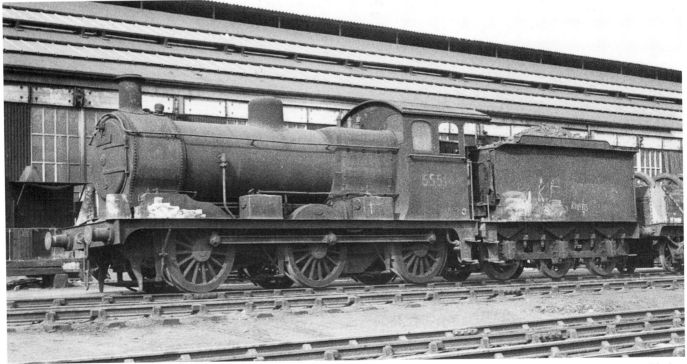

We built engines to last at Stratford..... Regrettably I did not keep a record of every engine I worked on but it is a fair bet that at some point in my career, I had something to do with the engine illustrated above which served its company for something like sixty years. Some of the class, including 65514, were fitted with short tenders suitable to the small turntables in parts of the Norwich district. The engine is on the 'bank' at Stratford, in a pretty filthy state, with parts of the blastpipe and smokebox brick lining resting on the running plate.

CHESHIRE LINES

A couple of Stanier 3MT 2-6-2T's were allocated to Heaton Mersey for the sheds share of the Midland suburban service between Stockport (TD) and Manchester (Central). One suspected that someone in authority bore a grudge against the Manchester suburban district: prior to the Stanier regime most trains had been handled by 0-6-4 'Flatiron' tanks - which no-one else would have - whilst their replacements - the 3MT's - could hardly make enough steam to brew a can of tea. 40203 of Liverpool (Brunswick) is seen in the Kentish Town roundhouse.

I left Stratford in the autumn of 1943 to take up my first salaried appointment on the LNER after acting in salaried grades for many months and whilst I was delighted at my promotion I could not help reflecting on the rigours of the grading system on the LNER which prevented any of my earlier service from giving me any credit towards my pension.

The shed to which I was appointed was one of which few people had any knowledge and was located on the Cheshire Lines Committee a mile of so west of Stockport (Tiviot Dale). The CLC was a joint LMS and LNER concern with Heaton Mersey shed being situated next to the Godley Junction - Liverpool route with the Midland line to Manchester via Chorlton-cum-Hardy branching off a short distance from the shed. Both routes were heavily used by freight trains although prestige passenger services gave Heaton Mersey a wide berth. Great Central expresses passed well to the north in Manchester whilst the Midland workings from St Pancras to Manchester Central took the Cheadle Heath route to avoid Stockport. In peace time GC excursion traffic had used the line to by-pass Manchester but everything that remained was of a fairly lowly character.

The main flows of passenger services - those which remained following the war-time cuts - consisted of stopping trains on the Midland between Manchester Central and Chinley or Derby plus the remnants of the GC service between Stockport and Liverpool. As passenger trains had been excised from the timetables, additional freight trains filled the gaps so what had been lost from the right hand was well and truly made up by the left.

In spite of the war reasonable standards had been maintained in the Stratford district, especially where the operation of trains and the condition of track was concerned, and I was therefore totally unprepared for the state of affairs which greeted me at Heaton Mersey when I arrived there.

Especially bad was the Cheshire Lines Committee permanent way and on my first visit to the depot I was astonished by the sight of a Midland 3F on its knees outside the Foreman's office having burst the road. Poor as the track was in the shed limits, that of the adjacent sidings was even worse.

Operation of the railway from the depot seemed to be as wayward as the condition of the track. No-one seemed to be particularly concerned about the punctual departure of engines from the shed, something we strove very hard to excel in at Stratford in spite of the Blitz. About twenty wagons of engine ashes stood at the side of the shed, some of which had been there so long that grass was growing on them - and this in the middle of a war when every

wagon was desperately needed. I started to understand for the first time what the expression 'North-south divide' meant.

Fortunately I was not the only new appointee at Heaton Mersey at that time as a very conscientious new shedmaster started on the same day as myself: Geoff Ford who was to end his time (and die in harness) as the Divisional Maintenance Engineer at Norwich.

At my interview for the job I was surprised to hear that not only had I to take charge of the LNER engines allocated to the shed but an equal number of LMS locomotives as the two companies had negotiated closer working arrangements to effect staffing economies during the 1930s.

Not allowing ourselves to become despondent at the apparent neglect of the CLC, Geoff Ford and I wasted no time in getting down to improve the performance and appearance of the shed, a task in which we were assisted by two outside foremen appointed by the LMS. The wagons of ashes went within the first few days and right-time starts for engines leaving the shed became the order of the day. There was some resistance to this, especially from some of the footplate staff, but with the support of the supervisory staff we were able, in a short time, to overcome this recalcitrance.

Although we were in fact a joint shed, the engines of the two companies were kept apart

STOCKPORT (TIVIOT DALE) : 1938/9			
TRAIN	ARR	DEP	DESTINATION
22.05 MARYLEBONE	03.52	04.00	LIVERPOOL (05.20)
00.05 St PANCRAS	05.25	05.48	MANCHESTER VIC (06.12)
		05.50	Liverpool (07.07)
05.50 Liverpool	06.21		
06.05 Manchester	06.31	06.34	BUXTON (08.02)
		06.40	St Helens (07.56)
		06.45	Manchester (07.10)
		06.51	Godley Jcn (07.09)
		07.10	New Mills (07.35)
07.19 Chorlton-cum-Hardy	07.29		
07.33 Godley Jcn	07.46	07.48	Liverpool (09.12)
		08.12	Manchester (08.33)
07.58 New Mills	08.17	08.28	Manchester (08.53)
08.15 Manchester	08.39		
08.38 MANCHESTER	08.57	08.58	St PANCRAS (13.00)
		09.12	Manchester (09.36)
07.15 MATLOCK	09.46	09.48	MANCHESTER (10.05)
09.23 Millers Dale	10.21	10.23	Manchester (10.47)
09.33 Liverpool	11.15		
10.55 Manchester	11.23	11.26	Chinley (12.08)
08.55 HULL	11.40	11.41	LIVERPOOL (12.30)
		11.47	Warrington (12.32)
12.06 Manchester	12.31		
12.25 Chinley	12.55		
		13.00	Marple (13.16)
		13.10	Manchester (13.35)
12.38 Manchester	13.02		
11.35 Liverpool	13.22		
13.04 Manchester	13.32	13.33	Chinley (14.10)
13.15 DERBY	13.35	13.37	MANCHESTER (14.02)
		13.50	Liverpool (15.54)
13.18 LIVERPOOL	14.03	14.05	HULL (16.45)
		14.08	Manchester (14.33)
14.05 Marple	14.18		
14.00 Warrington	14.38	14.41	Godley Jcn (14.59)
14.42 Manchester	15.09	15.10	Chinley (15.50)
14.30 Warrington	15.22		
15.10 Godley Jcn	15.23	15.24	Liverpool (16.49)
15.08 Chinley	15.35	15.37	Manchester (16.02)
15.41 Chinley	16.09		
15.55 Manchester	16.21	16.23	Chinley (17.00)
		16.25	Halewood (17.57)
		16.36	Manchester (17.03)
16.34 MANCHESTER	16.50	16.51	NOTTINGHAM (19.11)
16.38 Manchester	17.03		
		17.18	Manchester (17.42)
17.08 Manchester	17.32		
		17.41	Manchester (18.05)
16.57 Warrington	17.43		
		17.48	Marple (18.00)
14.45 HULL	17.49	17.50	LIVERPOOL (18.47)
17.38 Manchester	18.00		
17.55 MANCHESTER	18.10	18.11	BUXTON (19.21)
		18.15	Liverpool (20.04)
16.33 Liverpool	18.22	18.26	Godley Jcn (18.44)
18.05 Manchester	18.29		
18.20 Marple	18.32		
17.40 Buxton	18.52	18.53	Manchester (19.16)
18.32 Manchester	18.53	18.58	Millers Dale (20.09)
18.45 Manchester	19.09	19.11	Chinley (19.50)
		19.49	Manchester (20.15)
19.50 Manchester	20.14		
16.30 St PANCRAS	20.39	20.41	LIVERPOOL (21.38)
20.12 Chinley	20.39	20.50	Manchester (21.14)
20.50 Manchester	21.09	21.10	Buxton (22.22)
21.05 Marple	21.18		
19.12 DERBY	21.35	21.38	MANCHESTER (22.02)
20.50 Liverpool	22.28		
22.09 Chinley	22.34	22.36	Manchester (23.02)
22.40 Manchester	23.04	23.10	Marple (23.24)
00.00 MANCHESTER	00.25	00.32	St PANCRAS (06.00)

The passenger service from Stockport Tiviot Dale never recovered from the wartime cuts and until the closure of the station in the late 1960's it did little more than serve the infrequent service of local trains on the Manchester (Central) - Chinley axis. The two tables show the difference between the service using the station pre-war and after the wartime cuts.

from each other, the LMS engines being given the four shed roads nearest to the river Mersey whilst the LNER locomotives took the four nearest to the running lines. The LMS allocation was a mixed bag and consisted of two Stanier Class 3 2-6-2 tanks for working the suburban services, two 7-foot 2P 4-4-0s (ostensibly) for assisting freight trains up to Peak Forest), a solitary 3F of Midland origin, three 2F 0-6-0s for local freight and shunting and a number of 4F 0-6-0s and 8F 2-8-0s.

The LNER stock had rather less variety and comprised of a D9 4-4-0, three B9 4-6-0s together with some J10 0-6-0's and N5 0-6-2 tanks.

In his time at Heaton Mersey Geoff Ford effected a considerable improvement in working, not the least of which was the provision of a decent Running Foreman's office instead of the former dirty cubby hole in the oil stores which I and my colleagues had had to use when I arrived. Unfortunately he was not destined to remain long at the depot and within a short space of time I found myself stepping - temporarily - into his shoes and having charge of the depot.

The maintenance facilities at Heaton Mersey were almost non-existent and consisted for the most part of some handtools, a pair of shear legs (LNER) and a few jacks. In spite of this it was seldom necessary to send a locomotive to another depot for heavy repairs except that, for LMS engines, I had to send them to Sheffield for their 30-36,000 mile examinations.

The Heaton Mersey breakdown train was an object of derision. It comprised two ancient vehicles dating from the Crimea (at least); one of which was a brake-van in which the staff rode whilst the other conveyed tools and apparatus. The outfit was known internally as Sangers Circus and externally (by the trainspotters) as the Dum Dum Train. Both names were equally appropriate.

It will be understood that the range of mishaps which could be dealt with using such primitive equipment ought to have been strictly limited but such was the state of the permanent way that the services of the Dum Dum were relied upon to a far greater extent than its appearance and age warranted.

The usual method of rerailing was to employ ramps and packing which, because it could cause further damage to the track, was none too popular with the permanent way department who themselves had problems in obtaining supplies necessary for maintaining the track in the first place. It was something of a vicious circle.

On one occasion we were called to the derailment of a loaded coal wagon at Godley Junction. The vehicle had come to rest some distance from the siding on which it was supposed to be and the only means of rerailing it was to pull it with a long chain until it could be guided back onto the track. The local permanent way ganger turned up as I was preparing to attach the chain and, when the procedure was explained to him, he became most upset, threatening me with all sorts of dire consequences if the track was at all damaged. I told him to stand back, wait, and then do his reporting.

The chain was attached and the haul began. The wagon jumped and danced all over the place and in fact did just about everything but turn over. Fortunately the hand of providence was with me and by some miracle I got it back on the track without a single chair be-

PASSENGER SERVICE : STOCKPORT (TIVIOT DALE). 1944			
TRAIN	ARR	DEP	DESTINATION
22.00 MARYLEBONE	04.52	05.10	LIVERPOOL (06.25)
		05.40	Liverpool (07.08)
06.05 Manchester	06.32	06.35	Buxton (07.55)
05.05 Liverpool	06.38		
		06.35	Glazebrook (07.12)
		06.45	Manchester (07.13)
07.09 Chorlton-cum-Hardy	07.27		
		07.40	Liverpool (09.13)
		08.12	Manchester (08.40)
08.00 Manchester	08.27		
		08.34	Manchester (09.02)
08.30 Manchester	08.54	08.55	Sheffield (10.44)
07.02 Sheffield	08.54	08.56	Manchester (09.24)
07.10 DERBY	10.03	10.10	MANCHESTER (10.38)
10.55 MANCHESTER	11.22	11.27	DERBY (14.17)
12.06 Manchester	12.33		
10.10 DERBY	12.55	12.57	MANCHESTER (13.25)
13.04 Manchester	13.31	13.32	Sheffield (15.15)
11.35 Liverpool	13.25		
		13.37	Manchester (14.05)
12.45 Sheffield	14.31	14.33	Manchester (15.01)
14.42 MANCHESTER	15.09	15.10	DERBY (17.31)
		15.23	Liverpool (16.54)
13.20 DERBY	15.57	15.59	MANCHESTER (16.26)
15.55 Manchester	16.22	16.24	Sheffield (18.08)
17.00 Manchester	17.27	17.28	Chinley (18.08)
17.08 Manchester	17.35		
		17.43	Manchester (18.10)
16.57 Warrington	17.55		
		18.15	Liverpool (20.12)
18.05 Manchester	18.32		
16.33 Liverpool	18.36		
18.45 MANCHESTER	19.12	19.14	DERBY (22.12)
17.30 Sheffield	19.31	19.35	Manchester (20.03)
19.56 Manchester	20.23		
17.48 DERBY	20.36	20.38	MANCHESTER (21.05)
		21.10	Manchester (21.38)
20.45 Manchester	21.12	21.13	Chinley (21.50)
22.47 Chinley	23.14	23.16	Manchester (23.32)

The most important service linking the CLC with the Midland was the Northwich - Peak Forest circuit of workings which consisted of fully braked hoppers conveying limestone between Tunstead and the various ICI works in and around Northwich. When the service started in the 1930's the workings were shared between Northwich and Heaton Mersey although from the time of nationalisation the entire service was based upon Northwich. 8F 2-8-0's monopolised the trains and 48135 of Northwich climbs towards Chinley North Junction with a train of empty hoppers for Great Rocks Sidings, Peak Forest, in 1950.

ing broken. The ganger shook his head and said he never would have believed it........

Some accidents were well beyond the scope of the Dum Dum and one that could have been particularly nasty took place not long after Geoff Ford had left me in charge of the depot.

At the time large numbers of American troops were disembarking at Liverpool and being taken, via the CLC and Woodhead, to LNER destinations where they formed the spearhead for the invasion of Normandy, whilst at the same time vast quantities of petrol were being moved from Stanlow oil refinery to the East Anglian airfields by the same route.

Naturally the troop trains had a higher running priority and one night the signalman at Brinnington Junction, faced with a petrol train closely followed by a troop special, signalled the first train to take the Reddish branch, the idea being that it should reverse back onto the main line and resume its course after the passage of the troop special. Unfortunately when the petrol train came to a stand on the branch, someone misjudged matters and the brake-van was still obstructing the main line; something the signalman, who had no track circuits to rely on, was unaware of.

The gradients between Stockport (Tiviot Dale) and Godley Junction are severe and because of this the troop trains tended to be assisted over the section, in this case the K3 2-6-0 working the train being assisted by a J10 0-6-0. Both engines were working hard when they ran full tilt into the brake-van, the force of the collision throwing the 0-6-0 right

round the way it had come and onto its side. The K3 was derailed but managed to stay upright whilst the passenger stock suffered very little damage. Similarly one or two of the petrol tankers were derailed but mercifully there was no fire which was as well since the troops in the passenger train had been locked inside their carriages.

By equal good fortune neither of the train crews was seriously hurt whilst the guard had left his van shortly before the moment of impact.

Being a major crash (or pitch-in as we styled them on the railway) both the Gorton and Newton Heath cranes were summoned to the scene, the former being in the charge of breakdown maestro Ernest Maugham who, much to the horror of the fire brigade, proceeded to burn through the drawbar between the J10 and its tender.

Having separated the 0-6-0 from its tender, Maugham proceeded to lift the engine bodily with the Gorton crane alone, a procedure I have never again witnessed. The Newton Heath Foreman was astonished, declaring under his breath that Maugham was an optimist. Nevertheless the lift proceeded without a hitch.

Soon afterwards another J10 was again in trouble, one of the class taking a diamond crossing and attempting to go round it rather than across it, such was the state of the track. The Dum Dum managed to sort that one out which was more than it could do with a wagon laden with concrete blocks which shed its wheels and axleguards not far from the shed inlet. The best we could do was to jack up the wagon body clear of the main line and wait for the Gorton crane to come to the rescue.

Thick fog frequently prevailed in the Manchester area, especially in winter, and on one particularly thick night we were

LMS 5XP 'PATRIOT' 4-6-0. 5533 'LORD RATHMORE'. 11:358/385 TONS. 1937						
m.ch	Point	1/in	WTT	Actual	mph	dbhp	pc
0.00	EUSTON	-	0.00	0.00	-	-	
5.36	Willesden Jcn	656	9.00	9.31	61.5	902	3
8.06	Wembley (C)	852		12.08	62.0	791	5
11.31	Harrow	339		15.14	62.5	1158	7
16.01	Bushey	554		19.35	67.2	1077	7
17.37	WATFORD JCN	4049	21.00	20.45	69.2	1146	8
20.75	Kings Langley	586		23.56	67.7	837	5
24.39	Hemel Hempstead	429		27.22	63.0	734	4
27.76	Berkhamstead	335		30.39	59.2	928	6
31.53	TRING	408	35.00	34.10	59.2	1013	6
36.08	Cheddington	-356		37.55	79.0	1029	7
40.15	Leighton Buzzard	-644		40.49	80.5	713	6
46.53	BLETCHLEY	-1075	47.00	45.49	77.5	485	4
52.33	Wolverton	-1014		50.10	72.5	390	3
54.60	Castlethorpe	800		52.10	67.2	456	3
59.72	ROADE	353	59.00	56.51	60.0	894	6
62.66	BLISWORTH	-709	63.00	60.09	-	-	0

The LMS was, in the view of the author, rather a scruffy railway and lacked the ability to command the respect of its staff in the way that the LNER did. Prior to arriving at Heaton Mersey his experience of it, however, was limited to occasional visits as a passenger although there was one instance when a particular performance made him sit up and take note. The effort by 4-6-0 5533 on the 16.35 Euston - Birmingham was something that the GN would have been pleased with.

Heaton Mersey MPD on 2 May 1948. LMS engines kept to the right hand side of the shed, LNER to the left.

called to a derailed brake-van in Cheadle Sidings. Arriving at the scene after feeling our way in five yard visibility, we found it was a six-wheeled vehicle derailed cross-cornered, a situation which conjured up all sorts of difficulties. In view of the weather and our desire to get the job done quickly (and easily) we decided to try and rerail both ends at once by using both left and right ramps at opposite ends of the vehicle. Once again luck was with us and the van sidled up the ramps and sat itself on the rails at the first attempt, an operation I was never able to do successfully again.

Whilst the Dum Dum was kept busy with regular incidents on the main line, derailments inside the shed limits were even more frequent and scarcely a day went by without me involved in some sort of rerailing exercise. I recall one particular day when I had a visitor from Derby who stared at astonishment at the sight of two N5 0-6-2 tanks, both with derailed radial wheels in different parts of the depot at the same time. The Luftwaffe could have come and blitzed Heaton Mersey and we would probably never have noticed the difference.

Another peculiar derailment concerned the Stanier 2-6-2 tanks which had a tendency to derail their driving wheels over the inner edge of a sharply curved section of track near the coal stage. Such was the rigidity of these long wheel base engines that I had quite a struggle to get them back on the rail without further damage to the permanent way.

One of the rostered turns for the B9 4-6-0's was to work a freight train to Northwich in the early afternoon. On one instance the engine was about to come off shed for the turn when it became derailed at the points between the turntable road and the main outlet road, not by Heaton Mersey standards an uncommon occurrence. However on this occasion just as the engine was being eased back onto the road the large laminated spring on the bogie jumped out of its hanger on the right hand side. To have jacked the engine up would have been a long and laborious matter causing serious delays to other engines coming off shed and so I decided that the easiest course was to deliberately derail the engine again, replace the spring

and rerail it once more, an operation completed in just a couple of minutes.

Even relatively routine incidents took on a complexity of their own at Heaton Mersey. Every shed in the country has seen a wagon pushed too far down a siding resulting in the stop blocks being shoved back a yard whilst the leading wheels of the wagon either bury themselves in the ballast or mount the stop block.

We had such a case at Heaton Mersey and to rerail it I had first of all to clear the siding of all the other wagons standing in the way and then to connect a length of chain to an engine and the wagon which had to be drawn back away from the buffer stops. I told the driver to move back smartly and the wagon literally leapt into the air, landing with one pair of wheels on the track. Meanwhile the stop block, rotten with age, collapsed in a cloud of red dust......

Sometimes the rather depressing catalogue of mishaps could be tinged with humour as was the case with an O4 2-8-0 which, as it was going off shed, broke the leading section of its right hand rod and came to a stand completely blocking the shed outlet. A quick inspection revealed that dismantling the rods in order to tow the crippled engine away would be a lengthy business during which time nothing would be able to leave the shed resulting in delayed trains all over the system. After some quick thinking I decided on the novel solution of moving the locomotive by skidding it out of the way. I arranged for a couple of fitters to oil the track under the engine and had another engine attached to the cripple. When this had been done I applied the steam brake on the 2-8-0 and waved for the assisting engine to do its stuff. At first it worked marvellously as the engine slid along nicely with the fitters walking alongside pouring oil under the driving wheels. The problem was that my scheme was too efficient and the engine picked up speed, leaving the oilers behind. As it hit the unlubricated section of track, the leading wheels began to turn and, being out of phase, the crankpin caught the crosshead, bending the slidebars thus putting the 2-8-0 right out of

commission. Looking for compensation I mused that at least my unorthodoxy had succeeded in clearing the shed outlet.

Some incidents were the result of good intentions such as the time my leading fitter was on holiday and his deputy decided to remove the valves on our solitary D9 4-4-0. He attempted the removal by uncoupling the valve spindle and placing a block between it and its driving block (a curious GC gadget which dated back to the days when the engines were converted to piston valves). He then tried to push the valves out of the cylinder liner by winding the engine into forward gear with the result that the weighbar shaft arm bent and bent until the engine had taken as much forward gear as it could. The die block was still showing mid-gear, the same position it had been when the operation started.

At this point the alarm was sounded and I was brought to inspect his handiwork, the result of which had been to cripple a perfectly good locomotive. I could see at once that if I took the weighbar shaft down for despatch to Gorton there would be some pretty awkward questions to answer whilst on the other hand Heaton Mersey was not equipped for repairs of this magnitude. I mentally rummaged through the various pieces of useless equipment that some well intentioned soul has sent us in the hope that it would serve the war effort. Very little of it had ever been used but I thought I recalled seeing a Wells Heater - a sort of giant blowlamp - at some point in the past before it had been consigned to store-room oblivion. I sent someone round to see if they could find it - which they did - and rigged it up next to the D9 where I was able to heat the shaft arm until it became red hot. With the thing red hot I wound the engine back into mid-gear and was relieved to see the shaft resume its familiar shape without fracturing.

Material for LNER locomotives was usually obtained by road from Gorton works, unloaded by engine cleaners onto handbarrows and wheeled through a small public park where a steeply falling path crossed the Mersey, and into the depot. Some items (unlike Wells Heaters) were in constant demand and yet were dif-

I had two Midland Railway 2P 4-4-0's in my charge at Heaton Mersey, one being 544, pictured above, the other being 453. Whilst just about competent to meet my local needs, they could not be relied upon for special trains and forced me to beg and borrow more suitable engines from colleagues at adjacent sheds.

ficult to obtain, one particular specimen being the large diameter coil springs which formed the buffing gear between the engine and tender of our J10 0-6-0s.

One day one of these valuable springs was unloaded from the van and, on the point of being transferred to the barrow, the lads decided it would be easier (or more fun) to roll it down the path. They quickly discovered to their peril (and eventual pain) that playing hoop-la with a sizeable section of a J10 required more than a passing knowledge of Newton's principles, something that may have flashed through their minds as the coil spring gained momentum, dashed down the path, missed the bridge and plunged with a mighty splash into the river.

Recovery was out of the question - a replacement was eventually received - and I hope I was not too hard with the miscreants since the incident was followed by a spell of exceptionally dry weather which caused the level of the Mersey to fall revealing the lost spring which was immediately hauled out, cleaned and placed in the loco stores.

Thanks to the pranks of a couple of idiots I was the possessor of a spare coil which saved quite a bit of requisitioning the next time a J10 came in for attention.

My drivers at Heaton Mersey were the usual mixed bunch that you find at any large shed, ranging from the best you could possibly hope to work with to the downright unco-operative. There was one particular example of the latter who, out of sheer cussedness, would not take an engine off the shed punctually and would resort to all manner of excuses in order to effect a delay. This was especially true of

his performance on afternoon turns of duty, the reasoning being that the greater the delay the greater the amount of overtime whilst the evenings entertainment had been lost anyway.

I went to some lengths to trip him up and, one afternoon with my nose for trouble was working overtime, I quietly had three engines prepared and made ready for his working. He climbed aboard the first and, predictably, found some reason to fail it. I introduced him to the second engine with much the same result but when I produced a third, all ready and waiting, he got the point and, for once in his life, left the depot on time.

At the other extreme there were drivers who realised their responsibilities at a time when others were fighting for our freedom and would do whatever was asked of them without question. One such was an LMS driver, Arnold Scott, who, because of his reliability, was always the favourite for any especially important LMS job. I knew that with him on the turn there would be no late starts, inexcusable delays en route or complaints about the fitness of his engine although we always tried to give him the best engine available.

There was a story doing the rounds concerning a freight train he once worked from Cheadle Heath to Chaddesden (Derby), a distance of fifty three miles, which was let out at Cheadle in front of a following London express. Apparently Arnold kept ahead all the way - he must have intimidated the signalmen with his whistle - and was tucked safely away in Chaddesden before the express reached Derby. The firemen at the depot staunchly defended him against any suggestions of recklessness,

claiming that no matter how fast Arnold ran, he always had absolute control of his train.

V.I.P. specials on the LMS were always a worry because the only passenger engines I had were the two old (and rather doubtful) 2P 4-4-0s which meant I had to borrow suitable engines from other sheds whose offerings were usually engines they would prefer not to have used themselves. This beg and borrow policy once threatened to bring me to the attention of Field Marshal Montgomery (which would have been almost as bad as an uncomfortable meeting with L.P.P.) when Sheffield met one of my requests for assistance with a compound 4-4-0 which I took the precaution of giving the once over before entrusting it to Monty's train. It was as well I did for a cursory inspection revealed an unworkable steam brake cylinder whilst a more detailed look brought to light a steam leak on the ejector steam valve caused by the union nut being split on one side. Time was of the essence - there was no other engine available - and working against the clock we cleaned and replaced both brake cylinders for good measure before discovering that we had no replacement ejector nut. Packed with copious amounts of asbestos string the original nut was tightened up as much as I dared and to my relief did the trick. For a while I knew how Rommel must have felt in North Africa but there were no repercussions, the compound evidently having held together at least for Monty's purposes.

Suddenly the war was over and with the VE bells ringing in our ears I was 'loaned' to the Gorton District office with the responsibility of drawing up plans for the improvement of CLC depots which, needless to say, were never put into effect.

My links with Heaton Mersey were not completely severed and occasionally I used to return when, for any reason, the regular incumbent was away. It was on one of these visits that the Running Foreman burst into my office absolutely convulsed with laughter. I asked him what the joke was and he told me that the LNER directors had decided to hold an inspection of the CLC by running their special saloon over the line. When it arrived on the district at Guide Bridge the signalman, not knowing anything about it, shunted it into a loop whilst someone tried to locate the special traffic notice for the working. When this had been located it was discovered that no pilot driver had been provided to take the train forward to Manchester Central thus more delay ensued whilst a substitute made his way from Gorton. Eventually the party made their inspection of the Central and rejoined the train which promptly pulled out for Liverpool leaving Sir Charles Newton, the Chairman, on the platform and having to run for his train. The Liverpool element of the trip passed without incident but when the party alighted at Bidston for a walk around, the heavens opened and soaked the lot to the skin.

All this, however, was a mere prelude to what was to happen anon and as the special was passing Mickle Trafford, its - newly outshopped - J11 decided to part company with its tender. The fire had to be thrown out - utilising the District Inspector who was in waiting to the Board - and another engine sent for. On any other day assistance could have been given by the Mickle Trafford banker, which

was close at hand, but it turned out that on this occasion the banker had no leading drawgear and could only be used to push goods trains from the rear. After a long delay a filthy shambling J10 0-6-0 came to the rescue from Northwich and eventually got the party, hours late, back onto GC metals proper at Godley where an ex-works A5 4-6-2T took over as far as Sheffield. (Everyone expected the 4-6-2T to run hot bit it didn't although I later heard that the Atlantic booked to take over at Sheffield Victoria failed before leaving Darnall shed).

I have to say that I joined in the laughter.

There were two postscripts. The first was that we received D3 4-4-0 No. 2000 (in pristine livery) for the working of future officers specials and whilst it was unlikely - according to its drivers the best feature about it was its green paint - to match the feat of the unfortunate J10, it looked very pretty. The second was that I happened to meet Sir Ronald Matthews some time later and mentioned his disastrous trip. His comment was to the effect that it showed the Board what could go wrong.

During my days at Gorton the LNER started to feel the influence of the new breed of locomotives, the Thompson and (later) the Peppercorn classes; one of the A2 Pacifics which had been developed from the Gresley V2 design being sent to take its turn in the Manchester - Marylebone links.

The engine was No. 3697 and as a prelude to its career it had to be worked up to London for an inspection by the Board at Marylebone. Since I had a promotional interview in the Capital the next day, someone decided that I ought to accompany the engine.

What an engine and what a trip. The engine had been fitted with all the latest Thompson gadgets - steam reverse, steam brake and a quadrant type regulator with a great long handle which stretched right across the footplate; the latter being as far removed from the tidy Gresley regulator that we were all used to.

All went well for the first twenty miles until we ran into the single-bore Woodhead tunnel - three miles of it - when the engine started to slip. The driver closed the regulator and immediately there was an almighty blowback with flames blasting out of the firebox into the cab almost reaching the tender. Mercifully none of us were injured, good fortune having the Inspector and myself sitting on the fireman's side whilst the fireman happened to be standing immediately behind the driver.

The driver tugged the regulator open and the flames subsided into the firebox whilst the engine ceased her tricks having given us a thoroughly frightening experience. There were no further alarms of this nature but for the rest of the journey, whenever 3697 got the opportunity to show its paces, the riding was appalling and I for one was heartily glad to get rid of it at Marylebone.

At the time I imagined that the rough riding was due to the state of the track which was still suffering from a lack of maintenance. Later experience with the class revealed that the trouble lay fairly and squarely with the locomotive.To add insult to injury I did not get the job I was being interviewed for.

In the midst of the hurly-burly of playing my part in keeping trains moving on the wartime CLC there were occasional instances when I looked back to times before world wars played havoc with the railways and my indigestion. Brought up in the era of Pacific and eight coupled engines it was difficult to realise that the Great Northern used its 'singles' for something like forty years and that scenes such as that of G class 4-2-2 leaving Peterborough with an express for Grimsby were commonplace. The engine, 886, was built at Doncaster in 1882 and drew attention to itself by running from Kings Cross to Grantham in 101 minutes during the races of August 1888.

Winters in the Pennines could be severe with heavy snowfalls calling for special measures as is the case with this Austerity 2-8-0 which has been sent out to clear Totley tunnel in 1963.

ing that the site was too small for the number of engines using it. Most engines arriving or departing from the shed were required to work trains from Sheffield whilst the exit roads from the shed faced to the east so that almost all engines leaving the depot had to make an awkward 'W' movement before reaching their starting point.

Similarly engines arriving on the shed from Sheffield had to make a number of shunts, which could often conflict with the movements of other engines, as they came in to fill up under the coaling plant, went to the wet pit for ash disposal and fire cleaning and had to reverse yet again in order to reach the shed roads. None of it made for a very efficient way of servicing engines.

My appointment to Darnall was as senior shift Foreman of which there were

In the autumn of 1946 my efforts on the CLC were rewarded with a return to a mainline worthy of the name, and I was given the rank of Running Foreman, grade 1, at Sheffield Darnall. It was a relief to find myself back on a line that was generally recognised and to have been elevated to quite a senior rank. The lowest salaried position on the railway was class 5 - a starting grade - whilst the majority of staff retired as a class 4. Those who made the grade to 3 were quite comfortably off whilst a 2 lived like a King. As a class 1 at the age of only thirty I could reasonably expect to achieve the dignity of first class free travel at the next grade: Special A.

Darnall was a new shed - which alone made a change from Heaton Mersey - with an allocation of just under 100 locomotives. Previously the main Sheffield (GC) shed had been at Neepsend on the Manchester side of Victoria station, Darnall being a short distance on the London side.

The duties for which Darnall provided power varied considerably. Many of the engines set out to power the freight workings which started from the various yards in the Sheffield area although we had a significant role to play in the working of passenger trains. The bulk of the GC goods traffic tended to avoid Sheffield Victoria, the heaviest flows of traffic were from the South Yorkshire coalfield, around Barnsley, to the Manchester and Liverpool districts and these joined the main line at Barnsley Junction, Penistone, some miles to the west. Similarly traffic from the south to the north - our main marshalling yard was at Wath, to the south of Barnsley, - avoided Sheffield leaving traffic which either started from Sheffield (the princi-

pal depots were at Bridgehouses, just to the West of the station, and Bernard Road to the East) or services from London and the Nottingham pits to Manchester which had little choice but to be routed through Victoria.

Although we were on a trunk route to London, there was always the impression that the Marylebone workings - the extension as it was known - were something of an afterthought and that the principal services were the rather slow trains which ran, not infrequently, between Manchester and Lincolnshire, chiefly Cleethorpes. We also a respectable series of local trains to places such as Barnsley and Penistone together with a number of stopping trains to points on the extension such as Nottingham and Leicester.

The cream of our motive power consisted of Great Central 4-6-0s with a sprinkling of V2 2-6-2's and B17 4-6-0's although the older types were rapidly being replaced by the new Thompson B1 4-6-0s. Power for the Manchester - London trains was provided by Gorton and Leicester and took the form of A3 Pacifics or V2 2-6-2s although B1 4-6-0s were not unknown as substitutes. The heaviest goods traffic was worked by the 04 2-8-0s, of which we had about 30 whilst J11 and J39 0-6-0s took care of more local workings. Suburban passenger trains were divided between a couple of C13 4-4-2 tanks and a sizeable allocation of N4 and N5 0-6-2Ts.

Although it was a very modern depot, Darnall was far from being an ideal shed to work, the root cause being

TRAFFIC MOVEMENTS : SHEFFIELD VICTORIA (1936)			
TRAIN	ARR	DEP	DESTINATION
		22.00	RETORD
		22.05	CHESTERFIELD
18.15 SWINDON		22.09	YORK
19.50 Ardwick		22.24	Marylebone
22.07 Deepcar		22.31	Sheffield (Bernard Rd)
16.55 Huskisson		22.42	Kings Cross
		22.55	DONCASTER
23.00 Bridgehouses		23.02	Ardlsey
		23.10	RETFORD
21.30 Godley		23.25	Marylebone
21.08 Ardwick		23.30	Marylebone
19.25 Huskisson		23.37	Whitemoor
22.30 MANCHESTER	23.49		
22.30 MANCHESTER (C)	23.57	00.17	MARYLEBONE
21.16 Deansgate		00.18	Colwick
15.10 Kings Cross	00.33	00.43	Deansgate
19.50 Trafford Park	00.43	00.50	Lincoln
22.20 Nottingham		00.58	Liverpool
23.00 Godley		01.01	Annesley
23.59 Barnsley Jcn		01.04	Worksop
22.55 HULL	01.09		
22.52 Dewsnap		01.10	Leicester
00.05 YORK	01.17		
23.15 Colwick		01.23	Mottram
23.35 Lincoln		01.31	Mottram
01.35 Bridgehouses		01.37	Marshgate
21.05 SWINDON	01.21	01.42	YORK
00.50 Staveley		01.44	Mottram
22.05 MARYLEBONE	01.55	02.05	MANCHESTER
23.15 Ardwick		02.20	Grimsby
		02.35	MANCHESTER
21.10 Grimsby		02.37	Ardwick
02.10 Holbrook		03.00	Sheffield (Bridgehouses)
01.40 MANCHESTER	02.50	03.03	CLEETHORPES
21.50 Marylebone		03.05	Ardwick
01.50 LEEDS	03.18		
19.00 Brunswick		03.20	Rotherham Road
01.12 Lincoln		03.20	Sheffield (Bridgehouses)
00.01 Ashton Moss		03.46	Grimsby
23.45 Hull		03.53	Sheffield (Bridgehouses)
00.10 Godley		04.01	Kirkby in Ashfield
01.30 Colwick		04.03	Sheffield (Bridgehouses)
02.25 Colwick	04.06	04.14	Liverpool
		04.20	LEEDS
01.27 Annesley		04.20	Mottram
02.45 Colwick	04.25	04.32	Mottram
00.33 Ardsley		04.36	Sheffield (Bridgheouses)
23.42 Deansgate		04.39	Colwick
03.25 Lincoln		04.52	Ardwick
		05.05	NOTTINGHAM
02.00 Godley		05.06	Retford
01.20 Dringhouses		05.10	Sheffield (Bridgehouses)
		05.15	CLEETHORPES
01.55 Mansfield		05.32	Mottram
04.28 Staveley		05.40	Mottram
22.20 Marylebone		05.48	Mottram
02.32 MARYLEBONE	05.54		

Any doubts about the importance of the GC should be dispelled by the accompanying tables which show the volume of traffic which passed through Sheffield Victoria. Although the timings are those for 1936 the density of traffic remained constant almost until the closure of the route as a through entity between Manchester and London.

three, one on each shift, each being responsible for the depot when the shedmaster was not on duty. For some reason we did not operate from the general offices but from the 'wet pit' office which would normally have been the location for the junior foremen at any other depot. This was a mixed blessing for while the wet pit office gave us a far better view of what was going on in the shed than we would have had from the main offices all communication from the district control and the outside world generally had to be relayed, second hand, by someone in the main office; something that was only occasionally an advantage.

The heavy repair shop was also on the far side of the shed and was governed by a colleague, Colin Scutt, who was later to become CM&EE of the Eastern Region of BR. Repairs were also carried out on two of the shed roads on the west side of the main running shed to make matters worse, when I arrived, these roads were blocked to the west end by queues of withdrawn engines which meant that the possibility of removing engines from the Sheffield end of the depot was nil. After a struggle I managed to get these engines moved to the far end of the stores road outside the shed altogether, a move which greatly facilitated the more efficient movement of engines in the shed and allowed me to use the Sheffield end of the establishment relatively freely.

I had hardly settled in at Darnall when we, and the rest of the country, was hit by the 1947 winter which, by any standards, was extreme and has yet to be repeated. Life in the wet pit office was made thoroughly miserable by the fact that whenever anyone opened the office door all the preciously conserved heat from our coal-fired stove would instantly dissipate leaving the floor awash with black melting snow.

One of the peculiarities of the weather during that particular winter was that it would give occasional signs of improvement which lent a false sense of security. People would relax and withdraw the permanent way staff from snow clearing duties after which the snow would return again, stronger than ever, and block everything. Several key places such as Woodburn Junction and Sheffield Victoria were caught napping.

From my position in the wet office with its limited communications I had little idea of what was happening beyond the range of my eyesight and it was only with the co-operation of an excellent signalman at Darnall box, who went to great pains to keep me advised of events as they happened, that I managed to keep the shed working. Both he and I agreed that, improvements in the weather or not, we would keep our snow clearance staff on continuous duty and thanks to this policy we were never caught out.

Curiously absenteeism was not a problem, a blessing for which the Corporation can be thanked since although the streets were piled high with three-foot drifts of snow, they managed to keep the tram service operating throughout. Fortunately most staff lived within a local radius of the shed where the trams could take them to and from work. What absences there were resulted from genuine illness because of the extreme conditions and in fact I succumbed myself for a short period.

TRAFFIC WORKING : SHEFFIELD (VICTORIA) 1937			
TRAIN	ARR	DEP	DESTINATION
		06.03	PENISTONE
		06.10	NOTTINGHAM
05.20 DONCASTER	06.20		
05.40 CHESTERFIELD	06.25		
04.28 Worksop		06.25	Mottram
05.00 Dunford		06.28	Aldewarke
		06.30	LINCOLN
06.35 Sheffield (Bridgehouses)		06/37	Birdwell
		06.38	BARNESLEY
03.51 Dewsnap		06.39	Mansfield
05.08 Staveley		06/40	Guide Bridge
05.52 RETFORD	06.43		
06.40 Sheffield (Bernard Rd)		06/48	Oughty Bridge
		06.50	DONCASTER
06.00 BARNSLEY	06.52		
		07.06	MANCHESTER
03.25 Hexthorpe		07/06	Sheffield (Bridgehouses)
03.30 Mansfield		07/18	Mottram
01.10 Immingham		07/21	Dunford
04.05 Banbury	07.23		
03.25 Ashburys		07/26	Lincoln
		07.30	MARYLEBONE
05.25 MANCHESTER	07.20	07.33	CLEETHORPES
06.50 RETFORD	07.40		
		07.48	CLEETHORPES
03.57 Godley		07/48	Annesley
		07.55	NOTTINGHAM
03.53 Ashburys		08/02	Warsop Junction
		08.05	YORK
06.00 HULL	08.08	08.15	HULL
06.25 NOTTINGHAM	08.18	08.20	RETFORD
		08.23	PENISTONE
07.55 PENISTONE	08.24	08.34	LINCOLN
		08.40	MANCHESTER
06.06 NEW HOLLAND	08.43		
03.05 Frodingham		08/43	Barnsley Junction
08.00 BARSNLEY	08.51		
07.32 LINCOLN	08.56		
07.22 LEICESTER	09.01	09.06	MANCHESTER (CENTRAL)
07.22 NOTTINGHAM	09.16		
08.32 DONCASTER	09.21		
08.36 RETFORD	09.28		
08.20 MANCHESTER	09.31	09.35	MARYLEBONE
		09.38	CLEETHORPES
		09.43	HULL
		09.52	NOTTINGHAM
08.02 LEICESTER	09.53	09.58	MANCHESTER (CENTRAL)
07.35 HULL	10.07		
03.40 Grimsby		10/08	Mottram
09.35 RETFORD	10.11		
		10.20	BARNSLEY
10.03 PENISTONE	10.30		
08.55 HULL	10.33	10.37	LIVERPOOL
08.30 LIVERPOOL	10.45	10.50	HULL
08.28 CLEETHORPES	10.46	10.50	MANCHESTER
		10.53	LINCOLN
09.09 NOTTINGHAM	10.57		
08.25 Warsop Junction		10/58	Mottram
06.30 Dewsnap		11/01	Warsop Junction
10.24 BARNSLEY	11.03		
10.03 MANCHESTER	11.08	11.12	CLEETHORPES
10.00 BRADFORD EXCHANGE	11.15	11.20	MARYLEBONE
		11.25	LINCOLN
07.10 Huddersfield		11/34	High Hazels
10.51 DONCASTER	11.35		
10.10 YORK	11.22	11.37	BOURNEMOUTH
07.20 Lincoln		11/39	Mottram
06.50 Ashton Moss		11/40	Worksop
10.53 RETFORD	11.45		
		11.47	NOTTINGHAM
08.55 Bulwell		11/47	Mottram
08.00 Godley		12/11	Holbrook
10.35 HULL	12.13		
10.50 LINCOLN	12.17		
08.45 MARYLEBONE	12.23	12.27	MANCHESTER
11.22 MANCHESTER	12.36	12.41	BARNETBY
07.25 HARWICH	12.41	12.45	LIVERPOOL
		12.50	FELIXSTOWE
12.50 Sheffield (Bridgehouses)		12/52	Rotherham Road
11.05 NOTTINGHAM	12.54		
09.35 NEWCASTLE	12.51	13.01	SWANSEA
12.16 BARNSLEY	13.11		
12.28 DONCASTER	13.16		
10.00 MARYLEBONE	13.21	13.25	MANCHESTER
		13.27	HULL
		13.28	PENISTONE
		13/31	Bidston
09.00 Stanton Junction			
10.50 CLEETHORPES	13.40	13.46	MANCHESTER
12.40 MANCHESTER	13.54	13.58	CLEETHORPES
07.33 SOUTHAMPTON	13.51	14.00	NEWCASTLE

SHEFFIELD MPD : 1937 (MSX)	
TIME	TO WORK
00.05	02.00 Orgreaves - Annesley
01.10	01.35 Sheffield - Marshgate (Doncaster)
02.00	Bridgehouses pilot
02.15	03.00 Sheffield - Lincoln
02.20	03.03 SHEFFIELD - CLEETHORPES
02.30	03.20 Sheffield - Woodford
02.35	03.35 Sheffield - Frodingham
02.40	03.15 Broughton Lane - Mottram
03.20	04.10 Sheffield - High Hazels
03.30	04.02 Sheffield - Huddersfield
04.00	05.15 Sheffield - Woodhouse
04.00	04.30 Sheffield - Deepcar
04.50	05.15 SHEFFIELD - CLEETHORPES
04.50	Sheffield Victoria Pilot
05.00	Ickles trip engine
05.15	Rotherham Pilot
05.20	Holbrook Pilot
05.20	06.58 Holbrook - Grimsby
05.40	Meadow Hall Pilot
05.45	06.03 SHEFFIELD - DONCASTER
05.50	06.10 SHEFFIELD - NOTTINGHAM
05.50	06.40 Sheffield - Oughty Bridge
06.00	06.35 Sheffield - Birdwell
06.00	06.53 Broughton Lane - Langwith Junction
06.05	06.30 SHEFFIELD - LINCOLN
06.15	06.38 SHEFFIELD - BARNSLEY
06.30	Harvest Lane Pilot
06.45	07.10 SHEFFIELD - MANCHESTER
06.50	Ickles Pilot
07.00	Ballast Engine (As required)
07.15	Sheffield Victoria Pilot
07.35	Broughton Lane Pilot
07.35	08.05 SHEFFIELD - YORK
08.00	08.50 Sheffield - Wath
08.00	Meadow Hall Pilot
08.05	08.23 SHEFFIELD - PENISTONE
08.25	08.40 SHEFFIELD - MANCHESTER
08.45	10.30 Orgreaves - Lincoln
08.58	Brooughton Lane Pilot
09.10	09.35 SHEFFIELD - LEICESTER
09.10	09.48 Sheffield - Whitwell
10.05	11.30 Ecclesfield - Stanton Jcn
10.20	10.37 SHEFFIELD - LIVERPOOL
10.57	12.17 Ickles - Worksop
13.40	14.15 SHEFFIELD - CHESTERFIELD
13.40	14.05 SHEFFIELD - LEICESTER
14.55	15.10 SHEFFIELD - YORK
14.55	15.16 SHEFFIELD - DONCASTER PILOT
14.55	15.16 SHEFFIELD - HULL
15.00	Bridgehouses Pilot
15.15	15.35 SHEFFIELD - LINCOLN
15.20	15.43 SHEFFIELD - HEATH
15.55	16.30 Sheffield - Eckington (LMS engine)
16.20	16.45 SHEFFIELD - LIVERPOOL
16.30	Bernard Road Pilot
17.12	18.13 Broughton Lane - Meadow Hall
17.45	18.21 SHEFFIELD - LEICESTER
18.10	19.18 Deepcar - Sheffield
18.37	19.35 Holbrook - Attercliffe
18.45	19.30 Sheffield - Grimsby
18.45	19.25 Sheffield - Wath
20.40	21.30 Sheffield - Dringhouses (York)
20.40	21.16 Sheffield - Banbury
21.25	22.25 Broughton Lane - Guide Bridge
21.25	21.53 Sheffield - Mottram
21.45	22.09 SHEFFIELD - YORK
22.09	23.20 Broughton Lane - Annesley
22.09	23.08 Broughton Lane - Mexborough
22.30	23.00 Sheffield - Ardsley
22.50	21.30 Godley - London
23.55	00.35 Sheffield - Hull

The engine departure list for Sheffield (Neepsend) shed before the war. Interestingly most of the workings are for the Cleethorpes - Manchester route, the express workings to Marylebone being worked by throughout by Gorton and Neasden locomotives.

TRAFFIC WORKING : SHEFFIELD VICTORIA (1937)			
TRAIN	ARR	DEP	DESTINATION
		14.05	NOTTINGHAM
		14.10	HULL
12.30 LINCOLN	14.12		
		14.15	CHESTERFIELD
14.08 PENISTONE	14.36		
		14.39	BARNSLEY
13.45 DONCASTER	14.42		
11.1- ardwick		14/46	Annesley
07.40 SWANSEA	15.03	15.10	NEWCASTLE
13.18 LIVERPOOL	15.06	15.16	HULL
14.38 BARNSLEY	15.17		
12.35 LEICESTER	15.25		
14.20 MANCHESTER	15.25	15.30	MARYLEBONE
		15.30	PENISTONE
		15.35	LINCOLN
12.22 CLEETHORPES	15.36		
12.25 Barnsley Junction		15/37	Sheffield (Darnall)
		15.40	HULL
		15.43	HEATH
14.05 HULL	15.44		
10.28 Dewsnao		15/45	Staveley
12.15 MARYLEBONE	15.50	15.54	MANCHESTER
		15.57	PENISTONE
14.20 LIVERPOOL	16.16	16.21	HARWICH
15.00 YORK	16.13	16.26	SOUTHAMPTON
		16.30	CLEETHORPES
15.05 Dunford		16/41	Sheffield (Bernard Rd)
14.45 HULL	16.37	16.45	LIVERPOOL
16.20 PENISTONE	16.48		
15.50 MANCHESTER	16.57	17.02	MARYLEBONE
		17.05	NOTTINGHAM
15.25 LINCOLN	17.09		
		17.15	DONCASTER
15.08 NOTTINGHAM	17.15		
12.47 Dewsnap		17/20	Worksop
		17.30	RETFORD
14.20 CLEETHORPES	17.20	17.31	MANCHESTER
		17.35	BARNSLEY
15.52 MANCHESTER	17.35		
16.44 DONCASTER	17.37		
		17.40	PENISTONE
		17.45	RETFORD
16.57 BARNSLEY	17.48		
		17.55	CHESTERFIELD
16.30 HULL	17.55		
09.40 Neasden		17/59	Guide Bridge
16.00 LIVERPOOL	17.57	18.02	HULL
10.55 BOURNEMOUTH	17.40	18.07	NEWCASTLE
17.00 HEATH	18.00		
16.00 CLEETHORPES	18.09		
17.00 MANCHESTER	18.06	18.12	CLEETHORPES
17.00 BRADFORD	18.16	18.21	MARYLEBONE
15.20 MARYLEBONE	18.26	18.30	MANCHESTER (CENTRAL)
17.46 DONCASTER	18.42		
18.11 PENISTONE	18.38	18.44	HULL
15.00 Ashburys		18/48	Grimsby
17.57 RETFORD	18.50		
		18.55	PENISTONE
		18.55	NOTTINGHAM
15.40 Warsop Junction		19/02	Mottram
18.30 Staveley		19/16	Mottram
18.35 DONCASTER	19.23		
14.15 ashburys		19/26	Warsop Junction
19.30 Sheffield (Bridgehouses)		19/32	Grimsby
18.25 YORK	19.37	19.44	SWINDON
19.04 CHESTERFIELD	19.49		
		19.50	GAINSBOROUGH
19.18 Deepcar		19/55	Sheffield (Bernard Road)
18.31 MANCHESTER	19.58		
16.55 MARYLEBONE	20.01	20.05	MANCHESTER
		20.05	CHESTERFIELD
18.15 Worksop		20/09	Barnsley Junction
14.05 FELIXSTOWE	20.13		
18.12 Oughty Bridge		20/25	Sheffield (Bernard Road)
20.03 PENISTONE	20.30		
18.32 HULL	20.24	20.31	LIVERPOOL
		20.35	PENISTONE
18.18 NOTTINGHAM	20.45		
		20.51	HULL
19.22 MANCHESTER	20.45	20.54	LEICESTER
		21.00	DONCASTER
19.50 Ickles		21/05	Mottram
18.50 Deansgate		21/12	Colwick
17.51 NEW HOLLAND	21.18		
21.16 Sheffield (Bridgehouses)		21/18	Banbury Junction
19.15 Ardwick		21/23	Marylebone
21.30 Sheffield (Bridgehouses)		21/32	York
21.15 PENISTONE	21.41		
18.20 MARYLEBONE	21.38	21.43	BRADFORD
		21.48	BARNSLEY
18.48 CLEETHORPES	21.44	21.50	MANCHESTER
20.00 NOTTINGHAM	21.57		

The train service was, of course, in chaos with every workable engine on our books pressed into service. On one particular day I recall a GC compound Atlantic rolling into the shed in dire straits due to a severe blow in the smokebox at a time when the only engine I had in steam was a run down J50 0-6-0T which was due for shoppings. The driver of the 4-4-2 requested a fresh engine with which to work back to Grimsby and the loss of steam was such that it was hopeless to pretend that the Atlantic would get anywhere near its destination. The J50, of course, would hardly have got as far as Victoria.

On the verge of desperation, out of the blue - or white - appeared a Retford J11 which had arrived for firecleaning and coal. Taking a foreign engine off its diagram was of course forbidden but needs must when the devil drives and I sent the two engines out coupled together, the 0-6-0 acting as pilot at least as far as Retford and the last I saw of them was as they passed the shed eastbound in a blizzard. What happened when they got there I never heard nor can I recall what was done with the train the J11 was supposed to work. Anyway, I received no complaints.

Engines were not the only thing I ran short of. We had two Great Central tenders which had been fashioned into snow ploughs. They were called out at the commencement of the bad weather and that was the last I ever saw of them. By the time they got back, assuming they ever did, I had been sent on to another shed.

The weather apart, a thorn in my side was the loco coal train which would arrive unannounced in the early hours precisely when engines for important passenger trains were getting ready to leave the shed. With the loco coal on the scene the shed was completely tied up and resulted in strong complaints from the operating side about delays due to engines arriving late for their workings. Counter complaints from me that the delay was due to the traffic department blocking the shed with one of their trains - even though it had loco coal on - fell on very stony ground and eventually I hatched a plot with my friend in Darnall box, arranging for the loco coal to be held on the main line until I was ready to accept it. This produced howls of rage from the district control but resulted, eventually, in someone agreeing to hold the train back and not to enter the local area until I was happy for it to enter the shed.

One of the more colourful members of staff - in more ways than one - was a Nigerian firedropper named Albert Binney who sticks in my mind for at least two reasons. The first was that coloured immigrants were a rare sight in the country in those days, more so in Sheffield, and Albert of course had to bear a considerable amount of badinage from the footplatemen, all of which he took in good part. The second was his kindness during the severe rationing that was in force then. Albert, when he wasn't firedropping, ran a smallholding upon which he kept pigs and I was delighted when, one day, he presented me with a large piece of pork.

Another interesting man was a driver by the name of Harold Jones who occasionally acted as a deputy Running Foreman but who had been a fireman at Kings Cross before the war and had fired trains like the Leeds Pullman with firebreathing drivers such as the well known 'Slasher' Payne. Although he was an excellent deputy Foreman he had no wish to come off the footplate and after nationalisation he transferred as a driver to Millhouses shed on the Midland. I lost touch with him which was a pity as I should very much liked to have heard him discourse on the relative merits of B1s -versus - Black 5s, etc.

Although my career was going well - as mentioned I was already a class 1 whilst being barely thirty years of age - there were disadvantages about the job I was in. One of these was the relentless cycle of shifts that it was necessary to work; the worst being the twelve hour 18.00 - 06.00 on Sunday nights returning for duty at 14.00 on Monday simply so that the three of us could have a week end off every third week. Another was that you were not the captain of the ship but a chief officer whose responsibilities and interests had to be shared by others which, of course, placed severe limitations on the breadth of improvements that an individual could introduce. Thus I started looking around for a Shedmasters post so that I could run a depot of my own for which I would be fully responsible and, after what now seems a very short search, I was fortunate enough to be granted my wish.

SHED MASTER

C13 4-4-2T 67414 leaves Northwich for Manchester (Central) in 1948. Looking perhaps a little down at heel, the class at the timer had given nearly fifty years useful work which included a successful stint on the tightly timed Manchester - Liverpool CLC services at the time of the grouping - not bad for a suburban locomotive. 67414 was a Chester engine and spent most of its career on the eastern fringes of the CLC, being withdrawn from Wrexham in 1955. The last survivor of the class remained in traffic until January 1960, fifty-seven years after the first appearance of a C13.

After years of shift work and being at someone else's beck and call, I was now the master of my own kingdom. There was no advance in grade - I was still a class 1 - but the main thing was that I was now the captain of the ship. The other side of the coin was that I had been returned to the Cheshire Lines Committee - perhaps my time at Heaton Mersey had been regarded by some sort of guardian angel as a devilish apprenticeship - and thus I was prepared, to some extent, for what I found when I arrived to take control of Northwich.

The winter had yet to pass and on my way west from Sheffield I passed a number of goods trains which had been abandoned in goods loops and all but buried in snow drifts. It had been a winter without parallel, before or since, and not only had there been a record number of trains immobilised by snow but at one point matters had become so severe that a jet engine had been mounted onto a flat wagon in an - unsuccessful - attempt to clear snow. (Recollection of this experiment still causes a smile. The machine blew away the snow effectively enough - it also blew away the permanent way).

Once through Woodhead tunnel however matters seemed to be less severe and I recall seeing green grass for the first time in about three months.

Northwich lay on a different section of the CLC from that which I had previously worked on, the town being situated about half-way between Manchester (Central) and Chester (Northgate) on what was the secondary route between the two cities. Our passenger service

consisted of a series of train between the two points interspersed with a rather infrequent LNWR motor train to and from Crewe. On the goods side matters were very different since Northwich was in the heart of ICI country with its salt and chemical interests. In addition I also had control of the sub-shed at Chester Northgate which in turn had one of its engines outbased from Wrexham.

The allocation at Northwich amounted to about thirty LNER locomotives plus a further four at Northgate. These included the last two D6 4-4-0s left in service, two D9 4-4-0s (one of which was in works), one J11 0-6-0, two L3 2-6-4 tanks plus a miscellany of N5 0-6-2Ts and J10 0-6-0s. Chester had three C13 - and one C12 (ex GNR) 4-4-2 tanks. I also had charge of three old friends (Stanier 8F 2-8-0s) from Heaton Mersey which worked the limestone trains between Winnington and Tunstead on the Manchester - Derby main line of the Midland Railway. (Later on - after my time - these workings were transferred in their entirety to Northwich and the shed ended up with an allocation of twelve 2-8-0's for the Tunstead workings).

Reviewing the state of play from my office the realisation dawned that there were two ways to run a railway: It could either be done with a pencil or attacked with a spanner. I preferred the latter method whilst my predecessor had obviously done the opposite. One could hardly blame him for it since a shed's standing in the eyes of authority was based upon the percentage of engines you could declare avail-

able for traffic on the daily return. To achieve this state of grace the policy had been to have as many engines as possible at work irrespective of their mechanical condition. Of course they eventually degenerated into the running wrecks which I inherited although, on paper, everything seemed to be in good order. This suggested to me that paperwork as a pointer to performance had its weaknesses.

I decided to adopt a completely different attitude and to get my engines into good and reliable working order which at the end of the day would result in availability statistics that would be fully meaningful. To begin with I made a start with the two most severe cases on my books, a pair of Chester C13 4-4-2 tanks, one of which was confined to yard shunting because of a hot driving axlebox whilst the other, 7413, had some chronic valve ailment which resulted in two very loud exhaust beats alternating with two normal ones. I also earmarked a J10 0-6-0 which had its axlebox brasses so badly worn that it had bent its siderods. (Someone had attempted to straighten them out without attacking the problem at source and of course the rods had simply bent again on its first trip out).

The two C13s were attacked first, the one with axlebox trouble being remetalled and refitted by hand, given a spell of shunting to bed the box in and then sent out into main line traffic whilst the other had its valves removed when it was discovered that the left hand valve had had its laps worn completely away due to lack of lubrication. Fortunately the port bars were undamaged so with a pair of new valves and attention given to the lubricating mechanism I made two serviceable engines out of a pair of cripples.

The J10 was in a near terminal state and I had to send its motion and side rods to Gorton for a thorough overhaul. In the meantime we stripped the engine down, fitted new axlebox brasses and, when the rods returned from the works, had a locomotive fit for a further 20,000 miles before any further attention was needed.

I had to admit failure with one engine. The D9 4-4-0 that had been in Gorton when I took over, came back to us and immediately broke its left hand big end strap (the bolthole had been reamed out too much in the works) and smashed the cylinder casing. I simply sent it back to Gorton, a visit from which it never returned.

During these frenetic repairs nationalisation took place and it was decreed - whether in connection or not I never knew - that our two D6 4-4-0s had to go. 2106 was in good condition and I thought it a pity to let a useful engine be scrapped although its partner, 2101, I was glad to see the back of. At the same time our remaining D9 4-4-0 was posted elsewhere and as replacements for all three we were sent a trio of D10 Director 4-4-0s, engines which for many years before the war had been the mainstay of the Marylebone - Manchester expresses. These were excellent engines and handled the Chester - Manchester service with ease remaining on these turns until well after my departure from Northwich in 1950.

The three Directors concerned were 2650 Prince Henry, 2652 Edwin A. Beasley and 2655 The Earl of Kerry; the first two being fitted with Tropinoff piston valves. This type of valve was loose on its spindle and, the D10s having outside admission, the stop discs pushed them to the end of the stroke when steam was shut off. This allowed free communication between each end of the cylinder and resulted in very free coasting. When steam was applied the pressure forced the heads against their stop discs (with a distinct 'ping') and the valves then performed like conventional piston valves. This ingenious arrangement originated in Russia but was not widely adopted in this country since, in certain conditions, the valve spindle became carbonised causing the valve heads to become stuck out of position and immobilising the engine. On the Northwich turns no such troubles manifested themselves although this may be that the nature of the workings - short runs between stations - meant that the spindles did not accumulate enough deposit to give trouble. The Tropinoff engines were preferred over 2655 which had ordinary piston valves and could not coast as freely as the other two and had, as a result, a markedly higher coal consumption.

Valve and piston examination of the D10s was facilitated by removing the bogie and lifting the engine under a pair of sheer legs. On one occasion 2652 was going through this operation - which took several weeks - when, to my horror, it was noticed that the left hand main frame had a long crack in it, stretching from the front driving horn block which was also fractured.

In my mind's eye I could see the wrath of Gorton descending upon me for having had an engine out of service for so long locally only to have to send it to works for frame repairs. Questions were likely to be asked in the house.

In something of a state of shock I had the engine lowered from the sheer legs onto its bogie and whilst this was being done, noticed that the fracture had closed up so as to be invisible and it looked as though the frame was somehow holding itself together. I put the engine on our easiest diagram for a few days, during which time it was carefully watched but no trouble was experienced and subsequently proposed it for a shop visit for a casual frame repair as though it was a perfectly routine shopping proposal.

The amount of work I had put into reshaping the Northwich fleet had the result of temporarily increasing the number of engines unavailable for work, figures that had to be included in the dreaded return. Sure enough this attracted the attention of authority and shortly afterwards I received a visit from the District Superintendent in person who wanted to see for himself the reasons for our fall from statistical grace as indicated on the availability returns. I told him straight that I was not at all concerned about engines on the 'stop list' but rather with those that were running about in a

PASSENGER SERVICES (SX) : NORTHWICH (1950)		
TRAIN	TIME	DESTINATION
	06.25	MANCHESTER (07.29)
06.15 CREWE	06.43	
05.55 MANCHESTER	06.54	CHESTER (07.40)
	06.59	CREWE (07.25)
06.37 CHESTER	07.12	
	07.20	MANCHESTER (08.17)
07.45 HARTFORD	07.49	
	07.55	MANCHESTER (08.50)
07.32 CREWE	08.02	
07.17 MANCHESTER	08.11	CHESTER (08.51)
07.35 CHESTER	08.18	MANCHESTER (09.12)
	08.35	CREWE (09.02)
08.19 ALTRINGHAM	08.50	
08.15 CHESTER	08.58	MANCHESTER (09.53)
08.40 CHESTER	09.22	MANCHESTER (10.03)
08.55 MANCHESTER	09.48	
09.23 CHESTER	10.03	MANCHESTER (10.41)
	10.20	MANCHESTER (11.11)
09.48 MANCHESTER	10.42	CHESTER (11.23)
11.16 CHESTER	11.58	MANCHESTER (12.54)
11.58 MANCHESTER	12.52	CHESTER (13.34)
12.48 CHESTER	13.30	MANCHESTER (14.22)
13.40 MANCHESTER	14.31	CHESTER (15.11)
14.45 CHESTER	15.25	
	15.29	MANCHESTER (16.22)
15.45 MANCHESTER	16.39	CHESTER (17.23)
16.39 SANDBACH	16.55	
16.15 CHESTER	16.59	
	17.05	MANCHESTER (18.02)
16.31 MANCHESTER	17.13	CHESTER (17.54)
	17.15	CREWE (17.42)
16.42 MANCHESTER	17.33	
	17.49	MANCHESTER (18.41)
17.20 CHESTER	17.59	
	18.04	MANCHESTER (18.58)
17.08 MANCHESTER	18.08	CHESTER (18.50)
17.40 MANCHESTER	18.24	CHESTER (19.00)
17.55 CREWE	18.38	
	18.50	CREWE (19.21)
18.15 MANCHESTER	19.09	
18.44 CHESTER	19.25	MANCHESTER (20.23)
18.39 MANCHESTER	19.37	CHESTER (20.18)
	20.30	MANCHESTER (21.25)
20.13 MANCHESTER	21.07	
	21.12	CHESTER (21.52)
20.37 CHESTER	21.18	MANCHESTER (22.12)
21.20 CREWE	21.45	
	21.55	CREWE (22.21)
21.38 MANCHESTER	22.32	CUDDINGTON (22.43)
22.35 MANCHESTER	23.25	

Once the pride of the Great Central, the D11 4-4-0's had been displaced from the Manchester - Marylebone services after the grouping by B17 4-6-0's and were put to work on Nottingham - Sheffield, Manchester - Liverpool and Manchester - Chester stopping trains. 5502 'Zeebrugge' was one of the locomotives allocated to the Cheshire Lines around the time of nationalisation although most of its latter career was spent at Lincoln working over the Midland Railway to Derby. It was the last GCR express locomotive to remain in BR service.

Although officially withdrawn in 1941, M1 0-6-4T 6145, I resurrected it as the Gorton MPD shunter never dreaming - or intending - that it should remain on the duty for something like seventeen years. It was never, however, given a BR number.

potentially dangerous condition. Much to my surprise the Superintendent accepted my argument and I had no further trouble especially as, once the effects of my private blitz became felt, the statistics resumed their previous good level but with a more meaningful foundation.

The two Great Central L3 2-6-4 freight tanks were huge machines weighing 94 tons and were used on the I.C.I. traffic up and down the Winnington branch. Outgoing traffic started from the Exchange sidings, known as the gridiron, with a gradient of 1/53 which taxed these engines to the limit and made the frequent use of sand essential. Unfortunately the front sand-boxes were all but useless due to the fact that the operating rods had so many pins and joints in them that, after a bit of wear and tear, all motion had been lost by the time they reached the sand valves.

Someone somewhere had the bright idea of alleviating the problem of damp sand by fitting a steam supply to a pipe through the sand boxes which would keep the sand dry and the L3s were so fitted as they passed through the works. An obvious extension to this idea was to get the same steam to operate the steam sanders using spares from J10s and N5s - which had steam operated sanders - and I had no difficulty in getting the modification done locally. Whilst it worked most successfully I had to bear in mind that it was an unofficial alteration and therefore had to be removed from each locomotive when they were called up to go into Gorton for general overhaul. (The penalty for altering a locomotive without the Chief Mechanical Engineer's authority was said to be severe).

The maintenance facilities at Northwich, like most CLC sheds, were almost non-existent and it is probable that the average do-it-yourself enthusiast had as good an array of tools in his garage. The only fixed machine we had was a hand-operated pedestal drill with which we managed to carry out such jobs as boring out piston packing. The only other useful tool was a portable electric drill for which, after a pile of paperwork some six inches thick, I managed to obtain a pillar stand and thereby made routine drilling jobs a great deal easier.

Having no lathe meant that overheated axleboxes could only be dealt with by re-metalling and fettling by hand until a satisfactory bearing was obtained. Strange as it may seem in the light of the

crude machinery at our disposal very little trouble was experienced with bearings treated in this manner provided the precaution was taken of thoroughly running the engine in on shunting or similar slow work before allowing it back on its normal workings. Hot bearings were never a serious problem at Northwich, a feature I suspect was due to the habit of enginemen at the depot being very conscientious about siphoning out water from axlebox oil reservoirs.

In spite of the lack of repair facilities, Northwich occasionally performed wonders as in the case of the C13 4-4-2 tanks which gave troubles with loose motion plates, something that was probably the result of inadequate lubrication of the slide valves after the engines were superheated. When the trouble first made itself apparent, I had the engines sent to Gorton but the effectiveness of the repair hardly justified the length of time the engines were out of service so our boilermaker, Hopkins, decided to set to and do the job in the shed. Extemporising where he had to, such as using hot rivets instead of the cold that Gorton would have used, Hopkins succeeded so well that no more of these engines had to be sent away for motion plate repairs. We were able to do them ourselves.

This was not the only surprise that Hopkins produced. Our J11 0-6-0 came back from a general repair at Gorton with one of the injectors which would not work. Try as we could, we could not get it to work until Hopkins, who was a boiler maker and not a fitter, wondered if Gorton had connected it properly to the delivery clack on the boiler. His suggestion was followed up and sure enough the pipe from the injector to the combined steam valve/clack box had been incorrectly coupled up. We had to cross the pipes over (literally) to get the injector to work - it could not have been tested properly at Gorton - after which the engine ran perfectly.

After I had been at Northwich for about nine months the railways were nationalised which resulted in the CLC being allocated to the London Midland Region and the shed coming under the auspices of Trafford Park, Manchester. This was a neat arrangement from the point of view of the administrators but denied us a concentration depot where major repairs and examinations could be done with the result that I was completely at the whim of other LM districts as to when big jobs could be undertaken.

Soon after the take-over, I was visited by a head office mechanical inspector, Bill Thorley whose memoirs, incidentally, were written about twenty years ago and are well worth reading. A man very much after my own heart, he was a down to earth running shed man and there was very little disagreement between us over the way that periodic examinations should be carried out.

My time at Heaton Mersey had made me familiar with the LMS examination schedule which was basically right except that it was too rigid in its application. On the other hand the LNER schedules were not faultless, at least so far as sheds like Northwich were concerned; the mileage between valve and piston examinations of 20,000 mile for J10 and N5 engines being a complete waste of time. Big-end brasses were also set to run 20,000 miles before examination and this allowed too much wear to take place before refitting was undertaken. I had therefore to set my own system of examinations with big ends being done at about

CHESTER NORTHGATE (SX) : 1948			
TRAIN	ARR	DEP	DESTINATION
		05.15	Connahs Quay (05.40)
06.06 Connahs Quay	06.32		
		06.37	Manchester Central (08.17)
		06.45	Wrexham Central (07.49)
06.15 Wrexham Central	07.23		
		07.32	Connahs Quay (07.52)
		07.35	Manchester Central (09.12)
07.19 Connahs Quay	07.43		
05.55 Manchester Central	07.49		
		07.50	Connahs Quay (08.11)
		08.15	Manchester Central (09.53)
08.00 Connahs Quay	08.22		
		08.32	Connahs Quay (08.54)
		08.40	Manchester Central (10.03)
08.25 Connahs Quay	08.45		
07.17 Manchester Central	08.51		
08.03 Wrexham Central	09.09		
		09.23	Manchester Central (10.41)
		09.50	Connahs Quay (10.12)
10.26 Connahs Quay	10.48		
		11.16	Manchester Central (12.54)
09.48 Manchester Central	11.23		
		11.40	Connahs Quay (12.02)
12.15 Connahs Quay	12.37		
		12.48	Manchester Central (14.22)
		13.05	Buckley Junction (13.38)
11.58 Manchester Central	13.34		
13.35 Connahs Quay	13.54		
		14.02	Wrexham Central (15.00)
14.04 Buckley Junction	14.38		
		14.45	Manchester Central (16.22)
13.40 Manchester Central	15.11		
		16.00	Wrexham Central (17.01)
		16.15	Manchester Central (18.02)
16.20 Connahs Quay	16.40		
		17.10	Wrexham Central (18.13)
		17.20	Manchester Central (18.58)
15.45 Manchester Central	17.23		
16.25 Wrexham Central	17.36		
		17.45	Connahs Quay (18.04)
16.31 Manchester Central	17.54		
18.13 Connahs Quay	18.35		
17.08 Manchester Central	18.50	18.44	Manchester Central (20.23)
		19.00	Wrexham Central (20.01)
17.40 Manchester Central	19.00		
18.10 Wrexham Central	19.32		
		19.45	Connahs Quay (20.01)
18.39 Manchester Central	20.18		
20.10 Connahs Quay	20.32		
		20.37	Manchester Central (22.12)
		21.05	Wrexham Central (22.09)
21.02 Connahs Quay	21.25		
20.13 Manchester Central	21.52		
		21.45	Connahs Quay (22.04)
		22.30	Connahs Quay (22.52)
22.18 Connahs Quay	22.39		
23.05 Connahs Quay	23.21		

Who now remembers the LNER at Chester yet Northgate station remained in service until the late 1960's - one of the last blows of the Beeching axe - whilst the CLC service to Manchester continues to function from the LMS station, Chester General. 4-4-2 tanks were used on most trains although ex-works A3 Pacifics were often put onto Manchester - Northgate services as running-in turns.

It is easy to understand why manipulation of the availability figures could be the preferred option it was possible to work wonders with the minimum of equipment. The last D10 4-4-0 62653 'Sir Edward Fraser' has its bogies removed with the assistance of the very primitive apparatus available at Northwich.

10,000 miles and a complete overhaul of pistons, valves and motion at 35,000 - 40,000 miles with any worn parts being sent to the main works for refitting. Under the Somers system engines would run without trouble until called in to the works for general repair. I discovered soon after 1948 that I had unwittingly introduced a procedure that was very close to the LMS system of maintenance which, in time, became standard on BR.

The LMR influence was gradually extended. Chester CLC was detached and placed under the supervision of the LNWR shed whilst our J11 was replaced by a 4F 0-6-0 from Crewe South. Whether Crewe were trying to pull one over me by sending the worst engine on its books, I do not know, but its condition did nothing to enhance CLC/LNER opinion of the LMS and their standards of maintenance. It took Hopkins and his staff a week to clear the sludge and scale out of the firebox water-spaces after

which we discovered a badly leaking firehole ring. On discovering the latter I decided to conform to LM practice and had the engine sent to Springs Branch, Wigan, for attention. When it twice came back little better, Hopkins decided to undertake the work himself, a decision which threatened to put us on a collision course with the new authority - garage depots like Northwich did not do major jobs for themselves. Somehow I managed to persuade the powers that be to let me have the materials

A number of the original D10 Director 4-4-0's were to be found on the CLC during my time on the line. 62650/52 and 55 were under my control at Northwich whilst others were based at Brunswick and Trafford Park. 62656, one of the Merseyside engines, turns at Manchester Central in 1949 before working back to Liverpool Central.

and, up to his usual standard, Hopkins made a first class job of the repair which put an end to the trouble we had been suffering with the engine.

The Northwich initiative came in useful with one of the L3 2-6-4s which arrived back from the works with its valves so far out as to make the locomotive almost useless. I sent it back but it returned without anything seeming to have been done so I elected to overlook the instructions and do what we could ourselves. What the works had done to get the valves setting so badly wrong I had no idea but we had to pack out one of the eccentric rods to the limit of the securing studs and whilst the exhaust beats were far from right, at least I had an engine that could do some useful work.

The Northwich breakdown train was little better than the Heaton Mersey Dum Dum although its use was less frequently required. Even so I found plenty of examples of the vagaries of breakdown work such as the rerailing of a J10 0-6-0 at Mouldsworth which took about five hours whereas the rerailing of an L3 titan, derailed all wheels except the trailing bogie, was accomplished in a single pull albeit at some cost to the rerailing ramps.

Some of the incidents were of an unusual nature. An up passenger train had come to grief when the tender of its engine became derailed near Mobberley. The trouble had been caused by the left leading wheel which had shifted on its axle. As luck would have it the engine had come to a stand within a few feet of an overbridge, something I took advantage of since by moving the engine forward (rather gingerly) we were able to jack the tender up, using the bridge abutment as a fulcrum, and thrust the wheel back into position on its axle. In order to convince a sceptical authority of the cause we left just enough sign of movement as evidence of what had happened.

Another peculiar incident concerned a B7 4-6-0. A message had been received to the effect that the engine had failed at Hale on the down line with its valve events having gone wrong. This information - which was probably third hand - did not give us much of a clue as to what had happened but we made our way to the scene of the mishap and found the engine in rather a sorry state with the crankaxle having broken right up against the left leading driving wheel boss. This was a situation rather beyond our limited resources whilst to call for additional help would cause the line to be blocked for many hours. Looking at the

engine I noted that the wheel was still on the rail and that the engine had come to rest a short distance from a conveniently placed siding. I sized up the situation and instructed the crew of our breakdown engine to shunt it (carefully) into the siding, hoping - praying - that the wheel would not drop off the rail in the process. It wobbled ominously as the engine inched along but, thanks probably to the heavy Great Central side rods, the wheel kept in line with the others and the locomotive made it to safety.

It was unusual for a vehicle to become derailed because of the unsatisfactory condition of its tyres but I was called out to one such instance which involved a Black 5 4-6-0 which had a left leading tender flange so razor-sharp that it could not be relied upon to negotiate pointwork. I took another chance and sent the engine light to Crewe for repairs with instructions that it should run tender-first on the reasoning that with the defective flange trailing there was less likelihood of a derailment occurring.

At the time I was at Northwich the celebrated locomotive exchanges were being held and whilst I took no part in them directly I did enter into the spirit of the fiesta by sending a K3 2-6-0 to Crewe on a weedkilling train - probably the first time they had ever seen such an animal. The reason was that the engine which set out in the working was an LNWR 0-8-0 which managed to lose a coupled wheel spring - a commonplace problem with the class - which necessitated a change of engines. The 2-6-0 was the only substitute available and probably made a few train-spotters happy when it approached Crewe.

Although no-one complained about the K3 from Crewe (which made me wonder what sort of engines they were used to given that the Jazzers were one of the roughest-riding engines in Christendom) a similar swap when I had to substitute a J10 0-6-0 for another LMS failure caused considerable consternation at Mold Junction, Chester, and it was several days before a crew could be found who were willing to bring it back to Northwich.

Ingenuity was the basic tool of keeping steam engines on the move and one trick I used on the D10 4-4-0s proved to be especially useful. When one of the class was due for a valve and piston examination I used to arrange for it to work the diagram which finished up with the 20.13 Manchester Central - Chester Northgate, the last train of the day. The en-

gine's final duty was to run light from Chester to Northwich and upon arrival a fitter was instructed to mount the smokebox and pour a gallon of paraffin down the blastpipe. The result was that the valves were nice and easy to remove the following day.

Shortly before I left Northwich it was decided to renew the shed roof, half of each side of the building being done in turn leaving the other half as covered accommodation under which running repairs could be done. The contractor stripped the slates from the roof, dropping them into wagons shunted onto the shed road, leaving a skeleton of supporting beams which, somehow, had to be removed from the side walls. To have unshipped each beam would have been both dangerous and time-consuming and therefore we decided between ourselves to use a locomotive and pull the whole lot down in one go.

A long chain was attached at one end to a Stanier 2-8-0, the other being fixed to one of the cross beams and at a given signal the 8F gave a good tug and brought the whole lot crashing down, after which it was a simple business to saw the beams up into manageable sections. Versatile engines, the Black 8!

Northwich, like all sheds, had its human side and one of these was manifest in a number of photographs, hung in the office, displaying bygone days on the CLC. One, I recall, showed a Sacre outside framed 0-6-0 at Helsby whilst another - of more recent date - illustrated one of my predecessors at the shed who bore a striking resemblance to King George V. The likeness was so close that on more than one instance he had been mistaken for the Monarch travelling incognito.

Above all I have a special regard for Northwich shed because, in addition to it being situated in the pleasant Cheshire countryside with a good staff under me, I married and set up my first home there. My fiancee prior to our wedding had been a teacher/missionary in darkest Africa - some sort of equatorial Heaton Mersey by all accounts - and in accordance with the custom of the order had to announce our engagement formally at one of the periodic meetings of the mission elders.

"What," she was asked, "does he do for a living? A minister, perhaps, or a doctor?"

"No," replied Mrs Somers-elect, "a railwayman" and proceeded to propagate at length the fact that not everyone who worked for the railway was a ticket collector.......

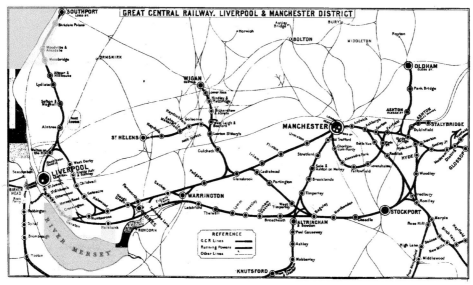

GREAT NORTHERN

The Great Central and the LNER went to lengths to describe the Sheffield - Cleethorpes trains as expresses although in reality they were stopping trains, calling at most stations on the line. Whatever they lacked in speed they made up for in motive power and stock as the above view shows as D10 4-4-0 5434 'The Earl of Kerry' pulls out of Retford with a Cleethorpes - Manchester train in 1938. The locomotive is passing over the access road to the GN loco. B1 4-6-0's took over most of these services from nationalisation.

From the relative obscurity of the CLC I moved to the East Coast line, a route very much in the public eye, taking charge of the two sheds at Retford; one serving Great Northern requirements and the other covering services on the Great Central, each shed operating in isolation of the other as though the grouping, let alone nationalisation, had never taken place.

Nowadays Retford has receded into near insignificance, the goods traffic having disappeared whilst the GN and GC routes have been separated to the extent that the casual observer would hardly credit that it was once an important cross-roads. Until the mid-1960s the GN and GC crossed on the level at the south end of the station, the up platform serving the east coast route at one end and then sweeping round at a right angle to serve the Great Central. Down GC trains ran into the down GN platform and then boxed the compass to continue running towards Sheffield. GC goods traffic avoided the station by running straight across the GN line on the level crossing at the south end of the station. A generation ago it was a

complex and highly interesting place - now even the fast line platform on the down side has been done away with.

Although Retford is recognised by the enthusiast as being a GN location, in fact the amount of traffic dealt with locally on the East Coast route was minimal and consisted of no more than two local trips which ran to Harworth colliery (Scrooby) and Ranskill plus a main line working to New England which returned to Retford via Scrooby. Passenger operations were entirely in the hands of other depots and in fact the local stations between Grantham and Doncaster, of which there were eleven, were served by two trains in the up direction and one in the down. Not for nothing was the GN contemptuously regarded as a 'green fields' railway by other systems.

The atmosphere was very different on the Great Central side where there was a relatively frequent series of trains between Sheffield/ Manchester and Lincoln or Cleethorpes together with a heavy programme of goods trains and although we provided power for a number

of GC passenger services the bulk of my responsibilities lay with freight traffic for which no less than 30 engines a day were booked off the GC shed.

The Great Northern shed was a small tidy affair situated in a tangle of lines on the down side of the GN line where the GC connection curved away towards Sheffield. It housed our six B1 4-6-0s, the last GN two-cylinder 2-8-0, then classified O3, several O2's, J39's and a solitary O4 2-8-0 which worked the 07.20 trip to Scrooby and Harworth Colliery. The shed also maintained the J3 and N5's that were outbased at Newark and which came in when required for periodic examination.

The remainder of the allocation of about 70 engines were shedded at Thrumpton, the local name for the GC shed which was located about half a mile from the GN shed on the GC line to the east of the station.

The cream of my fleet were the B1 4-6-0s of which I had six for GC passenger duties to Lincoln and Cleethorpes. At the time of my arrival it had been proposed to reduce their

In contrast to the Great Central services, only semi-fast and slow GN workings called at Retford; most trains running non-stop between Peterborough or Grantham and Doncaster. A4 4-6-2 4493 'Woodcock' approaches at speed with an up east coast express in 1938.

numbers by one; something I took exception to stating that although the sixth engine appeared to be engaged in station shunting, in fact it served an invaluable purpose as a mainline pilot, ready to take over from any ailing Pacific, something that would be out of the question with an 0-6-0T, the proposed replacement. At the end of the day I got my way which was just as well since the prospect of an express failing at Retford and having to wait for assistance to come from either Grantham or Doncaster did not bear thinking about.

A particular problem with my B1's concerned their manning since although all six engines were based at the GN shed, their workings were to Lincoln and Cleethorpes which were covered by GN and GC links respectively. This was an unsatisfactory arrangement because there were twelve sets of men divided between the two sheds whilst the engines were only allocated to one of the sheds. This resulted at times in one set of men having a different engine each day of the week, a state of affairs not conducive to careful handling of the locomotives.

I was a strong advocate of allocating engines to individual drivers and it took no breadth of vision to see that a little reorganisation would give two sets of men their own engine each. To achieve this I had to make some changes to the sanctity of the local link working but, on presenting the argument to the drivers' representatives, found sympathy for the proposal which was quickly put into effect. The results were almost magical and the time engines were stopped for out of course repairs almost disappeared as did failures in traffic. In addition the crews of the B1s took every opportunity to take pride and care in their engines, with footplates spotless and shining.

One fireman, who had had a reputation for being difficult, was so proud of the condition of his footplate that he insisted my wife came to inspect it.

Nothing would have given me greater pleasure than to have extended the scheme to freight engines but this proved to be impossible. Goods engines had, of course, to be booked off the shed on time but one could never be sure when they would get back thus it would have been impracticable to allocate engines to individual crews as I had done the B1's. I did however compromise by allocating the same engine, so far as it was possible, to the same working, day in day out, so that the drivers would have a good idea of the engine they were going to get and would stick with it for a week at a time. Whilst this made a considerable improvement to the way each engine was looked after, it also reacted upon the maintenance staff who had to abandon some of their old slipshod ways and deal with repairs promptly in order to get engines back into traffic for their nominated trains. They knew that if they didn't do a job when it was first booked, it would be waiting for them the next day - there was no way in which the engine would be swapped onto another job.

Most of the goods trains worked by the GC engines did not originate in Retford - there were only eight workings that started locally (although a great many through trains called for crew relief) - the remainder being based upon Worksop, seven miles towards Sheffield, for whom we provided motive power. Engines usually ran light from Retford to pick up their trains after which they ran to all sorts of far-flung places such as Annesley, Whitemoor and New England as well as Manchester and Cleethorpes. I think that we were probably

unique in that the shed was such a distance from the traffic centre and, with the continuous and hourly changes that were inherent in the working of coal trains, efficient communications were more essential than usual. For example at times of crew shortage an engine for a short distance working might be sent to Worksop with a set of men who had already done half a days work on another diagram. If, however, it was decided by the control to divert the train, say, to New England - a long journey which required a fresh crew - and the intention had not been communicated to the loco in good time, then all sorts of problems could arise. Where yards and engine sheds were next to each other there was a strong bond of co-operative working which did not always exist where the loco and traffic centres were separated by distance.

The late running of trip workings to and from the collieries in the Worksop district was always a headache for Retford shed. Typically an engine would leave Retford at about 06.00, run light to Worksop, take a train of empties to a colliery and return with a load of coal. It would then run light to Retford for relief before repeating the operation in the afternoon. Frequently, however, the morning trip would run so late that the afternoon crew would sign on long before their engine was likely to get back, thus a second engine had to be given to them to ensure a right time start, something that was a source of irritation to the running foremen who grieved over their dwindling supply of engines.

To alleviate the problem I made an analysis of the workings and eliminated some of the light running between Worksop and Retford, sending the crews passenger to Worksop instead. This move placed the responsibility on

O2 2-8-0 3483 winds an up goods train over the slow road and round the back of Newark (Northgate) in 24th May 1947. The number of wagons littering the sidings on both sides of the line testify to the amount of shunting that was required at even relatively small locations.

the traffic department for ensuring that the morning delays were minimised if they were not to place the afternoon leg of the workings at risk. The scheme also had the benefit of saving a great deal of light engine running and although the worst of the 1947 coal shortage was over, supplies were still a little uncertain and any saving was more than worthwhile.

In addition to the uncertainty of coal supplies there were occasions when we received fuel that was completely unsuitable. On one occasion coal used to light up a B1 turned the firebox into a retort producing no steam but with long stalactites of tar hanging down from the stays. It turned out that the fuel sent was actually gas coal.

Another wagon sent to us labelled as loco coal was found to be half full of slack and had actually been marked for consignment to colliery boilers. Although the coal was burnable I objected strongly to paying the full price for something that didn't fulfil the meaning of the act. At some point someone in authority put pressure on the locomotive department - not just Retford - to utilise coal that had been spilt in shunting yards. Most of my colleagues would not touch the stuff but I felt it might be usable in our coaling crane boiler and on some of the local trip engines. This proved to be the case and for some time I was in favour for being able to use up so much spilt coal.

The BR standard schedule for periodic examinations - which I had pre-empted at

Northwich - was already in operation when I arrived at Retford and to ensure that these examination were carried out my mechanical foreman, Harry Bills, devised a simple but effective scheme to see that the new system worked correctly. The main difficulty in keeping to a schedule of maintenance was in getting the engine into the shed at the right time. If, for example, 63608 for due in on a Thursday then it was asking for trouble if, earlier in the week, it was put onto a working which took it well beyond the limits of my local authority. Sending it, for instance, to New England, raised the possibility of the engine being taken out of diagram at Peterborough and used for a week on trips between New England and Ferme Park or Whitemoor.

Harry therefore devised a scheme whereby our engine numbers were stamped onto discs which were hung on hooks, set out for three months ahead, over a chart showing the dates and details of examinations due in that period. It therefore became simple to see at a glance which engines were going to be required over a given period and that allowed us to ensure that engines were readily to hand as their time for examination approached.

The GC/GN divide which operated on the footplate side also extended to the mechanical staff in a way that was far more difficult to resolve. Historically the GN men had worked under conditions negotiated by the National Union of Railwaymen whilst the GC had ar-

rangements agreed under what was known as the Manchester Agreement - an agreement between certain engineering unions and the Great Central Railway - the terms of which in times past had been superior to those of the NUR. By 1950, however, the positions had been reversed, with the NUR conditions being superior to those of the Great Central.

Not unnaturally discontent at the GC shed grew until it culminated in a strike which was initiated by the GC shop steward, a blacksmith. Had it not been for an element of farce this could have developed into something rather serious but as it was the withdrawal of labour only effected Sunday working which the shop-steward did not take part in anyway. When it dawned upon the rest of the staff that they were being exploited for the sake of one man's political ambitions the strike collapsed although the matter did receive sufficient publicity to encourage the Railway Executive to review the position and negotiate standard rates at national level.

In addition to the two sheds at Retford, I had three outstations, Newark, Worksop and Kirton Lindsey which all required visiting from time to time. Newark had six engines of which five were N5 0-6-2 tanks, which shunted in the local yards, plus a J3 or J6 0-6-0 that worked the 20.55 goods to Sleaford, returning at 01.00. The shunting locomotives presented something of a logistical problem since the five engines covered only three daily workings, the

Although they were never prohibited from express passenger duties, a number of incidents around the time of nationalisation raised questions as to the suitability of V2 2-6-2's being employed on Pacific duties. One of the class came to grief in a spectacular manner at Carlton on Trent when it failed on the main line with defective motion in 1951. The tortured remains of the valve gear, etc, were salvaged and placed on display. For all the misfortunes the class suffered in the late 1940's their reputation for reliability and good steaming remained untarnished and to the end many toplink drivers considered them to be the best engine ever produced at Doncaster although their employment on express passenger services diminished with the arrival of the Peppercorn A1 Pacifics.

low utilisation resulting from the fact that a boiler washout had to be done after every third day because of the poor water at Newark. Eventually the treatment chemist at Doncaster was persuaded to examine the difficulty - which was caused by foaming - and was able to provide anti-foaming compounds which cured the trouble and allowed me to reduce the allocation by one N5.

It was my practice to visit Newark on a weekly basis which, apart from anything else, got me out of the office for a day. Because of the vagaries of the train service I was unable to travel direct but had to go first to Grantham and then double back for fifteen miles. Normally this arrangement worked quite well although I got caught out one holiday time at Grantham as I stepped aboard my service for Newark. Too late I noticed that the train was

formed of odd stock and was obviously a special of some sort - and away I went non-stop to Doncaster. I never did get to Newark shed that day.

Kirton Lindsey was a very small depot, supervised by the driver in charge, with an allocation of one N5 0-6-2T, was changed by Retford as required, and used to bank goods trains up the incline to the summit tunnel.

Worksop, curiously for such a significant location, had no engines allocated to it, the depot existing as a signing-on point for a handful of footplatemen who worked shunting and some local trip duties.

An interesting responsibility of mine at Newark were the water troughs at Muskham, which allowed trains to run for long distances on the East Coast without having to stop to fill their tenders. I was aware that prior to my

appointment the troughs had been a source of trouble; complaints being received from enginemen alleging a shortage of water in the troughs which meant the risk of trains having to make an out of course stop, the delay from which raised the ire of the traffic department.

The complaints had been serious enough to warrant consideration being given to the renewal of the pipe-line from the water softener to the storage tank, a proposal that would have cost a considerable amount of money and kept the troughs out of action for some time whilst the work was being done.

As it happened, I was poking about in the float chamber underneath the storage tank one day when I noticed a curious hissing sound coming from the stop-valve in the supply pipe to the tank and it dawned on me that the valve might not be fully open. I peered more closely and sure enough the valve was partly shut, restricting the flow into the tank which in turn effected the volume of water available for the troughs themselves. I simply opened the valve to full and our troubles at Muskham were resolved without a farthing being spent.

The episode provided a prime example of the adage 'leave well alone'. In our standing orders - LPPs famous book of instructions - it was laid down that the levelling valve, which controlled the level of water in the troughs, was to be overhauled periodically. Unfortunately every time this was done at Muskham we had great difficulty in getting the valve to settle down and function correctly with the result that the troughs either received insufficient water or - as happened more often - were flooded out. After putting up with this nuisance a couple of times, I decided that once we had made a perfect adjustment, the valve would be left to function on its own and from that moment all difficulties at Muskham vanished. Indeed for the last eighteen months of my tenure at Retford, no overhauls were carried out and the troughs functioned as they were supposed to do.

The breakdown train at Retford was one stage better than that at either Heaton Mersey or Northwich but only because it had a crane. Not, be it noted, some mighty steam crane with which Pacific locomotives could be casually lifted and moved but a 15-ton hand crane which, whilst it was better than nothing, could hardly be said to be consonant with the running of the Great Northern main line and I was fortunate, not long after my arrival, to procure for myself something more appropriate when a general redistribution of cranes resulted in a 15-ton steam crane becoming spare.

Although it had been earmarked for Frodingham, I put in a bid for the thing to be sent to Retford and was successful in having it diverted. However, when it arrived I was not sure what sort of a bargain I had won since it arrived with a hot axlebox and - this is probably how I got it so easily - with a jib which could only be moved by hand and was therefore to all intents and purposes fixed.

I sent the crane to Doncaster works who modified its axleboxes so as to enable it to run at a moderate speed without overheating although the difficulty with the jib remained. To alleviate matters I had a plate fastened at the end of the jib against which the lifting pulley could rest and this allowed the jib to be raised and lowered mechanically. However, owing to the acute angle of the rope, the strain must have been considerable but I decided it was

It was during my stay at Retford that I first came into contact with the Peppercorn A1 Pacifics. They were powerful engines and able to run great distances between examinations but at times were horribly rough riding and not to be compared with a Gresley Pacific. On the other hand the relatively short tube-length in relation to the firebox area made them prodigious steamers and the A1's could raise steam in record time. They never achieved the acceptance of Gresley engines but nevertheless were the most frequently seen express passenger engine south of Doncaster and the Copley Hill allocation almost monopolised the West Riding services.

not in my interests to find out by how much. The jib came up easily and that was all that was wanted.

As it happened the crane did not see a lot of use and was not kept in steam. Perhaps, after all, it might have been of more benefit to Frodingham.

Both Retford and Newark had their fair share of main line failures to deal with, some of which were almost spectacular. It should be remembered that this was a time when we were still attempting to run engines on long turns of duty, as we had done before the war, although, as it turned out, we were not ready for such a step and the result was a high number of failures in traffic. A year or so later the problem was solved by reducing the sphere of operations by changing engines at Peterborough, Grantham or York in order to ensure that engines remained under the watchful eye of their parent depot. (This was one of the reasons that stopping trains such as the London - Grantham services more often than not had a Pacific on the front. In order to keep engines

close to their home depot it was often necessary to diagram express engines to work local trains as a balancing arrangement thus most of the humble workings which called at places such as St Neots and Biggleswade were worked by A4 Pacifics).

The V2 2-6-2s - the engine which won the war - had to shoulder more than their fair share of express passenger work in the early 1950's and I recall one of these engines coming to grief on an up express south of Tuxford after having broken its left-hand connecting rod in such a way that it went on to strip virtually all the motion on that side of an engine. The driver's report stated that everything on the left-hand side had been broken except the side rods.

The driver of another V2 reported that he had heard a loud bang as his engine took the crossover into the up platform at Retford but couldn't find anything wrong when the rain stopped in the station. I ran over and gave the engine a quick going-over and found that the right-hand leading side-rod

TRAIN WORKING : RETFORD North (BABWORTH) : 1949			
TRAIN	Up	Down	DESTINATION
19.35 Kings Cross (Pcls)		22/04	York (23.26)
19.25 Colwick		22/17	Hull (03.02)
17.10 Thirsk	22/29		New England (03.00)
21.05 York (Fish)	22/37		Kings Cross Gds (02.14)
17.30 Kings Cross Gds		22/39	York (00.14)
19.08 New England		22.41	Doncaster (23.45)
20.00 Leeds	22/55		East Goods (02.30)
17.25 COLCHESTER		22/56	EDINBURGH (05.36)
21.05 Hull	23/11		East Goods (03.23)
19.30 NEWCASTLE	23/33		KINGS CROSS (02.55)
20.20 KINGS CROSS		23/42	EDINBURGH (06.20)
00.30 Aberdeen (Fish)	23/43		Kings Cross Gds (03.15)
18.40 Kings Cross Gds		23/51	Leeds (03.47)
22.00 LEEDS	00/01		KINGS CROSS (03.55)
01.40 Aberdeen (Fish)	00/10		Kings Cross Gds (03.36)
21.40 Hull	00/21		Colwick (02.00)
20.10 Kings Cross Gds		00/24	Niddrie (11.34)
20.10 Hull (Petrol)	00/33		Colwick (02.26)
00.15 Scrooby	00/38		Retford (00.39)
22.45 Colwick		00.51	Hull (03.56)
22.15 KINGS CROSS		01/04	EDINBURGH (06.50)
19.00 Gateshead	01/06		East Goods (04.42)
00.15 Newark		01.06	Doncaster (01.40)
22.30 Ardsley	01/13		Colwick (04.57)
22.30 KINGS CROSS		01/24	EDINBURGH (07.25)
22.35 NEWCASTLE	01/32		KINGS CROSS (04.50)
02.10 Aberdeen (Fish)	01/42		Kings Cross Gds (05.55)
22.40 KINGS CROSS		01/44	BRADFORD (04.20)
15.25 Glasgow	02/00		Marylebone Gds (09.55)
21.10 Leeds	02/14		New England (06.20)
18.50 Finsbury Park		02/18	Doncaster (03.05)
19.50 EDINBURGH	02/35		KINGS CROSS (06.05)
23.30 KINGS CROSS		02/44	NEWCASTLE (06.11)
00.18 York (Pcls)	02/44		Peterborough (05.55)
00.20 Colwick		03/00	York (05.23)
01.50 LEEDS	03/10		LINCOLN (04.50)
21.28 Grantham		03.12	Doncaster (04.05)
22.00 EDINBURGH	03/21		KINGS CROSS (06.20)
21.10 Kings Cross Gds		03.30	Leeds (07.32)
02.10 Doncaster	03/35		Grantham (10.43)
20.00 DUNDEE	03/40		KINGS CROSS (06.40)
01.00 KINGS CROSS		03/47	EDINBURGH (09.40)
23.30 Kings Cross Gds		04/02	York (06.21)
01.00 Colwick		04.06	Doncaster (06.15)
18.55 ABERDEEN	04/14		KINGS CROSS (07.15)
18.30 Niddrie	04/23		Kings Cross Gds (09.38)
00.25 Kings Cross Gds		04/27	Doncaster (05.00)
22.50 Kings Cross (Pcls)		04/44	York (06.45)
02.10 High Dyke		05/02	Frodingham (08.26)
21.15 GLASGOW	05/21		COLCHESTER (11.15)
05.20 Scrooby	05/39		New England (10.05)
05.05 Doncaster	05/55		Grantham (09.30)

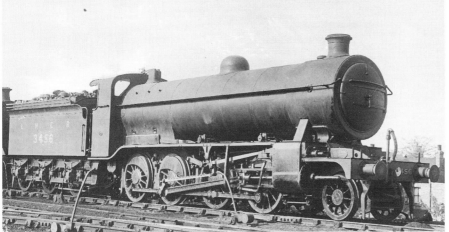

The last O3 2-8-0 (63484) was retained at Retford for reasons of litigation well after its classmates had been withdrawn. 3486 is pictured above.

One particular headache associated with Retford was the problem of providing assistance to any trains that failed on the GN mainline. There were no pilot engines between Grantham and Doncaster and a cry for help meant losing a B1 4-6-0 which had serious consequences for the booked workings from Retford. The above tables shows the number of trains at the north end of Retford (Babworth) on the night shift.

After years of Gresley elegance the postwar breed of pacifics took some getting used to and none more so than 60113, the Thompson replacement of the original Great Northern Pacific. Although powerful, it was rough riding and had an unhealthy appetite for coal. It did little work of importance, spending most of its time as a spare engine at Grantham and working the occasional stopping train to Kings Cross.

cap bolt had broken and that the cap was missing. The bang heard by the driver was the displaced side-rod catching the slide bars.

The engine had to come off its train and the easiest place for it to go was the GC shed. Unfortunately it meant traversing a very sharp left hand curve which tended to bring the rod off the crankpin. I told the driver to proceed at extreme caution whilst I walked alongside pushing the rod back into place each revolution of the driving wheel.

Another failure, unique in my experience, occurred to an A3 which was working an afternoon Leeds Central - Kings Cross express. The train had just passed through Retford at speed and was preparing to attack Gamston bank which started a couple of miles south of the station; the first bit of hard-collar work to be done since the engine had taken over at Doncaster. The A3 had recently been overhauled in Doncaster works but a superheater element, which had obviously been insufficiently expanded in the header, blew out and caused a blowback in the firebox.

The crew were lucky and escaped injury but the engine was a complete failure and had to come off the train. I managed, by opening

Visits by individuals from higher authority were not usually occasions to be relished - cupboards tended to open revealing unwanted skeletons - but on the 16 November 1951 the hierarchy from Liverpool Street HQ arrived en masse in order to open the BR social club at Retford. C.K.Bird, General Manager and a former Cambridge wrangler, is seated and is being introduced by the speaker. L.P. Parker sits on the extreme left whilst I keep a low profile, second from the right.

Muskham troughs looking south on 14th April 1960 with the connection from the down goods loop being replaced. The water tower and pump house are just visible from behind the down main home signal. The zig-zag sign is prominently placed on the up side to indicate the commencement of the troughs to firemen although the sign was situated - for the majority of trains - on the drivers side of the engine.

Thompson was very keen to extend the performance of the Great Central J11 0-6-0's and in 1942 rebuilt a number of the class with long-travel piston valves. One of the modified engines, 64450, came to Retford GC from Gorton and is seen working a local goods service in the district.

On 28th September 1952 I left Retford in style, travelling to take up my appointment as Assistant Motive Power Superintendent at Liverpool Street HQ in the Gresley beaver-tail saloon. O.S.Nock and his wife are seated on the right opposite to Sir Nigel Gresley's daughter on the left. Sir Ronald Mathews sits pensively in the rear, wondering, perhaps, what damage his protege can do to this special.

and shutting the regulator in short bursts, to get the engine out of the way in a convenient siding whilst the pilot, one of my B1 4-6-0s, took the train forward to Grantham. I remember that to ensure the express got up the bank without too much trouble I used an O2 2-8-0 to give (very vigorous) assistance in the rear until the B1 had got hold of its train. The train, incidentally, included in its formation the unique GNR quintuple restaurant car set.

Not all my troubles involved anonymous V2 and A3's. I was at Newark one day when the illustrious A4, 60022 Mallard, came to grief with injector trouble whilst working a northbound express. I had nothing better as a replacement than an old J3 0-6-0 - which was quite useless for the job - and the best I could do with it was to shunt the disabled train clear of the main line whilst waiting for assistance in the form of the Grantham Pacific pilot.

Revisionists - especially those too young to have had an involvement - are very keen to denigrate the Gresley 2-1 conjugated gear yet I have to say that in those days of difficulty I only came across one case where it caused a failure and that was on an A3 Pacific - again fresh from works - where the gear suffered a seized pin which had either been inexpertly fitted or been improperly lubricated. In my experience the conjugated gear was both sound and reliable.

New arrivals on the scene at the time were the Peppercorn A1 Pacifics and my journeying between Retford and Newark gave me my first opportunity to sample one. Used to the good riding of the Gresley engines I can still remember being far from impressed by the riding qualities of the new locomotives. They were

very powerful machines and were capable of exceptional mileage's between overhauls but the hunting due to the middle cylinder driving on the first axle had to be experienced to be believed.

It was as Shedmaster at Retford that I first came to know Alan Pegler - of Flying Scotsman fame - and his colleague Brian Hinchcliffe who was them a leading light of the Gainsborough Model Railway Club.

The club had set up an exhibition of model locomotives in some premises adjacent to Retford GC shed so, on my own initiative, I decided to add interest to the proceedings by having an engine in steam in the nearby goods yard, on which visits to the footplate were permitted. Although the footplate was generally a hallowed shrine so far as most people were concerned, we existed in an age when initiative was not always frowned upon, and considerable public relations work was done for no cost. I judged that the probability of anyone coming to harm was remote although, I have to say, had there been an accident my railway career might have ended there and then.

Alan Pegler arranged a works outing to Blackpool for his staff at the Northern Rubber Company whilst I was at Retford and, having some influence, managed to persuade the railway to let him have 60113 Great Northern - the rebuilt A3/A1 - for the train. I was invited to join the train which provided an interesting instance of an East Coast Pacific running on unusual metals. My strongest recollection is of the ascent of Copy Pit incline for which the LM provided a banker in the shape of a Crab 2-6-0. 60113 was well and truly opened out to the extent that the poor old Crab gave us as-

sistance to the tune of about one coach out of the thirteen.

I mentioned earlier that Retford housed the last remaining 03 2-8-0, the rest of the class having been withdrawn some time earlier. The reason for the survival is interesting, if not unique, and had its origins in an accident at Worksop in which a shunter had been killed. Although it had been established that he had been negligent, his widow thought otherwise and instructed her solicitors to make a case for compensation against the railway. The action took an unduly long time and, until it could be settled, the engine had to be retained in the event of it being required for the purposes of evidence. In the event the legalities dragged on to such an extent that the engine was eventually withdrawn and scrapped with an 02 being substituted in its place when the action was eventually heard.

It turned out to be rather a waste of time (and probably money). At the time of the incident the fireman had been driving and the prosecution thought that they might use this as material evidence. Unfortunately for them they made the mistake of calling the driver as their witness who - being the star turn of the Drivers Mutual Improvement Classes and an expert in rules and regulations - ran rings around their counsel and demolished the case.

Such matters included, I think that the most melancholy happening in my time at Retford was the passing of the last Ivatt Atlantic which I and my two-year old son witnessed from the down platform as it passed on its last trip in November 1950. It was the end of an era.

HEADQUARTERS

In September 1952 I was taken away from the rough and tumble of shed life and installed in the relative comfort of our headquarters at Liverpool Street (which oversaw the GE, GC and GN as far as Shaftholme Junction, north of Doncaster) as the assistant for mechanical matters. I took up the appointment in style, travelling from Retford on an RCTS special commemorating the centenary of the direct route from Peterborough to Doncaster; riding for some of the way in the beaver-tail saloon in the company of such notables as Sir Ronald Matthews and Sir Nigel Gresley's daughter, Mrs Godfrey. The well known amateur enthusiast O.S.Nock was also present. (It was during this trip that I reminded Sir Ronald of his unfortunate survey of the CLC. Thankfully he didn't hold it against me).

At Liverpool Street I was the assistant to Mr E.H. Ker who in turn was an assistant to LPP for whom, in spite of his reputation as a martinet, I was glad to be working for again. The first instruction I received from LPP was to go and ride on a Britannia so, nothing loathe, that is what I did.

I found the engines - which were in command of the Liverpool Street - Norwich services - a complete contrast to the Gresley engines with which I was familiar. The riding was harsh in the extreme and it was almost as though they had no springs. However they rode steadily without any of the unpleasant lurching that was the hallmark of the Thompson and Peppercorn Pacifics.

By this time - 1952 - the early troubles such as driving wheels shifting on their axles and carry-over of water into the cylinders had been overcome and the engines were performing well. The Great Eastern men who operated them liked them and the only complaint I can recall came from an old Norwich driver who complained that the pheasants wouldn't stay on them. One reason for their acceptance by the GE - as opposed to some other parts of BR who regarded the Britannia's with a degree of loathing - was that they were much more powerful than anything they had ever had before.

One curious phenomenon I was unable to throw any light on was the impression one of the engines gave that it was slipping at high speed. I rode on it in an attempt to locate the cause but was unable to account for the problem. Sometime later someone - probably Bill Harvey of Norwich - diagnosed the trouble as being due to an axlebox sticking in the horns.

Just before my arrival at Liverpool Street some changes had been made to the hierarchical structure, of which I had become a part, with the GC and GN motive power interests devolving to LPP - who had formerly been responsible for GE affairs only - increasing his dominion to a considerable extent. This merging of interests was due to a retirement somewhere in the chain of command rather than any empire building ambitions on LPP's part and to compensate for the extra responsibility he was given an assistant, Mr J.S. Jones, who had formerly been deputy to Mr Musgrave who, until his retirement, been LPP's opposite

number on the GN and GC. Fortunately for me, since I enjoyed working closely with LPP, he made little use of his nominated assistants - he never had - and I was able to work more or less directly under him until his retirement in 1953.

A major part of my duties was to maintain the mechanical items in LPP's book of standing orders and in particular to devise new instructions for situations which had not arisen before. An example of this arose when the

Elizabethan (09.30 Kings Cross - Edinburgh non-stop) was having to stop out of course at Berwick because of water shortage en route.

I was given the job of deciding what should be done to improve matters - the non-stop coming to a stand 50 miles short of destination was a serious matter - and I produced some theoretical calculations which demonstrated that the amount of water which could be picked up en route was insufficient to allow the engine to perform the 393 mile non-stop run. I suspected

The first order I received at Liverpool Street was 'to go and ride on a Britannia'. These engines had been introduced to the Great Eastern only a year earlier and had a revolutionary impact, especially on the Norwich services which previously had been rather a moribund affair of infrequent and slow trains headed by B1 and B17 4-6-0's with a change of engines at Ipswich. In 1953 we extended the range of the Pacifics to similarly revitalise the Cambridge line expresses. 70011 'Hotspur' of Norwich pulls away from Liverpool Street in the summer of 1956 with the 15.30 express for Sheringham and Cromer.

The B17 4-6-0's had been Gresley's response to the need for an intermediate express locomotive to operate on routes unsuitable for Pacifics. Some of them did good work on the Great Central between Marylebone and Manchester before the war but most of the class were allocated to the Great Eastern where they were joined by the GC engines after nationalisation. Not always popular with enginemen - they could be very rough riding - most of the class survived on secondary expresses in East Anglia until dieselisation although the example depicted above, 61624 'Lumley Castle' seen at the head of a Cambridge - Liverpool Street service in its final days, was withdrawn as early as March 1953.

that the standard scoop dip setting was not deep enough and set up some trials over Langley troughs, near Hitchin, to confirm my calculations.

I used A4 60028 which was fitted with a Flaman speed recorder and carefully measured the intake of water at different speeds. The results were interesting to say the least and were as follows: 50 mph : 2000 gallons, 60mph : 1500 gallons, 70 mph : 1000 gallons and - to my astonishment - 80 mph : 2000 gallons. This was not the linear result I expected by

any means and upon investigation I discovered that the pressure of water at 80 mph was such that it had bent the scoop lip down by almost an inch.

As a result of the trials and the results obtained, the standing order covering the setting of water scoops was amended to provide for an additional three-quarters of an inch of dip for locomotives working the non-stop whilst the scoops themselves were given additional strength - a light stay - to prevent distortion of the type experienced with 60028.

Having found the cause and suggested a cure, my next duty was the acid test of riding on the non-stop to see if things had improved in practice. The down trip was quite satisfactory and went well but on the up trip water problems were obscured by those of coal, the tender being filled with rather poor quality Scottish coal, a considerable quantity of which literally blew away as we turned into the teeth of an easterly gale on the coastal stretch coming down to Berwick.

We carried on as best we could but by Newark were in serious trouble for steam and Inspector Jenkins, who was with me on the footplate, decided to whistle up for a fresh engine at Grantham.

Another A4 was provided and the delay in changing engines gave us the incentive to make a high speed dash for London during which I clocked my one and only 100 mph on a steam engine. (Having done so, disaster struck - I dropped my stop watch). Given that the load was the heavy 11-coach Thompson set of 411 tons, a three figure speed was not, in my estimation, a bad effort. In the rush at Grantham I failed to notice the engine we had been given but I believe it was one of the Kylchap locomotives.

The early 1950s was a period when the steaming of the A4 Pacifics was giving some concern and suggestions were made that a series of tests be carried out with a view to effecting an improvement. The exception to the rule were the four Kylchap-fitted engines - the remaining thirty had their original single chimneys and blastpipes - and this quartet had a reputation for excellent steaming. This being

In an attempt to bring the 'A4' look to the Great Eastern, two B17 4-6-0's were given streamlined casings in September 1937 and set aside for the East Anglian service between Norwich and Liverpool Street. In spite of the war both engines retained their streamlining until 1951 when they were supplanted as the principal GE express engines by the Britannia Pacifics, although both survived in service until the Spring of 1960. 61659 'East Anglian' backs off Norwich MPD a few months before losing its casing.

The biggest motive power scheme to take place whilst I was at Liverpool Street headquarters was the electrification of my 'old' line between Sheffield and Manchester, the wealth of steam variety being replaced by only two classes of engine, the EM1 for goods traffic (above) and the EM2 (below) for passenger services. At a time when BR thoughts tended to focus on mixed traffic locomotives, it was surprising that two distinct types had to be built for the project.

the case I was not a little surprised when a letter dropped on my desk from the BR headquarters asking if we wished to have the Kylchap equipment removed. I replied, rather forcibly, to the effect that the Kylchap engines steamed excellently and that if the remainder of the class were similarly equipped, no more talk of tests need be made. Three or four years later the remaining engines were fitted with Kylchap apparatus and it is satisfying to recall that I fired one of the first shells of the battle.

In this connection I should mention the credit which has been attributed to Mr Cook for rebuilding the A3 Pacifics. In fact the A3's were not rebuilt at all and the only improvement made to them was the fitting of Kylchap blastpipes; a feature that Mr Cook was far from enthusiastic about. Indeed it was only after an A4 had run trials with GWR smokebox and blastpipe proportions and shown them to be ineffective that the Kylchap apparatus was fitted as an alternative after Mr Cook's retirement. Once the A4's had been fully dealt with, attention was turned to the A3's, where it was

Peppercorn pacifics, Britannia's and electrics notwithstanding, the cream of the fleet remained the A4 Pacifics and the pride of the line was the Elizabethan or - as it was known on the inside - the 'non-stop'. Although only a pair of trains out of thousands, its prestige and importance was sufficient to warrant the employment of a senior officer to see why the engines were failing to obtain sufficient water for the run between London and Edinburgh. 60021 'Wild Swan' approaches Peterborough with the up train in 1959. The lines on the far left are those of the Midland to Leicester via Stamford whilst those next to them become the M&GN lines to South Lynn and Yarmouth. Westwood yard can be seen to the right of the train.

found they could be similarly fitted for very little cost whilst the performance of the engines could be appreciably enhanced. Mr Cook also fitted an A1 Pacific with a middle big-end of GWR design but to no positive effect.

The middle big-ends on Pacifics of all types were still giving a lot of trouble and, for my sins, I had to read a paper on the subject to an assembly of shedmasters, setting out ways and means, as I saw it, of avoiding big-end over-

heating. Sheltering behind the protection of over forty years since the talk I have to say that most of what I said was rubbish! I mentioned careful preparation, fitting of oil-vessel corks, etc., etc., whereas in actual fact the trouble was

The influx of Britannia Pacifics to Stratford and Norwich did not result in the mass withdrawal of older locomotives since with the Pacifics came a series of workings that had not previously existed. Other services remained in the hands of prenationalisation engines with B1 and B17 4-6-0's well to the fore. B17 61659 'East Anglian', one of the two that had been streamlined by the LNER, leaves Ipswich with a Yarmouth - Liverpool Street express in September 1954 whilst B1 61043 waits with a connecting train.

Amended October 1953.
(with effect from 4.10.53)

Allocation.

REPORTING OF LOCOMOTIVE CASUALTIES

Locomotive Casualties to be reported are as follows :-

Category A.1

All cases in which a locomotive in traffic by its unsatisfactory performance :-

(a) is prevented from completing its booked working
(b) causes a loss of time or late start of 5 mins. or over to a passenger train.
(c) causes a loss of time or late start of 10 mins. or more to a freight train.

For the purpose of this section the following are not casualties :-

(1) Changing an engine at a turn round point with less than 5 mins. delay to a passenger train or 10 mins. delay to a freight train.

(2) Changing an engine in the Motive Power Depot during a diagram working resulting in less than 5 mins. delay to a passenger train or 10 mins. delay to a freight train.

(3) Changing a diagrammed engine in the Motive Power Depot before the diagrammed working is commenced, providing there is less than 5 mins. delay to a passenger train or 10 mins. to a freight train.

Category A.2

All cases of the following defects, wherever they occur, whether time was lost or not :-

Cont'd....

Although an engineer by training, LPP believed in a tight administration, the foundation of which was laid by his standing orders (of which there were many). The following pages show SO 834 which set out the procedures to be followed whenever a locomotive failed in traffic or caused delay to a train - goods as well as passenger. The inference was that engine failures were the exception and that locomotives were routinely expected to do all that the traffic department required of them. Had SO 834 still been in force during dieselisation an additional division of clerks would have been required simply to do the paperwork.

Category A.2 (Cont'd.)

    (a) Hot engine or tender axle bearings where the bearings or wheels have to be removed for repairs.

    (b) Hot big or little ends.

    (c) Fusible plug failures and serious firebox defects.

    (d) Hot crankpins, crossheads, motion pins, die blocks etc.

    (e) Fractures or any part of the engine motion, cylinders, piston valves, or pistons, or an axle, wheel centre, tyre or drawgear.

    (f) Loose or detached parts where damage is caused or repairs required which involve stopping the locomotive, and necessitating its being shewn on the Availability Return as under or awaiting depot repair for at least one day.

NOTE: If in any of these cases the delay was 5 mins. or more to a passenger train or 10 mins. or more to a freight train the Casualty then comes under Category A.1.

All Casualties are sub-divided into those arising from Mechanical or Non-Mechanical causes.

Non-Mechanical Casualties are those in Category A.1. arising from :-

    (i) Overloading   The booked load and the actual load of the train in question must be stated. You must also say whether the correct or incorrect type of locomotive was provided.

    (ii) Priming   The approximate mileage run since the last boiler washing and water change must be given. You must state whether a blow-down valve is fitted to the locomotive, and, if so, whether it was in operation.

    (iii) Weather conditions   (only applies if mechanical performance is affected, e.g. frozen

Cont'd....

(iii) Weather conditions (Contd) injectors, frozen sanding apparatus, rain and heavy wind, snow and ice conditions - delays due to the application of the special instructions in regard to the working of trains during fog or falling snow are not locomotive casualties).

(iv) Mismanagement.

(v) Inferior Coal Confirmation must be obtained from a responsible person that the engine was in good mechanical condition and that the delay was in no way due to mismanagement.

∅ (vi) Slipping The condition of the sanding gear must be stated.

∅ (vii) Short of water in tank.

∅(viii) Short of coal.

∅ These cases may be due to one or other of the foregoing but it is required for them to be shewn separately on the 4-weekly return.

Submission of Casualty Report

The responsibility for the compilation of a Casualty Report rests with the person in charge of the Depot at which the enginemen who are working the locomotive at the time of the occurrence are stationed.

Mechanical Casualties in Category A.1 must be reported to me on Form No. BR.87315, those in Category A.2 on form BR.87315/1.

Non-Mechanical Casualties should be reported to me on a non-mechanical casualty form, a specimen of which is shewn in Appendix 'A' and you must obtain direct from other depots such information as you require for this purpose.

Reporting of Mechanical Casualties

(1) A preliminary locomotive casualty report should be submitted to me as soon after the occurrence as possible after it has been definitely established that this Department is responsible for any delay which has been incurred even though the full details are not known.

Cont'd..

(2)   When all the information has been obtained a
Final Casualty Report must be submitted to me endorsed
FINAL REPORT, and the space headed "Recommendations"
should always be filled in.

(3)   If a locomotive which has become a <u>Mechanical</u>
Casualty is repaired at your depot, and if you are
not responsible for the compilation of the casualty
report, the following information should be despatched
as soon as possible to the person in charge of the
depot who is responsible for the submission of the
report.

    (a) Engine number and class.
    (b) Depot to which the engine is allocated.
    (c) Detailed description of train.
    (d) Date and time of occurrence.
    (e) Nature of Casualty.
    (f) Cause of Casualty, with full explanation.
    (g) Details of repair work performed.
    (h) Any other relevant information.

    Form BR. 87315 or BR. 87315/1 should be used for
this purpose - the relevant portion to be completed.

(4)   If you are responsible for the submission of
<u>Mechanical</u> Casualty Reports on a locomotive which is
allocated to another Depot, you should obtain from
the owning depot all the following information to
enable the casualty form to be completed.

    (a) Date of last repair in shops when the
part affected received attention and
the estimated mileage since.

    (b) Date of last 'X' examination.

    (c) Date of last daily or weekly, as the
case may be, examination and where
performed, with name, grade and staff
number of Examiner.

    (d) Date of last periodical or mileage
examination, where performed, and
estimated mileage since this examination.

    (e) Particulars of any reports against
the part responsible for the Casualty
during any of the six previous working
days together with the name, grade,
staff number and Depot of men who under-
took the work and details of work done.

Cont'd..

(f) If relevant, name and grade of oil and fuel in use to be given.

(g) If staff at fault, name, grade, staff number and Depot of men at fault to be recorded with disciplinary action taken or recommended.

Form BR.87315 or BR.87315/1 to be used - relevant portion to be completed.

(5) If a man not stationed at your depot, books off at your depot, after having been in charge of a locomotive which has become a casualty, you should send immediately to me a report (Form BR.87315 or BR.87315/1) giving as much information as possible and forward two copies to the man's home depot. The person in charge of the latter will then be responsible for carrying the report to completion.

Material for inspection

As a result of a locomotive casualty it may be necessary for the parts concerned to be forwarded to the Motive Power Superintendent or Mechanical and Electrical Engineer for inspection.

The defective parts must be labelled with a special label (BR.87317) and the following information inserted thereon :-

> Locomotive No.
> Locomotive Tender No. where tender only is affected.
> Details of Casualty
> Description of parts
> Name of depot sending the parts
> Date of despatch

Material must be suitably packed and fractures covered by tinfoil or other suitable covering.

Advice or letter must be sent, prior to despatch, to the officers concerned advising them of the material despatched.

Special Reports

If any of the following cases occur at or near your depots, whether you are responsible for the submission of the casualty form or not, you must advise me by wire or telephone immediately whether time

Cont'd..

STANDING ORDER M. 834
G. N. Re-issue June, 1958.
N.M. 55/1

is lost or not :-

(a)   Failure of fusible plugs, serious firebox defects,
        boilers short of water, serious defects in the
        regulator valves or rods.

(b)   Fracture of any part of the engine motion,
        cylinders pistons valves or pistons, or an
        axle, wheel centre, tyre or drawgear.

(c)   Big and little end and crankpin failures resulting
        in serious damage or delay.

(d)   Serious derailments which may be caused by some
        defect in the locomotive.

(e)   Major loose or detached parts, e.g. brakegear
        water pick-up gear, buffers and whistles, etc.,
        where damage is caused or repairs necessitated
        which involve stopping the locomotive.

        I shall then advise the **Line Traffic Manager and the**
Chief . Mechanical and Electrical Engineer concerned, who may
send a representative to your depot to carry out an investigation.
Such representatives must be given every facility for the inspection
of the defective locomotive or part, and full access to all
relevant documents.

                                    District Motive Power Officer.

due to the use of bronze distance pieces between the strap and rod. The bronze was simply not strong enough to withstand the pressures expected of it and tended to crush. When Mr Harrison later changed the material to steel there was an immediate improvement which, coupled with the introduction of all-whitemetal bearing surfaces by Mr Cook, brought to an end the problems associated with middle big end overheating. It is a great pity that these alterations were not made prior to the 1948 exchanges during which the performance of the A4's was spoilt by several middle big end failures.

On the GN suburban services, the longer-distance trains - those to points between Hitchin and Cambridge - were worked by L1 2-6-4 tanks or B1 4-6-0s whilst the inner suburban workings were monopolised by the N2 0-6-2 tanks which also worked 'down the hole' to Moorgate and over the High Barnet branch, both of which were shared with London Transport.

Because of these incursions the N2s had to be fitted with trip cock apparatus which applied the vacuum brake in the event of a signal being passed at danger on LT lines. Since any particular N2 could spend weeks on GN lines before finding itself on a Barnet or Moorgate working, it was necessary to check the trip cock arms at intervals to make sure they had not been knocked out of alignment and this was done at the depot and again with a lineside device, both tests confirming the depth and sideways positioning of the trip arm.

The checks were rigorously carried out yet I was puzzled to receive repeated reports concerning engines failing the test as they were about to go onto the Barnet branch at Highgate whilst no problems were being experienced on engines going to Moorgate. This was curious, to say the least, since an engine failing one test should not be able to pass the other and vice versa. In the event it transpired that the fault lay not with the N2s but with London Transport who, then as now, was really a frag-mented organisation sheltering under a collective noun. The Highgate tester had been set to accord with the restrictions of the Northern line whilst that of the Moorgate road conformed to the Metropolitan gauge and both were different; our N2 tanks being the only vehicle common to both lines. I threw the problem back into the lap of London Transport and within a short space of time the matter was rectified.

As a welcome relief from the relative modernity of Pacifics and London Transport, in 1953 Allan Pegler managed to persuade someone in power that two GN Atlantics, 990 and 251, should be released from York museum and put back into traffic in order to power some enthusiast's specials and I went to Doncaster in order to monitor matters following approval for the scheme.

No difficulty was experienced with the small boilered engine, 990, but 251 had had its superheater removed and would not steam. I ran it to Lincoln on a trial and found the position hopeless - the familiar Atlantic beat having turned into a thin 'cheff-cheff-cheff' reminiscent of a saturated N1 0-6-2T. It was obvious that too much heat from the firebox was passing through the empty superheater flue tubes - reducing the steaming capacity of the boiler - and, after struggling back to Doncaster and thinking things over, I suggested that things might be improved by inserting dummy elements in the flue tubes.

A little later the engines were run in more thoroughly on the 17.00 Kings Cross - Cambridge/Peterborough and I have to say that 251 not only sounded a good deal better but steamed satisfactorily. The two engines double-headed the train with 990 being driven by driver Hailstone and 251 by Bill Hoole, which must have been my first contact with that well known driver.

The excursion to Doncaster went off well except that on the way back 990 smashed its scoop at Werrington causing anxiety over water on the run up from Peterborough since 251 was running as a saturated engine and could not be pressed too hard.

At Kings Cross we were met by Mr W.A. Carter who was building a 5" gauge model of a GN Atlantic and wanted to fit a whistle that imitated the tone of the real thing. He had with him some sort of tuning device and the drivers of the two engines, ever obliging, gave numerous whistlings which doubtless satisfied the model-maker but caused a few shaking heads amongst the travelling public.

During my time at Liverpool Street I was not called upon to deal with any major design features although I was instrumental in suggesting remedies for one or two minor design faults which had resulted in casualties. Broken whistle pipes on the A3 Pacifics caused a number of annoying failures and it was suggested that the steam supply pipe be lengthened to allow for movement between the boiler and the cab front, where the whistle was mounted. When this suggestion was followed up by the CME it was discovered that it had been authorised some twenty years earlier but had never, presumably because of the intervening war, been implemented.

Some of the improvisations that had been made during the war caused difficulties, one in particular being the welding on of bogie axlebox keep pin heads instead of the head being integrally forged. This wartime expedient had led to a number of failures and in the end I suggested that the single long pin be re-

The view from the fireman's side of an A4 whilst passing Helpston at the foot of the climb to Stoke summit. Riding on A4's was such an everyday occurrence that I did not bother to note which engine I was riding on.

After the war outer-suburban trains from Kings Cross to Hitchin and stations on the Cambridge branch tended to be the domain of the L1 2-6-4 tanks which were hardly an improvement on the GN 4-4-0's that they replaced. Their tanks leaked like sieves and their steaming was never as good as it ought to have been. Life would have been easier if the V1 2-6-2 tanks had been retained instead.

placed by two shorter ones in order to give a driver or examiner a chance to stop trouble occurring before any damage was done.

Post-war engines were not free of problems and I had to investigate several cases of serious overheating of the left-hand Cartazzi axlebox on the new A1 Pacifics. I identified the trouble as being due to the vacuum ejector drain pipe which discharged onto the top of

Contrary to popular belief, the Harwich boat trains were the prestige trains on the Great Eastern section and sometimes seemed to be accorded far more attention than the Norwich expresses. The regular engine for the night Continental from Liverpool Street was none other than Britannia itself, 70000, which although nominally allocated to Stratford was outbased at Harwich whilst the day train usually had a B1 4-6-0. In January 1955 61005 'Bongo' passes Ingatestone with the 08.55 Liverpool Street - Parkeston Quay, running over single line working because of engineering works.

The Thompson A2 Pacifics embraced (at least) four different types of engine which included six 2-8-2 rebuilds, four V2 developments plus thirty locomotives of the basic Thompson design of which there were three varieties. All were uniformly unpopular with traincrews and were soon shunted off to the backwaters of the North Eastern or North British where the amount of damage they could inflict was likely to be minimal. Unfortunately the passenger work covered by New England was of insufficient stature to warrant Gresley or Peppercorn Pacifics and I found myself with about nine Thompson engines, three of which were P2 2-8-2 rebuilds. Most of their work involved stopping trains to and from Kings Cross although they were used on one lodging turn to Newcastle, leaving Peterborough with the down Heart of Midlothian. In the view above A2 4-6-2 60527 'Sun Chariot' waits to be taken, ex works, from Doncaster to Dundee.

the axlebox, allowing water to wash the oil out of the keep. A simple extension to the pipe cured the trouble.

Weather was not something that might be expected to influence the functioning of a steam engine but the great London smog of 1952 certainly had an effect since the peculiar conditions allowed soot to accumulate to a greater extent than normal in the valve guide of the SJ vacuum ejector on the B1 4-6-0 engines. The degree of soot prevented the valve from working and allowed an excessively high vacuum to be created which eventually resulted in the brakes failing to release after an application or engine change.

The odd man out amongst the Gresley streamliners was the W1 4-6-2-2 which started life in 1929 as a high pressure water-tube compound but was converted into a conventional three-cylinder locomotive in 1937, utilising parts from the A4 programme which was under way at the time. Known as the 'hush-hush' or 'ten thousand' the rebuild was underutilised at Kings Cross and eventually I had it transferred to Doncaster where it replaced an A3 Pacific on a trouble-prone West Riding express. 60700 is seen here backing onto the 15.50 Kings Cross - Doncaster from an angle which displays to advantage the impressive lines of the locomotive. At least one Kings Cross footplateman referred to the W1 as a 'super-A4'.

Not only was it the longest nonstop railway journey in the world but it had become an east coast institution which told the world of the pride that the system took in its showpiece. It also exemplified the dislike that LNER men had for smoke and as 60027 'Merlin' backs onto the Elizabethan at Kings Cross only the merest haze of exhaust can be seen coming from the engine. Across the road at St Pancras the 'Thames-Clyde' express would also be getting ready for its departure, its Jubilee 4-6-0 blowing off furiously and making a smoke screen that could be seen in Euston Road.

The trouble did not occur with the older Dreadnought ejectors because their relief valve was simply guided by wings on the spindle, whereas the newer SJ type was cylindrical which allowed the soot to build up. A remedy was urgent - no-one knew whether or not the smog was going to recur and in any event about the most serious problem a railway can face is

brake trouble - and I arranged to have part of the SJ ring cut away, just leaving enough to guide the valve without leaving sufficient area for soot to accumulate and cause the valve to stick.

One engine that east coast enthusiasts of the 1950s looked out for in particular was the W1 4-6-4 (or 4-6-2-2 to be precise) which

closely resembled an A4 from a distance and which had been rebuilt from the Hush-Hush water-tube compound 10000 of 1929. In spite of its appearance it had never reached the heights of fame that the other Gresley pacifics did and much of its time was spent on the 16.00 semi-fast from Kings Cross to Doncaster which was not a working that called for anything like the full potential of the locomotive. At the same time 60700 was having an easy time of things at Kings Cross, I was being assailed by problems with the 10.06 Doncaster - Kings Cross, an A3 duty which was continuously losing time because of steaming problems. I suggested that the remedy would be to transfer 60700 from Kings Cross to Doncaster and utilise it in the A3 diagram which, as it happened, returned north with the very heavy 15.50 Kings Cross - Leeds. My proposal went through and the exchange was duly effected with the result that the frequent failures on the up train due to shortage of steam became a thing of the past.

I was glad to have found some useful work for a powerful engine and indeed it gave no trouble until 1955 when it succumbed to a fractured bogie frame at Peterborough and went over onto its side. I was sent to perform an inspection and found that the bogie frame had fractured through the bolt holes where it was secured to the bogie centre. The remarkable thing was that the last piece of metal to give way was just behind the paintwork rendering prior detection almost impossible. The driver involved in the mishap paid a generous tribute to the engine, saying that until the accident he

The 0-6-2 wheel arrangement which handled the Kings Cross inner-suburban services for more than half a century was introduced in 1907 with the N1 class which - still unsuperheated - remained in service until the summer of 1959. 69477, destined to be one of the last survivors, stands on Hornsey loco in 1954. In order to reduce the weight on the driving wheels, the water tanks were cut back and compensating water space built in to the sides of the bunker at the rear of the engine. Although succeeded to some extent by the N2 0-6-2T's from 1920, the N1's proved to be hardy survivors with withdrawal taking over twelve years to complete.

It was not just the procession of Pacifics that made Kings Cross such an attractive place to work at. The sight and sound of a train coming out of the 'hole' from Moorgate was not something easily forgotten and called for considerable skills on the part of the enginemen, a fact belied by the apparent nonchalance of the driver as N2 69548 emerges from platform 16 at Kings Cross with a train from Moorgate in 1955.

was having an enjoyable ride and being paid for it!

My advice did not always find fertile soil - the route between the genesis of an idea and its implementation was littered with devils advocates, some of whom resented ideas that they themselves had not thought of - and one such concerned the two daily Cleethorpes - Kings Cross services which probably represented the two most arduous daily workings for a 4-6-0 locomotive. The booked engines were B1 4-6-0's which, whilst generally excellent locomotives, were finding the job just a little bit too much for them. My proposal was to replace them with the high pressure (225lb) B17 4-6-0's which had been fitted with type 100A (B1) boilers on the ground that the 6' 8" driving wheels and the third cylinder should give the degree of reserve needed. Unfortunately the proposal died en route to LPP's office which was a pity since, given my knowledge of the man, I suspect that LPP himself would have told me to set up some trials.

An important part of my job at Liverpool Street was to analyse the daily casualty reports which highlighted delays to trains which were attributable to alleged locomotive shortcomings. All delays of five minutes or more for a passenger train or over ten minutes with a goods had to be followed up and I perused these reports looking carefully for the sign of a trend which could be attacked before the disease became an epidemic.

The action taken varied widely and ranged from some of the measures I have already outlined to taking disciplinary action against an individual for poor workmanship. In other cases design modifications or alteration to examination routines resulted.

In the case of material failure LPP insisted that the root cause be discovered as opposed to excusing defects as being due to 'wear and tear' (as was the practice in a number of other districts).

A league table was published by the Railway Executive (forerunners of the BRB) showing miles per casualty, district by district, which was invariably headed by the Welsh Valley districts whose demands on locomotive performance were far less than those of the main

line. The object of the report was to reduce or eliminate the causes of casualties although in fact it often had the opposite effect since it encouraged districts to try and climb the league table ladder by any means possible which included finding ways to avoid reporting failures. Inter alia, the Eastern Region districts did not show up well in the league since LPP stuck to his insistence that all failures be reported so that defects could be genuinely attended to. It was very much a question of integrity versus bureaucracy.

During the mid-1950s our energies were directed towards the improvement of passenger train speeds and not only those of the long distance expresses but also the timings of more humble trains which included the Liverpool Street Jazz service. Nothing was attempted with the heavy peak-hour 10-coach trains but the introduction of the Shenfield electric service released sufficient N7 0-6-2 tanks to replace the remaining 2-4-2T's and it was thought that as a result the off-peak 'half train' services could be accelerated. Trials were carried out with the engines being worked very much harder than usual and it was shown that the existing running times could be cut quite considerably.

I cannot recall the actual times achieved but I do remember comparing them with contemporary electric services on the North London and the Southern. The Chingford service achieved faster timings than the former - which had never been noted for speed - and was almost identical with those of the Waterloo - St Margarets schedule on the Southern Region. Neither can I remember whether the accelerated timings ever appeared in print although if they did it was not for long because of the increased coal consumption, wear and tear together with attention being diverted to the plans for the extension of the electrification.

LPP turned his attention to the London, Tilbury & Southend, which had come under his jurisdiction after nationalisation, and determined to do something about the loss of locomotive availability due to poor water quality in the Southend district. (It should be remembered that the LTSR retained its LMS atmosphere right up to the end of steam in 1961 and 2-6-4 tanks of Stanier design - plus others of a similar style - held sway until the electrics took over).

The accumulation of scale on the LTSR was so rapid that the boiler tubes had to be removed every 4 - 6 months for cleaning, a costly business in every respect. The ideal solution would have been to erect lineside water softeners at a number of locations but the cost and the forthcoming electrification forced us to think of an interim alternative. In the end it was decided to implement a system based on the French TIA on which the water was treated in the locomotives themselves and which proved to be very successful.

The introduction of Polyamide into water softeners allowed softening to be reduced to zero whilst preventing the foaming which had previously carried water into the cylinders. Thus the plan met not only our expectations but gave the added bonus of reducing the incidence of priming, allowing the engines to be worked much harder than had been the case before.

The 1950s were a time of labour shortage in certain departments and the recruitment of staff for jobs such as tube cleaning became very difficult. The London Midland had similar

Whilst the crack engines were without doubt the A4 Pacifics, many drivers expressed a marginal preference for an A3, the difference being that the cabs of the older engines were less prone to swirling coal dust. However 'the' engine for most top-link men was a V2 2-6-2 and if a substitute was required for an ailing A4, few complaints were heard if the replacement was a 'Green Arrow'. When examples of the type were sent to Nine Elms during the period when the Bulleid Pacifics had to be taken out of traffic in 1953 one of the class was sent out to work the 11.00 Waterloo - Exeter 'Atlantic Coast Express' with a GN loco inspector to hand for any help that might be needed. On leaving Waterloo the SR driver started the engine very gingerly, not at all sure that the engine would get as far as Vauxhall. The GN man glared at him, indicated the regulator and told him to 'pull the thing as far as it would go and to wind the lever well back'. The Nine Elms driver shook his head saying 'It'll never take it, never, never..'. "Oh yes it will" parried the Inspector and did it for him. The engine stood upon on its legs and proceeded to straighten out every curve between South London and Salisbury. The SR driver probably drank on the story for the rest of his life - the GN inspector certainly did. 60870, on a run from Doncaster after a visit to the shops, stands at Grantham ready to take over a northbound express on August 1956.

problems and had turned its attention to a chemical replacement, introducing a preparation known as 'Xit' which was a catalyst that reduced the temperature at which soot would burn. According to the LM the optimum time to use the Xit was to sprinkle it onto the fire when an engine came onto shed after finishing its diagram. My view was that whilst this would certainly get rid of some soot, most deposits in the tubes built up when the fire was first lit. To have introduced the Xit at that stage, however, would have been ineffective since there would be no draught to take it through the tubes whilst to add it when the engine was working would be equally useless since the compound would be taken through the tubes too quickly to do any good.

I.C.I. at that time were providing briquettes for water treatment purposes and they were persuaded to make some out of the Xit, the idea being that the compound would take effect over a longer period of time than it would in its powder form. The idea was a great success, two briquettes were put into the fire when it was made up in the shed so that the compound was taking effect by the time the engine backed onto its train. Drivers used to say that an engine would run a hundred miles before making any appreciable amount of smoke whilst very little, if any, tube cleaning was necessary.

LPP retired in 1953 and died the following year. I suspect that retirement was not something he enjoyed; he was totally immersed in his work, continually striving to improve the efficiency of his department right up until the very day he retired.

LPP was succeeded in the first instance by Mr Bernard Adkinson from the BR headquarters but there was some difficulty over his ap-

The N2 0-6-2 tanks of 1920 were designed as an improved version of the N1 of 1907 and, together with the older engines, handled most of the inner suburban work until the arrival of diesels. A number of N2's - generally referred to as 'Met Tanks' - had cutdown mountings to suit the Moorgate route, an alteration which lent them a rugged 'bulldog' appearance which matched their performance. 69584 is seen at Hitchin 1959, rather off its beaten track although odd representatives of the class did have diagrammed work which included the outer suburban area. The condensing equipment is clearly visible as is the trip gear around the rear bogie.

pointment and eventually Mr E.D. Trask took over the reins.

By this time BR was giving serious thought to dieselisation on a wide scale and had started with the introduction of diesel shunting engines in marshalling yards and railcars (DMU's) for branch and suburban work. I recall the arrival of the multiple units in 1954 since they were based at Bradford and came within my perview; my responsibility being to set their periodic maintenance schedules. I cannot say I was particularly well qualified to undertake this task but I remember arguing that these units should be able to run for more than one day without having to undergo a mechanical examination - as was laid down for steam engines. I lost the day then but it is accepted practice now.

I mentioned earlier the question of Kylchap blastpipes and their fitting to the Gresley Pacifics. What I wanted was an extension of the scheme so that the invaluable V2 2-6-2's would be included; thinking especially of the New England allocation which were so often called upon to deputise for Gresley and Thompson Pacifics. Eventually two of the class, 60817 and 60963, were given double chimneys of the LMS 'Royal Scot' type which were of no value at all as an improvement. Mr Cook had been replaced by Mr Miller by that time - I had also moved on - and I met the latter informally - in the Underground at Kings Cross - and put my case as forcefully as I could. The result was that five of the class were given the Kylchap arrangement and thrived on it - one example taking over a down express at Peterborough from a failed Deltic and hauling the 11 bogies over Stoke summit at 68 mph.

9F 2-10-0 92036 on the wheeldrop at New England. A fitter is in the process of removing the engine's motion whilst another stands by to take part in the main operation. Those who maintain that the steam environment was unnecessarily dirty should look at the floor - you could eat your dinner off it.

NEW ENGLAND

New England's claim to be the most important shed on the Great Northern was based on its activities in connection with freight workings, trains leaving the goods yards at twenty minute intervals throughout the day and running to all points of the compass. Part of the marshalling complex can be seen in the view looking north from Eastfield.

In October 1955 I left the headquarters at Liverpool Street to take up my first really senior appointment, that of Assistant District Motive Power Superintendent at New England, not only the biggest depot on the Great Northern but one that had several important subsheds.

The type of engines allocated to the shed and the variety of traffic dealt with was as varied as one could wish. At the top end of the scale I had a fleet of Pacific locomotives which powered a number of workings between Peterborough and Kings Cross whilst at the bottom there were a myriad number of 0-6-0s of one sort or another for the miles of sidings which made up New England yard and the other groups of sidings in the Peterborough district. In between I had 34 'Green Arrow' 2-6-2's for express freight and parcels duties (plus express work when my A2 Pacifics were not available or up to the mark) plus over 50 heavy mineral engines - Austerity 2-8-0's - for the heavy traffic to Colwick in the north and Ferme Park in the south. (Although the 2-8-0's remained very much a part of the New England scene until the 1960s, in 1956 they were supplemented by the new 2-10-0 'Spaceship' 9F's which took over much of the Ferme Park traffic). I also had a batch of LMS Ivatt 2-6-0 'clodhopper' 4MT's for working the M&GN line to Great Yarmouth.

At the time of my joining New England the railways were just entering the zenith of post-war operation. Maintenance had recovered from the war and its aftermath and the track had been improved so as to permit high speed running once again. The LNER atmosphere was very much to the fore with very little sign of nationalisation other than the new (and excellent) 2-10-0 locomotives plus a smaller number of 350hp diesel shunters which had taken over from the Stirling/Ivatt saddle tanks in the local yards. Absent from the scene were the standard BR engines - apart from the 2-10-0's - and mainline diesels.

Of the sub sheds, Grantham was the most important and whilst it had a relatively small allocation of engines - less than 40 - most of its fleet consisted of Gresley Pacifics which took the lions share of express workings to and from Kings Cross. The remainder of its allocation, apart from shunters and branch-line engines, were O2 2-8-0's which worked the High Dyke - Frodingham iron ore services.

In those days New England was not the only shed at Peterborough, the LMS having a depot at Spital Bridge for about 45 engines, most of which were 4F 0-6-0's together with about ten 4-4-0's for passenger work across to Leicester from Peterborough East. During LMS days Spital Bridge had come under the jurisdiction of Nottingham but in 1950 it was ceded to the Eastern Region and became a subshed of New England. No dramatic changes were made to the allocation which was allowed to retain much of its LMS flavour, at least un-

The most versatile engines under tmy control were the 9F 'Spaceship' 2-10-0's intended for the Ferme Park mineral trains but capable of a great deal more as I discovered during a motive power crisis. In addition to booked requirements the district control would call out, at any time of day or night, for a special of vans (or whatever) to London and we had to dig up an engine and crew from whatever resources were available at the time. In the scene above Doncaster-based 9F 92198, one of the double-chimney representatives of the class, heads south through Peterborough North with a train of vans for Ferme Park on 2nd May 1960.

New England's principal passenger diagram was a lodging turn to Newcastle - alternating with a Heaton engine and men - working the 13.20 Kings Cross - Edinburgh 'Heart of Midlothian' between Peterborough and Newcastle, returning with the up Aberdonian. A2 Pacifics from both depots were booked to cover the duty and 60505 'Thane of Fife' - a P2 rebuild - is seen setting out from Peterborough in 1958. I suspect that the crew probably had a few loose teeth by the time the train reached Newcastle.

til 1958 when it changed hands once again and came under the control of Cambridge, which made some sort of sense given that much of the traffic handled by the shed from Peterborough East came across from the Great Eastern. My other sub-sheds were located at Stamford and Bourne, the latter closed shortly after my arrival at New England.

Enthusiasts of the time remember New England as being the shed responsible for the down 'Heart of Midlothian' (13.20 Kings Cross - Edinburgh) between Peterborough and Newcastle plus the fact that, for a short time, we also worked the northbound Flying Scotsman with our engine which went up to London with the up Aberdonian. Doubtless there were images of me sitting in regal isolation pondering for hours on length, as a Mandarim might contemplate his next days dinner, on what engines to have selected for these august caravans.

In point of fact with goods trains leaving New England every fifteen minutes of the day my time for devotion to passenger workings - and that of my staff - was minimal since much of life consisted of the treadmill of getting engines off shed - in working order - to work these goods trains to most points of the compass. We also had to be on the alert for engines that left on trains - usually in the Doncaster direction - and never came back which, if it happened too often, left us short of power and with difficulties in meeting the needs of the operating department. Now and again I would get a letter from HQ enquiring why some passenger or other had lost a couple of minutes between

Sandy and Huntingdon and such was nothing compared to the volumes of paper which arrived concerning loss of time by goods trains. It had to be taken seriously and each complaint was investigated very thoroughly.

The fast freights which ran down from London in the evening and back in the small hours more often than not called at New England to change engines, usually a V2 replacing one of the same class, and the relieving engine had to be out on the road ready to take over some time before the train arrived. The changeover was made in a spirit of urgency and the train had to off on its journey immediately. Even a minutes delay would have the place ringing with threats of reprisals by the District Control - then located at Knebworth - whilst letters calling for the most detailed investigation would follow within hours.

Such attention to delays and the heart-burning it caused in the corridors of power was irksome at times and hardwork to complete but it did at least weld us into an efficient system with a proper horror of routine delay. I do not think that any other system in the country paid such attention to detail in this respect and this showed in the rather casual atmosphere that one detected when riding on their trains. I was proud of the way we did things on the Great Northern: you could not have any sort of a decent railway without proper discipline.

Whilst great improvements had been made by this time to the mechanical side of affairs and the permanent way, considerable difficulties remained with regard to staff discipline,

which had also been eroded during the war, and much of my time was spent dealing with complaints from the Operating Superintendent about delays that were (allegedly) caused by footplate staff or locomotives that lost time on the road.

One feature which was especially annoying, because in addition to being disruptive to the train service it was costly in overtime, was the practice of drivers of empty wagon trains going north to run as slowly as possible so that the Doncaster crews on the up loaded coal trains, and with whom they should have changed footplates at some point en route, did not meet as planned requiring all sorts of ad hoc methods to be implemented by the district control in order to keep things fluid. Doncaster crews were equally guilty of the same offence and would head south as slowly as they could thus forcing the complementary New England crew to work further north than they were booked. At the end of the day both crews amassed considerably more overtime than they were entitled to and it was therefore incumbent upon me to do something about it.

At this point it is appropriate to describe, briefly, how the railway dealt with serious disciplinary matters.

We had a system which had many similarities with the military courts martial except that on BR there was no provision for legal representation. If a man was to be charged with an offence such as that described in the previous paragraph, he had to be formally advised in writing on a letter known as a 'Form

O1 2-8-0 63652 approaches Peterborough East with a train from New England to Whitemoor in 1958. Peterborough East was the point at which the Great Eastern made an end-on junction with the LNWR (to Northampton and Rugby) and the Midland (to Leicester). However there was very little direct contact between the Great Eastern and the Great Northern especially where passenger trains were concerned, trains from the Eastern Counties to the Midlands passing by, but not calling at, Peterborough North.

1'. He could then plead guilty (by admitting the offence) or - as was more usual - to reserve his defence which he would give at a disciplinary hearing. At this hearing he could be accompanied by an advocate who could either be a railwayman from the same region or, more typically, a union official who specialised in such matters.

Although hearings lacked the weight of the law, they were nevertheless conducted with similar gravity and with equal integrity. It was therefore essential for me to ensure prior to the hearing - indeed prior to the issuing of the form 1 - that I had all the proof necessary to judge the charge as being found or proven. It goes without saying that the accused and his advocate would waste no energy in defending a charge and therefore disciplinary cases had to be conducted with great care and assuredness.

Having heard the defence and considered the evidence I would then pronounce judgement and administer a punishment which could range, according to the nature of the charge and the record of the defendant, from a reprimand to dismissal and this punishment would be handed to the culprit on a written advice known as the "Form 2". This was not the end of the matter since it could then be referred to a higher level of authority for appeal although - and this was rarely understood - the appeal was not against the finding of the hearing but the severity of the sentence.

Thus with my time-losing drivers, it was not enough to have a vague appreciation of the trouble, it was necessary to have a cast iron

case which would stand up to the scrutiny of a form 1 hearing and to withstand the argument of any defence.

Most formal disciplinary cases were therefore time-consuming exercises and the one in question, especially so, since I had to be more

than usually precise about my facts. To successfully prosecute a driver for deliberately losing time I had to ensure that all other causes were eliminated. Repair cards had to be perused to ensure that the engine was in good order whilst the coal situation had to be exam-

One of my successes was in pursuing the case for the V2 2-6-2's to be fitted with Kylchap blastpipes and double-chimneys. They had always been versatile locomotives, capable of a wide variety of duties, and I pressed my case on the grounds that the modification would make a good engine better. In 1960 two engines were equipped with LMS (Royal Scot) type double chimneys and this encouraged trials with the Kylchap arrangement. Six of the class were fitted thus, most of which were based at New England for the Peterborough pilot. Unfortunately dieselisation preventing the rest of the V2's from being similarly treated. 60881 stands in Kings Cross passenger loco in the course of being transferred from Doncaster to New England.

It cannot be said, alas, that New England had much of a reputation for clean engines, especially those used on mineral and goods services. (The usual instruction given to cleaners where Austerity 2-8-0's were concerned was to wipe over the number and leave the rest of the engine...). The condition of V2 60841 and 9F 92041 as seen on the shed in 1959 is, however, rather worse than the usual state of affairs.

ined to ensure that poor fuel could not be used as a defence. The most painstaking aspect was to ensure that the train concerned had had a clear run and not been delayed by any other services whilst the control records were not always to be relied upon, especially in the case of low priority mineral trains where miscellaneous running delays could sometimes be carelessly attributed to locomotive delays.

Finally I had what I believed to be a watertight case and instituted the formal procedure against the driver concerned. The case was proven upon evidence so strong that the driver when pronounced guilty - much to his surprise - did not think it worth while trying for an appeal. I cannot recall the punishment awarded but the important thing was that it sent a message to his colleagues in the link and delays due to deliberate late running diminished considerably from that time.

Another incident concerned a driver who would not accept authority of any sort and eventually refused to obey an instruction from the operating staff at Finsbury Park; something that resulted in serious disruption to the morning rush-hour into Kings Cross and Broad Street. Scrutiny of the man's past record revealed a state of affairs so bad that I took the view that he should be taken off the footplate without delay. The procedure was once again put into motion and, finding against him, I removed him from driving duties. Gratifyingly - since higher authority had a tendency to dilute punishments on appeal - the regional headquarters agreed that my action had been appropriate and the punishment was implemented.

C12 4-4-2T 67365, the up side pilot, positions stock for a southbound 'Parliamentary' to Kings Cross in 1955.

Other than the 9F 2-10-0's BR standard engines were not often seen in the Peterborough area and those that did appear were usually replacements for the Midland 4-4-0's which worked across from Leicester. On 17 August 1963 4MT 4-6-0 75061 (Leicester) winds the 08.55 Leicester - Peterborough under the GN main line shortly before running into the East station.

The result was dramatic. The individual concerned changed overnight from using threatening and abusive language to everyone in authority and became instead a cringing, tearful and rather pitiable mortal who spent the rest of his time on shed duties and well clear of the main line, which suited my purposes to the letter.

Not all staff troubles were appropriate to the full disciplinary procedure which, if used irresponsibly, could provoke industrial action. One particular problem, the details of which I have forgotten, brought to light a curious attitude amongst some drivers in relation to coal consumption. I questioned one driver who had lost time with a heavy train who defended himself by saying that if he had worked his engine so as to keep time he would have used up too much coal. Whether he was under the impression the cost of the stuff was in some mysterious way deducted from his wage or whether he felt some empathy with his fireman's back, I do not know but I remember letting him off with a flea in his ear, reminding him that a lot more coal had been wasted by other trains which had been standing, blowing off, in loops, waiting for him to go by.

The Peterborough district was blessed with three excellent locomotive inspectors - Messrs Dolby, Gilbert and Buxton. Of these, the last carried on the local tradition by transferring to the Nene Valley Railway upon his retirement. All three were thoroughly keen on good timekeeping and had no hesitation in speaking forthrightly to drivers or firemen if they thought that the best was not being done.

On one occasion Inspector Dolby was riding with a senior Grantham driver who had been given a V2 instead of his favourite A1 4-6-2. He complained to Dolby that the engine would not time the train. Dolby's retort (of course it won't, if you don't make it) was sufficient to sting the driver into a right time arrival at Kings Cross. (The driver's attitude on taking the V2 was distinctly unusual since most top link men were more than happy to take a Green Arrow as an alternative to anything - even an A4).

Inspector Gilbert was another expert at encouraging drivers to run at high speeds in order to recover lost time and was able to demonstrate this talent to good effect during the brief period that New England had the honour of working the ten o'clock (Flying Scotsman) between Kings Cross and Grantham.

The Suez crisis of February 1957 brought fears of petrol rationing and to ease matters at New England the 350hp diesel shunters were replaced for a time by J52 0-6-0T's. 68840 is prepared for a spell in the yards.

When the A4 Pacifics blew off it was like a bomb exploding and could be painful to the ears. The pop valves lifted suddenly at 250lbs but did not close until the boiler pressure had dropped well below the red line. To alleviate the problem I instructed my depots - and Grantham in particular - to pour cylinder oil over the safety valves on each engine's wash-out day - as was the practice with model steam engines. This ensured that the valves then closed as soon as the pressure had fallen under the blowing off point and prevented considerable waste. The valves lift on A4 60025 'Falcon' as it eases off for Peterborough with an up east coast express in 1959.

The diagram was unusual in that a New England A2 worked the up Aberdonian (05.43 ex Peterborough) sleeping car train to London, took the 10.00 Edinburgh as far as Grantham and returned light to New England. The reason for this curious and rather uneconomic working was obscure - it did not last long - although it did demonstrate that sheds other than Kings Cross and Grantham were capable of working the Flying Scotsman.

It was customary to use one of the best Thompson A2's on this turn but for some reason on this particular day none were available and rebuilt P2 60505 'Thane of Fife' had to be used instead.

Things started to go seriously wrong on the return from London, 60505 managing to slip to a stand on the bank at Belle Isle and being unable to restart the train. Eventually an N2 0-6-2T gave assistance in the rear and the train was restarted about ten minutes behind time.

Gilbert happened to be on board and as soon as 60505 was on its way again he issued the command - right time Grantham - later amending it to a challenge - right time passing Peterborough. Neither 60505 or its driver

failed the test and went like the clappers. Huntingdon was passed at 70 mph - after easing for the Offord restriction - and the cut-off gradually advanced on the climb to Abbots Ripton with the result that the summit was cleared with no reduction in speed. In the event Peterborough was passed only one minute to the bad whilst the train reach Grantham punctually in a net time that cannot have been much short of mile-a-minute.

Inspector Buxton brought his expertise to the notice of enthusiasts many years after my time at New England when a GWR Castle 4-6-0 was brought over for a special to York. Under his direction the firing of hard coal was managed so skilfully - and this in the days of diesels - that the engine was able to put up an excellent performance, especially in the ascent of Stoke. I imagine that his talents were especially welcomed by the Nene Valley Railway.

Occasionally the focus of my attention veered away from the Great Northern onto the foreign lines under my control and one train that bothered me for some time was the 06.58 from Peterborough East to Rugby which took a number of bogie vans on top of its passenger formation and loaded to about 400 tons which the LMS loading book claimed was within the capability of the Spital Bridge 4F 0-6-0 booked to the turn.

Time, however, was lost hand over fist whenever the load approached anything like 400 tons and I therefore arranged a test train of that weight, riding with the engine to see what happened. By the time we reached Nassington bank it was painfully obvious that time could not be kept with a 4F which could get up to about 50 mph on level track but slowed to a crawl at the first sign of an incline.

My conclusion was that an extra 20 minutes would have to be inserted in the 4F running times or else a class 5 should be used when the load reached 400 tons.

A small world...In 1957 the C12 4-4-2T's which had shunted the North station for years were replaced by Great Central N5 0-6-2 tanks, one of which was 69293 (above) which I had had charge of during my time at Northwich.

In the early 1960's some redundant N2 0-6-2T's were transferred to New England to replace the N5 engines on the station pilot workings. These turned out to be the last steam engines used for this task. 69580 shunts stock at the north end of the station in 1961.

Eventually some of the 4F and 2P engines were changed for J39 and D16s which brought a howl of protest from the Spital Bridge drivers. One consistent complaint was that the brakes on the Clauds (D16 4-4-0s) were very weak but, having been brought up on the Great Eastern and being familiar with the Westinghouse brake on the D16's, I soon found that the trouble was due to the air reservoirs not being drained of water, something a Great Eastern man always attended to before leaving the shed.

Another type of engine which was highly unpopular at Spital Bridge was the C12 4-4-2 tank, one or two of which were allocated for light passenger and carriage shunting work.

It was one of these C12 engines that gave us rather a spectacular morning's work at Spital

For years the station pilots at Peterborough had been Great Northern C12 4-4-2T's, New England remaining a stronghold of the class until their withdrawal in 1958. Two of the class were generally on continuous duty at the North station, one dealing with up traffic and the other with trains at the down and excursion platforms. 67365 is seen as the up side pilot at Peterborough North in April 1955.

VALVE SETTING.

At every valve and piston examination the setting of the valves must be checked by the following method :-

PISTON VALVES.

(a) Preliminary.

Examine the axlebox wedges and adjust if necessary. Examine Examine the valve gear pins, bushes and die blocks for excessive wear; examine the valve gear motion for defects. Remove the valves, clean and examine, fit new rings. Clean and examine the steam chest liners; check that movement has not taken place, clean the ports.

(b) Mark the Relative Positions of the Steam Cut-Off Edges on the Valve Spindle.

From the front end of the steam chest insert the front port trammel gauge against the steam cut-off edge of the front port. Place the straight edge across the front steam chest face and scribe a mark across the trammel gauge (Diagram No.1).

Repeat this operation with the back port trammel gauge which should be placed against the steam cut-off edge of the back port. (Diagram No. 2).

With the valves removed from the steam chest, place the front port trammel gauge in the same direction along the valves, with the stop in line with the front valve steam admission ring (or the head if the valve is head controlled). With inside admission it is necessary to use the Stop Guide in order to line up with the correct edge of the ring. Adjust the sliding valve spindle bush until it is square by the line on the trammel gauge and scribe the valve spindle. (Diagram No. 3).

Cont'd......

All you need to know about valve setting on LNER locomotives....... The following pages show L.P. Parker's Standing Order 300 concerning the instructions to be followed for setting valves on engines fitted with the Gresley conjugated gear and Walschaerts motion.

Repeat this operation for the back port trammel gauge.
(Diagram No.4). The marks on the front valve spindle
shew the distance from the front and back steam cut off
edges to the front steam chest cover straight edge.

Check that the distance between the two scribe marks on the
spindle is equal to twice the steam lap.

Replace the valves with the front port edge mark on the
valve spindle in line with the steam chest straight edge.
Mark the back valve spindle with a standard length bent
trammel from the centre pop in the cylinder casting. In
a similar manner mark the back valve spindle again, with
the back port edge mark on the spindle in line with the
steam chest straight edge (Diagram No.5).

(c). Check the Cut Off Position Indicator Plate

Place the reversing lever in the indicated mid-gear
position; and remove the eccentric rod pin from the foot
of the radius link. Swing the radius link backwards,
and forwards by hand and observe whether there is any
movement of the radius rod. If movement is observed the
reversing lever must be altered until the movement is
eliminated, and either the pointer on the reversing lever or
the indicator plate must be adjusted accordingly.

(d) Obtain the Maximum Port Openings.

Couple up the valves, and with the reversing lever in 25%
Cut Off move the engine forwards through one revolution
either by means of pinch bars, or revolve the wheels by
electric jigger where this is provided. Scribe the back
valve spindle with the standard length bent trammel until
the port opening reaches its maximum. Care must be taken
to move the engines always in one direction when the
scribing is done. Repeat for each valve, and check for
port opening in the reverse direction of running.

(e) Check the Readings Obtained

Transfer the measurements obtained to a marking plate and
check them for equal opening, taking into consideration the
allowances for expansion given in the table.
Adjust the effective length of the appropriate eccentric
rod or valve spindle where necessary.

/cont'd......

SLIDE VALVES.

(a) Preliminary Examination

Examine the axlebox wedges and adjust if necessary. Examine
the valve gear pins, bushes and die blocks for excessive wear;
examine the valve gear motion for defects. Remove the valve;
clean and examine, renew when necessary Clean and examine the
steam chest faces and ports.

(b) Mark the Relative Positions of the Steam Cut Off Edges on
the Valve Spindle.

Measure the distance between the steam cut off edge of the
front port bar, and the steam cut off edge of the back port
bar. Determine the total valve lap by substracting this
measurement from the total length of the valve.

Replace the valve in the steam chest with the front port just
opening to steam, proving with a .002" feeler gauge. Check
that the edge of the valve is parallel to the port bar.

With the valve in this position, the back valve spindle must
be scribed with the standard length bent trammel from the
centre pop in the cylinder casting.

Move the valve in the appropriate direction a distance equal
to the total lap of the valve; and again scribe the back
valve spindle with the trammel.

In a similar manner as described for Piston Valves :-

(c) Check the Cut Off position indicator plate.

(d) Obtain the maximum port openings.

(e) Check the readings obtained.

ALLOWANCE TO BE MADE FOR EXPANSION ON PORT OPENINGS.
For locomotives not fitted with Gresley 2 : 1 Valve Gear

Outside admission

Front port 1/16" bare more than the back port.

Inside admission

Back Port 1/16" bare more than the front.
(N.B. No expansion allowance should be given to the inside
cylinder valve of A. 1 Class locomotives).

For locomotives with Gresley 2 : 1 Valve Gear (2 : 1
lever at the back of the cylinders.

Unlike the Midland which diagrammed Class 5 engines to some of its best workings, the GN was so well provided with class 7 and 8 locomotives that the sight of B1 4-6-0's on top link workings was unusual and only two daily express services in and out of Kings Cross were worked by them. These were the pair of through workings based on Cleethorpes and travelled via the East Lincs which was restricted to Pacifics. Otherwise the B1's were only to be found on outer-suburban trains to Cambridge and the occasional 'Parli' to Peterborough although the class were well in evidence on some of the night goods services from Kings Cross. The North Eastern were similarly well stocked with Pacifics and 61338 finds itself on a rather humble, albeit well loaded, goods between York and Scarborough in 1958.

An A3, newly fitted with a Kylchap blastpipe and double chimney heads north over Digswell viaduct between Welwyn Garden City and Welwyn North. This section of track was a two line bottleneck and much of the East Coast goods service, especially the New England - Ferme Park mineral trains, were routed over the 'new line' via Hertford North. The viaduct was very nearly the scene of an unpleasant incident in 1956 when an up express came to a stand on it during dense fog. The guard, thinking the train was in Welwyn North, walked along the parapet top to find out from the engine crew why they had stopped. When the fireman told him what he had done they had to carry him, a nervous wreck, back to London on the engine.

Outside valves, back port 1/16" more than front port.

Inside valves, back port 5/64" more than front port.

Gresley 2 : 1 Valve Gear (2 : 1 lever at the front of the cylinders)

Outside Valves, back port 1/16" more than front port.

Inside Valves, front port 11/64" more than back port.

Auj 7/4626 of 5.2.51

CHECK THE VALVE SETTING FOR EQUAL LEAD

The valves must be tried for the correct lead should any of the valve motion be repaired or renewed, or if in the event of the port openings being correct, the valve setting is still unsatisfactory.

Obtain Dead Centres.

Set the crank slightly above the dead centre, and with a straight-edge scribe a mark from the edge of the crosshead across the slide bar.

With the trammel from the pop mark in the frame or running plate, scribe a line on the outside face of the tyre in approximately a horizontal position.

Move the engine over the centre until the crosshead has reversed its movement, and again coincides with the mark on the slide bar.

Scribe another mark on the tyre with the trammel from the pop mark when the engine is in this position.

Bisect the distance between the two trammel marks on the tyre and move the engine so that the point of the bisection is exactly the length of the trammel from the pop mark. Care must be taken to move the engine in only one direction whilst the trammelling is being done.

Repeat the operation for the other dead centres.

Mark the Lead Positions on the Valve Spindle

With the engine set on the respective dead centre and the reversing lever in the full forward position, mark the back valve spindle from the pop mark in the cylinder casting with the port opening standard bent trammel; the distance between this mark and the adjacent steam cut off edge mark being the lead of the valve for this position.

For all valve gears these operations should be repeated for the front and back centres for each cylinder, and the leads

/cont'd.......

checked

checked for being equal. For Walschearts and other Radial
valve gears the reversing lever must be moved by stages
from fore gear to back gear, and by the use of the trammel it
should be ascertained whether there is any variation in the
lead.

Should the leads be unequal the defects must be reported
corrections at the Main Works.

District Motive Power Superintendent,

Much of the work formerly by the K3 'Jazzers' 2-6-0's was usurped by the Gresley V2 2-6-2's although the smaller engines survived until the end of steam. They were not especially popular with their crews, being notoriously rough riding but nevertheless continued to perform useful work on secondary goods trains until the arrival of diesels in the early 1960's. 61835 in need of a good clean beside the old coal stage at New England, 7th July 1960.

Double-chimney 9F 2-10-0 92168 leaves New England loco to work a mineral train to Ferme Park in 1958. On average a train left New England about every twenty minutes, day or night.

Bridge when it was backed just a little bit too finely towards the turntable pit - like most Midland sheds it was a roundhouse - and fell in. By great good fortune its driving wheels remained just on the track and I was able to arrange for a hawser to be attached to the front coupling, the engine being hauled back onto the track with an LMS 8F 2-8-0 whilst fitting staff packed and jacked the C12 as it was slowly drawn up. The time taken to rerail the engine - 100 minutes - was probably a record for such an incident but it has to be said had the engine gone an inch or two further and dropped its driving wheels into the pit, we should have been there all day whilst the turntable, which had housed a B1 4-6-0 whilst the fun was going on, could have been put out of action for some time.

By the mid-1950's there was little LNER influence evident in the mineral workings between Peterborough and London and trains were normally in the hands of either 9F 2-10-0's or Austerity 2-8-0's, although in 1956 a Stanier 8F 2-8-0 was tried out for a short time on the Tempsford coal trains. Austerity 90246 of New England pulls out of the yard with a Ferme Park mineral train in 1958.

Mineral trains from New England to the north - many of which ran via the joint line - were generally worked by older locomotives than those engaged in the New England - Ferme Park services. Great Central O4 2-8-0 63870 of Langwith Junction stands on the wet ashpit before returning home with a New England - Mansfield train.

Another complete recovery achieved in record time occurred at March, shortly after I had moved from Peterborough to Kings Cross. The driver of an O2 2-8-0 had dropped off the footplate at Twentyfoot drain, near March, to change some handpoints, his engine trundling slowly along. For some reason he failed to catch up with the 2-8-0 which then cheerfully ran through the trap points, became completely derailed and all but turned upside down. Although no longer attached to New England I was the only senior officer in the vicinity qualified to accompany the Peterborough 45-ton crane and so I was called out to attend the mishap.

There isn't much to cheer about when dealing with an inverted 2-8-0 but one blessing was the fact that it was a Sunday morning and we had the line to ourselves. When I arrived from Peterborough I was pleased to see that the local March gang had parted the engine from its tender and I had no difficulty in picking the tender up and dropping it onto the track.

By the time this had been done, the Norwich gang had arrived with their 36-ton crane to give assistance in rerailing the engine. Before lifting could commence, however, we had to dig two channels under the O2 so that heavy chains could be passed underneath the boiler, and this was one of the most trying parts of the operation since the bone-dry ashes forming the embankment kept falling in.

Both cranes held the engine whilst men were working underneath but I decided it would be safest to roll the engine upright using the 45-ton crane on its own. Having manoeuvred into position and connected the lifting hook to the chains, we started - carefully - to roll the engine over by winding in on the jib. It took all the crane wanted but nothing went wrong and soon we had the engine upright.

The Norwich crane was then attached to the cab end and we moved the New England crane to take hold of the front buffer beam, after which it was a simple matter to drop the engine back on the running line. The worst of the job came from the strong wind which carried in clouds of dust - I had to bath twice upon arriving home - but notwithstanding this the time from arrival to rerailing was only four hours and forty minutes.

Probably the most significant motive power change on the GN during the 1950s - or at least the latter half - was the fitting of Kylchap blastpipes to the A4 and A3 Pacifics. The improvement in performance, however, was not

Coming up for a half-century and still in steam, Great Northern J6 0-6-0 stands on New England MPD on 7th July 1960. These engines worked local trips to Huntingdon in the south and Boston in the north together with a good deal of transfer work between the GN and GE yards in the Peterborough area.

By the early 1960's sufficient diesels had been received to see steam engines performing tasks that would have been unthinkable a year or so earlier. On 8th August 1961 V2 60871 of New England was turned out for a Ferme Park working and is seen passing Crescent Junction on its way back to New England with a train of mineral empties.

without its price and we suffered a considerable increase in the number of reported injector failures with these engines. This was simply because the engines were working harder and more water had to be fed to the boiler at the full 220/250lb pressure.

My chief became quite concerned about this and I teased him a little when he asked me what was wrong with our injectors and I replied "nothing". He went on to say, quite correctly, that most injector trouble could be traced to the water supply and I then explained the root of the problem. There was nothing wrong with the injectors, they were simply starved of water.

After making sure that the strainers were not blocked, the first place I looked was at the feed-cocks on the tender and discovered, to my surprise, that they were as originally fitted to the engines when they had 180lb boilers. In

addition to this many of the engines had had the tapered plug ground in so many times that they had dropped down in the body, partially blocking the waterway.

Whilst carrying out these inspections I also noticed that the hole through the body of the cock and plug could be opened out considerably yet still allowing the cock to fully close. The cocks were therefore opened out on all the A3s in the district after which there was a considerable decline in the number of injector failures. No attention of this sort was required on the V2 class since they had a different type of cock fitted to their 4200 gallon tenders.

Because of its position just over an hour out of London and because we provided emergency passenger pilots, it was natural that New England should have to deal with an abnormal number of mainline casualties and, of these, a number concerned A4 and A3 Pacifics which had failed with overheated right-hand driving axleboxes. (The reason for the right-hand box giving more trouble than the left was never satisfactorily explained but my theory was that the 2-1 gear put slightly more stress on the right-hand side of the engine and thus it was that box which gave way first). These were remetalled and refitted at New England but I noticed that they seldom lasted very long before running hot again. This, and the fact that heating seldom occurred before the engine had run 40,000 miles since coming out of the shops, suggested to me that the trouble was caused by something other than a failure of the lubricating system.

Once an axlebox had run hot all evidence of heating prior to the problem was destroyed

Down goods trains normally avoided the North station by running over the goods lines which separated the GN from the Midland. Occasional trips which were light enough to be whipped through the passenger lines without the danger of delay to other services were sometimes routed through the station as is the case with J6 0-6-0 64210 which hurries through Peterborough North with a trip working from Holme to New England in 1955.

The machine shop at New England.

and so, on the basis that the condition of the left and right could not be so very different from each other, I decided to strip down the left-hand box of the first convenient A3 that failed and was horrified to find that the bearing inside the axlebox was so badly worn as to taper from .13" oversize at the wheel-boss to .38" at the inner edge. No wonder our repairs did not last long; the wracking of the axle in the badly worn left-hand box adding to the conditions which produced the trouble in the first place.

Having made this discovery, the practice was adopted of refitting both axleboxes when dealing with Pacific or V2 failures and this produced some improvement in the length of time that the bearings would run after attention. However unless the boxes were renewed at about 40,000 miles as was done with the Kings Cross A4s, overheating was always liable to occur.

Much has been written about the optical alignment of mainframes introduced at Doncaster by Mr Cooke in the mid-1950s although my experience was such as to make me something of a sceptic. Instead of improving matters, we suffered from a spate of overheating from coupled axleboxes on engines fresh from the shops because the tolerances insisted upon were too tight for the Gresley Pacifics. Adjustments were eventually made but in my view insufficient account was taken of the distortion to mainframes when the engines were rounding sharp curves. The length of the Pacifics did of course tend to make them an extreme case.

Although I had a job which many enthusiasts would have given ten years of their lives to have done for a week, the opportunity to go down in history did not happen on a daily basis. It did however present itself one summer when I ran up against an extreme shortage of V2 2-6-2s intended for the fast freights between Peterborough and Kings Cross but used for many of the special passenger trains required at that time of year. Under-utilised was the ample allocation of 9F 2-10-0's which had been sent to the depot for the working of the heavy coal trains to Ferme Park and though they spent most of their time creeping up to London at about 25 mph I saw no reason why they could not be used on something more exciting. They were, after all, excellently designed, modern locomotives and I saw no reason why they should not run at speeds of up to 60 mph.

The first trip with a 'Spaceship' on a fitted freight produced a cry of horror from the district control who thought that a mineral engine could not possibly time an express goods. I thought otherwise and the 9F performed the working with ease, bringing our power crisis to an end. Thus began the use of 9F engines on fast services; a period which culminated in

The first one. Silver Link at Grantham in 1950 during the six years it was allocated to that shed. In May 1950 the engine was transferred to Kings Cross where it remained until being withdrawn at the end of 1962.

Connections between the GN and the Great Eastern were few and far between although the few that did operate usually generated some interesting motive power. D16 4-4-0 62605 of March draws its stock into the up main platform at Peterborough North prior to departing with a Cambridge service in 1955.

their being used in the haulage of express passenger trains, something I should not have been quite so happy about.

Peter Townend, shedmaster at Kings Cross, has pointed out in his book 'Top Shed' how relatively trouble-free the Peppercorn A1 Pacifics were and in fact their only fault lay in their poor riding qualities.

However there were a few machines which, for some reason, were equipped with a French design of axlebox which fitted right round the axle by being divided vertically. These wretched engines seemed doomed to run hot at Peterborough although occasionally one would get through to Kings Cross and fail there instead.

We had a dreadful job dealing with hotboxes on these engines, having to get a bearing right round the axle and then to hold it in position whilst raising the wheels into the horns on the wheel drop. Once the thing had been put together I then arranged to have it returned to the North Eastern on the slowest goods train I could find, only to have the engine back, hot, a few weeks later. The experiment must have been a costly failure as their final mileage was well below that of the rest of the class. In the end the volume of complaints caused the CM&EE to alter them to the standard design.

Whilst rough to ride on, the A1's were exceptionally good steamers and it therefore came as a surprise to find one at New England shed which had been replaced by the pilot because of shortage of steam. It did not take long to diagnose the fault since the uptakes from the Kylchap were almost blocked with carbon deposits due to defective lubrication. It was not

an ER locomotive but one from north of the Don!

In 1958 Grantham shed came under review with regard to its allocation which, for express work, included a mixture of A1 and A3 Pacifics, it being proposed to replace the Peppercorn engines with some more A3's plus a handful of A4 Pacifics from Kings Cross for specific 8P workings. Realising, however, that the A3's were being fitted with Kylchap blastpipes and knowing the difference that it

would make to their performance, I thought it would be better to have nothing but A3s at Grantham - Kings Cross could retain its A4s - allowing scope for Grantham men to be allocated regular engines. I managed to get this through and until diesels caused the closure of Grantham in 1963, all its class 8 work was carried out by 7P locomotives without the slightest difficulty.

Although the Kylchap arrangement transformed the A3s, it did cause steam and smoke

The Somers touch. Sympathetic to driver's complaints regarding drifting smoke from the double chimneys of modified A3 Pacifics and frustrated at the lack of action, I arranged for some of the class to be fitted with angled plates which had no effect on the exhaust flow but persuaded drivers that notice was being paid to their representations. Two years later the class were fitted with German type deflectors which were wholly successful in diverting smoke away from the cab. One of the Somers rebuilds, shorn of its smokebox numberplate and in need of a good clean, passes Brookmans Park with a GN express.

J1 0-6-0 64176 shunts in New England Yard in 1955. As a memento of my days at Peterborough I retained - and still have - the worksplate from this locomotive.

A New England Austerity 2-8-0 stands at Woodwalton, between Peterborough and Huntingdon, with a ballast train on 28 March 1957 whilst the effects of a bank slip are put right.

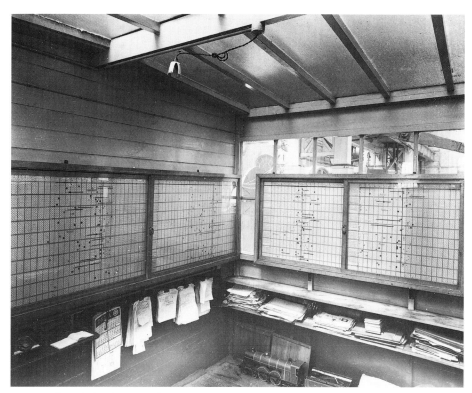

to drift down into the cab and this brought numerous complaints from the footplate staff. Although sympathetic I was fearful that the ugly and rather ineffective deflectors used on the Peppercorn Pacifics might be used on the A3's - 60097 had been disfigured in such a way some years earlier - and I suggested the fitting of small wing type deflectors, such as were in use on some A2 Pacifics, might be tried. I argued that they would not detract from their appearance too much whilst the enginemen would recognise that something was being done to meet their complaints. I have to say that I didn't have much faith in their effectiveness but, in the absence of any other ideas, I thought that appearances were worth preserving and it certainly reduced the volume of complaints from drivers who appreciated that notice was being taken of them.

Perhaps the most meaningful compliment came from a New England driver who remarked that the railway didn't want diesels - they needed more double blastpipes. (Another driver looking with one eye at the thirteen coach afternoon Scotch express and, with the other, at the new 2000hp diesel that he had been given, shook his head gravely and declared to the Kings Cross foreman "…that diesel will never move this lot. Better give me a Kylchap A3…").

In the end Peter Townend of Kings Cross came up with the clever and effective idea of using German-type deflectors which were eventually fitted to nearly all members of the class and I well remember a Grantham driver running into Kings Cross with one of these engines and saying "Here I am just about to retire and at last I can go home clean!"

Every depot had to design and operate a satisfactory system for planning locomotive maintenance so that as engines became due they could be retained locally so that they were to hand when needed. The system in use at New England during the 1950's is illustrated above, the details for each locomotive being shown graphically in the glass cases. From the evidence in the bottom of the picture, the author was not the only person at New England with an extramural interest in his subject. Someone on the staff was sufficiently interested in GNR history to keep a live-steam model of a large-boilered Atlantic in the office. What it was doing there is a mystery although when the running shed was reroofed, sufficient material was left over to enable a circle of track to be laid in the adjacent BR recreational sportsfield and it may be that the 4-4-2 was operated on the line and kept in the office when not in steam.

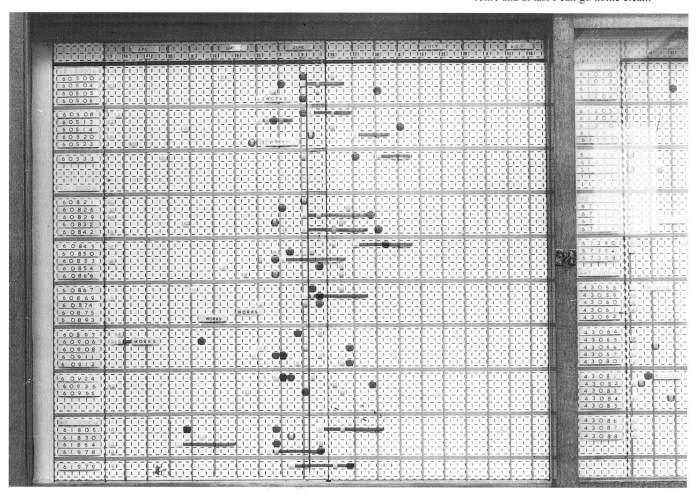

A closer view of one of the glass cases. The engines listed in the upper quarter of the display are the New England A2 Pacifics - note that no distinction is made between the sub-classes - and below, the V2, K3 and B1 locomotives. The markers under the months show the different requirements for each engine for some time ahead.

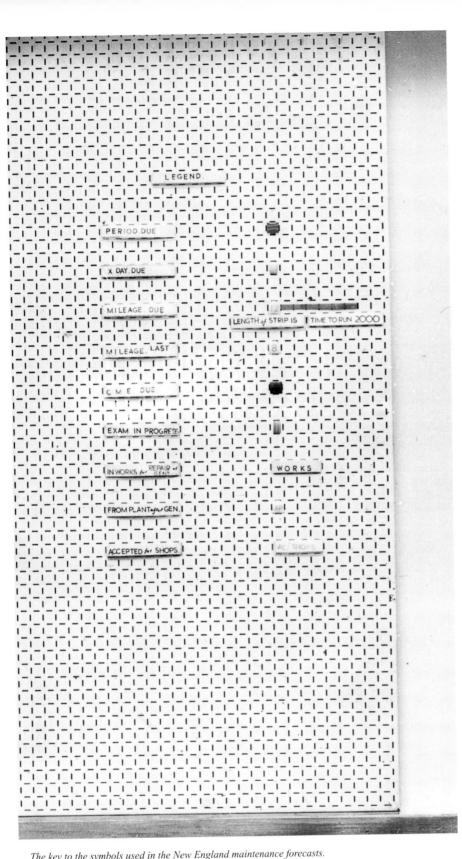

LEGEND

PERIOD. DUE

X. DAY. DUE

MILEAGE. DUE

LENGTH of STRIP IS [TIME TO RUN 2000]

MILEAGE. LAST

C.M.E. DUE

EXAM. IN. PROGRESS

IN WORKS for REPAIR of GEN.

WORKS

FROM PLANT for GEN.

AP

ACCEPTED for SHOPS.

AC. SHOPS

The key to the symbols used in the New England maintenance forecasts.

The effectiveness of the German smoke deflectors was quite remarkable. Working heavily through Gas Works tunnel coming out of Kings Cross they put all the steam and smoke on the tunnel roof and sides, leaving the cab quite clear, quite a difference to the choking conditions experienced on my Flying Scotsman trip before the war.

The A2 Pacifics, which formed the backbone of my express allocation at New England were deservedly unpopular machines and no doubt the reason for allocating them to Peterborough was because we had only a limited role in the working of express services, the Flying Scotsman period being an exception. One reason why they - or at least a particular member of the class - stick in my memory is because of their extremely bad riding.

I have rarely been nervous in my footplate riding but 60505 had had several serious complaints made by drivers and so I decided to investigate for myself. We set off for London from Peterborough, getting up to 70 mph on the straight stretch across Stilton Fen during which time the engine built up an oscillation of at least 6 inches either side of the centre-

line of the cab. The nose of the engine was hunting in a similar way and it was evident to me that, far from being guided by the bogie, the engine was being guided by the leading coupled driving wheel. I judged that this was due to the extreme weakness of the frames ahead of the outside cylinders which tended to nullify the guiding action of the bogies.

Mindful of the dreadful accident at Bihta in India, where a Pacific locomotive had left the rails - with heavy loss of life - due to lateral oscillation, I told the driver to part-close the regulator, increase the cut-off and to keep his speed down to 65 mph until we got to Kings Cross where I immediately failed the engine and had it sent to Doncaster works. What they did to it, I do not know but when it returned it made the extraordinary run referred to earlier in this chapter which suggests that its riding qualities had been improved very considerably - at least for a time.

A few years earlier Driver Hoole of Kings Cross had been involved in a fatal derailment at Cemetery tunnel, New Southgate, when his A2 turned over onto its side. The cause was put down to defective permanent way plus a hint of excessive speed but I have always suspected that the poor riding qualities of the A2 may also have contributed. Had the engine concerned been a Gresley Pacific I doubt if the accident would have happened.

I had a great many talented staff at New England although one I remember in particular was Horace Botterill, the Mechanical Foreman. We had difficulties with the 9F locomotives on the rare occasions that they ran hot and the driving wheels had to be dropped. Normally the wheels would be kept on a piece of track until the repairs had been finished but as the 9F's centre pair of drivers had no flange the very real problem of how to secure them safely arose. After some thought Horace then devised a temporary flange for these wheels by cutting semi-circular plates of steel a little larger than the diameter of the wheels, bolting them to a holding plate through the spokes, so that the wheels would remain in situ until needed. (The prospect of several tons of driving wheel falling into the wheel drop was not something that bore thinking about).

Horace was also a first-class man to have on a breakdown job and I remember going with him to clear up a jumble of wagons at Stamford where, first of all, we had to clear a path to the wreckage proper by removing all the undamaged wagons so that we had room to operate. Horace set his crane in such a way that all the derailed vehicles could be dealt with without it having to be moved again. To gauge things thus required a cool mind, experience and a skill for planning and under Horace's charge the mess was cleared relatively quickly and efficiently although it still took about three and a half hours to finish the job and get back to New England. As usual my boss complained that we had taken too long to deal with the incident. In defence I took some pleasure in pointing out to him that we hadn't made a single false move - something to be proud of alone - during the rerailing and therefore the job couldn't have been completed any faster.

Now and again we used the crane for matters other than derailments, one such occasion cropping up when the Gas Board was installing its trunk main for North Sea gas, part of which was routed alongside the GN mainline near Tempsford. The pipes were delivered by rail and arrangements made for the New Eng-

One of the New England A2 Pacific's waits for the right-away from Grantham in 1959. 60520 'Owen Tudor' was the engine involved in the Welwyn crash of 1956 in which it ran through signals with the up Aberdonian into the rear of a Baldock - Kings Cross semi-fast killing a passenger. The A2's were rough riding engines and were tolerated rather than liked at New England. Their survival at the shed was probably due to the fact that the passenger links was very much smaller in number than the core freight workings and needed a loud voice to be heard.

land crane to unload them from the wagons and position them in the trench next to the track.

It was more difficult than many of the derailments I had attended. For obvious reasons it had not been deemed feasible to remove the lineside telephone poles and wires and because of this the pipes and their guide ropes had to be lifted over the wires with no means of control whilst the pipes were aloft. Time and again the pipes were hoisted aloft only for the guide ropes to catch in the wind and be caught in the wires. Fun and games were had by all!

Some problems had an element of comic farce about them such as the instance when I was called out to an incident in the Sandy area where New England bordered with the Kings Cross district. A routine weekend possession was in progress; the up main line having been removed in order to allow the ballast to be renewed. There was, perforce, quite a trench where the track had been and for some reason a ballast train hauled by a tender-first J6 0-6-0 succeeded in being pushed by the weight of its train into the hole; the ancient GNR 6-wheeled passenger brake, in use as a ballast brake, plastering itself all over the engine's smokebox, knocking off the chimney and, besides filling the hole where the up line had been, completely blocking the down main line. To make matters worse, the brake van body had become detached from its chassis and was perched on the down road - a flimsy structure which would disintegrate if not removed bodily by the New England 45-ton crane which, as luck would have it, was engaged on a separate engineering job and could not be summoned to assist.

Armed with only the tool vans and only the haziest of reports as to what had happened, I set off and found quite a chaotic scene which I sized up as quickly as I could and then sent for the Kings Cross crane. I expected some considerable delay before it would arrive but fortunately someone, probably the district con-

trol, had alerted Kings Cross and the crane was ready to leave as soon as I asked for it.

However summoning assistance from another district - although on the border Sandy was still New England territory - was not something that was lightly done and it was sufficient to provoke my chief to leave his bed and come rushing down to the site, doubtless with the intention of castigating me for incompetence. When he arrived and saw the van body lying on the down main line minus wheels he cut short any criticism that he had ready prepared and made no comment, leaving me in peace to rerail the J6 with my Kelbus hauling gear as soon as the crane had lifted the remnants of the brake chassis off its smokebox. Calling out a 'foreign' crane struck a raw nerve with the boss yet displaced 0-6-0's, demolished brake-vans and several blocked lines were, presumably, routine. There's nowt - as they used to say at the far end of the GN - so strange as fowk!

One thing, in passing, that I was very proud of in all my dealings with mishaps and derailments was that none of my breakdown crews ever needed medical attention for injuries. Those days were many years before we developed a paranoia about safety - common sense was our guide - but a mishap scene was an environment where misjudgement could result in serious injury and I am grateful for the fact that the discipline I engendered saw no-one suffer any worse than the odd pinched finger or stubbed toe.

A useful legacy of war conditions were the examination sheds known as light tunnels which the LNER erected at several depots, including New England. Engines to be dealt with were run into a long shed, completely enclosed with doors at both ends, where examiners could get on with their jobs in relative comfort assisted by brilliant fluorescent lighting. The New England shed was still in use in my time and it was inside the structure that I came across a remarkable case of fatigue fracture.

A V2, which had just worked an express in from London, entered the shed for an examination and, as it came to rest, the radius rod fell in half. Clearly the fracture occurred with incredible rapidity - otherwise the engine would not have got as far as the depot - and I always called this instance to mind when future judgements were required on fractures where fatigue was suspected. The conventional wisdom of the day maintained that fatigue produced warning signs which could be spotted before any damage occurred: Thanks to the New England incident I knew better.

Like Northwich, New England had a number of old pictures displayed in the offices and I seem to recollect that the Inspectors office contained an original F. Moore painting of a GN Atlantic whilst in the little-used offices of the old North shed there were two very faded pictures of the boiler explosion in 1864 when 2-2-2 No. 98 blew up and wrecked the shed building, killing three of the workshop staff. What happened to these interesting views I have no idea but more than once I have regretting leaving Peterborough without them.

Imitation must be the best form of flattery, especially if it comes from the Great Western. Whether a Motive Power Officer from Paddington happened to see one of my 9F's at work on a fitted goods or whether it was pressure due to a chronic shortage of power, it was pleasing to see other railways adopt one's habits. A Ebbw Vale 2-10-0 passes Bath Spa at the head of a GW relief express.

DIESELS

From many points of view the 1950's were the best years of the twentieth century especially if one had been a railwayman. On the one hand many of the positive values of pre-war days still persisted whilst on the other we had the benefits of the social reforms that had been introduced during or soon after the war. Indeed the war-cry of most people during the 50's was to 'get back to 1939' and in some respects this was achieved by the end of the decade.

The railway itself of course had not changed greatly and the GN railwayman of, say, 1909 would not have found very much change half a century on - would that we could have said the same ten years hence - and there was a sense of stability upon which values and disciplines were built to be passed on to succeeding generations. Probably the most significant change - perhaps the only one - to the Great Northern had been the abandonment of our traditional way of running passenger trains in favour of the Midland system.

In years past we had run express services in blocks during the late morning, early afternoon, evening and night - gargantuan ensembles of seventeen coaches or more - which enabled the very heavy goods service to be fitted into the broad gaps between the flights of pas-senger workings. During the 1950's there had been a tendency to reduce the weight of the better established trains and to supplement them with additional services so that by the end of the decade trains of about ten or eleven coaches were leaving Kings Cross for Newcastle and Leeds at pretty well hourly intervals. Services to Edinburgh - beyond the edge of the world - had also been increased late in the decade with the former 10.00 and 13.20 services being augmented by departures at two hourly intervals from 08.00. All were steam worked - we saw nothing of the early diesels - with Peppercorn A1 Pacifics predominating on the Leeds trains and A4's taking most of the remainder. The goods service remained as heavy as ever and the increase in passenger trains saw the goods lines more intensively used than ever before with four or more freight trains, engine to brakevan, standing in a queue waiting to get through the bottlenecks at Huntingdon, Sandy and Arlesey.

Until 1959 modernisation was a word which appeared only in the columns of the Railway Gazette and it was not until that year I received my first taste of it and its associated term - reorganisation. The motive power organisation - like that of the permanent way and civil engineers - had been an industry within an industry and although we worked closely with the traffic department, the lines of responsibility did not meet until they came to the General Manager who was rather a remote figure. There were criticisms of this separation - or rather the results of it - and the opinion was sometimes voiced that we were rather conservative in our views of what an engine was capable of. A typical Kings Cross Pacific, for example, would not exceed much more than 400 miles a day - a trip to Edinburgh or a couple of returns to Grantham - and it may have been that we were a trifle unadventurous although in defence it has to be pointed out that the war-time arrears of maintenance had forced us to revise our strategies in the early 1950's by introducing engine changes at Grantham and we were only, by 1959, getting back to a position where we thought it probable that longer workings could be put into force without resulting in an epidemic of mainline failures.

For better or worse in 1959 it was decided to subordinate the Motive Power organisation to the Traffic Managers Department and from that time we ceased to exist as a separate entity. To my surprise - being in charge of the Great Northern's largest shed - I found myself out of work for a time and kicked my heels at Peterborough until being given an office in

Not all our anachronisms were steam engines. The gas wagons and inspection saloon are seen in the Nene carriage sidings - known as the wharf - to the south of Peterborough North on 26 April 1959.

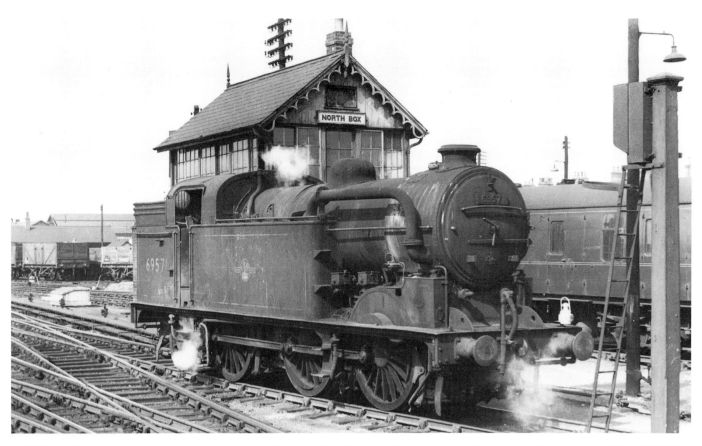

Whilst the Kings Cross suburban service had to make do with engines that didn't work, Peterborough was given some that did. Condensing N2 0-6-2T 69571 acts as the North station pilot on 19 April 1960.

Great Northern House - adjacent to Kings Cross - with the responsibility of assisting with the introduction of diesels to the division.

At that time our experience of diesels was minimal. In 1958 a handful of 2000hp English Electric (class 40) locomotives had been sent to us mainly to work the Master Cutler Pullman to and from Sheffield whilst a year later we received the prototype Deltic, which the LNW had rejected in favour of electrification, for trials. Lincoln had been selected as the central point for most multiple unit workings and a few of these appeared at Peterborough on Grimsby workings. For all these incursions, diesels were still a novelty on the GN in 1959 and I had no more idea of what the future would bring than anyone else.

For a time I travelled up to Kings Cross on the 08.12 from Peterborough (07.30 from Grantham) which was booked to one of my former charges, a Grantham A3, all of which had now been fitted with Kylchap blastpipes. The train also included a GNR 12-wheel Kitchen/Diner which did duty as a buffet car and although it dated back to 1906 it continued to give a faultless ride in spite of 53 years service.

One journey which sticks in my mind happened after heavy delays at Abbots Ripton due to an over-running permanent way possession when we ran the 59 miles from Huntingdon to Kings Cross in exactly one hour with stops at St Neots and Biggleswade. The driver was 'Benny' Kirk of Grantham who gained attention during the 1955 ASLEF strike by coming to work after an appeal by the Prime Minister, Mr Macmillan.

On a subseuent journey another Grantham driver, who did not have a reputation for being particularly enterprising, left Biggleswade and passed Arlesey, uphill, at 70 mph. He was probably taken by surprise by the A3 which

had recently been fitted with the Kylchap blastpipe.

When the diesels started to trickle in from the manufacturer, the first thing to do was to find somewhere to put them - we did not have a proper diesel depot until 1960 when Clarence Yard maintenance shed opened on the site of the down goods yard at Finsbury Park - and for the interim Hornsey was selected, an area of the steam shed being partitioned off to allow the new arrivals to be serviced in a tolerable degree of cleanliness.

No sooner, however, had the diesels started to arrive than the fitting staff at Hornsey decided to stage a strike which resulted in managerial and supervisory staff having to do their jobs. It was one way, I suppose, of getting to

the heart of the new locomotives but we also had to tend to the steam allocation, much to the amusement of the strikers - the affair was pretty good natured - who watched with glee as their lords and masters screwed and hammered and generally got their hands dirty. (So far as the steam engines were concerned, our efforts appeared to have been appreciated by the drivers who stated that we had put to rights a host of defects which had been ignored for years by the regular staff).

It was fortunate that the diesels were new and needed little in the way of heavy maintenance. By the time anything serious was called for the fitters were back at work.

Reliability apart - which was terrible - the planners appear to have sorely underestimated

Old friends and familiar sights were under siege by the early 1960's. The N7 0-6-2T's which had monopolised the Great Eastern Jazz service from Liverpool Street and held sway on the GN branches from Hatfield disappeared very quickly and by 1962 it was difficult to believe that only a few years earlier they had been a very familiar part of the landscape. 69713 sits at Stratford in the shadow of an English Electric type 3 diesel-electric.

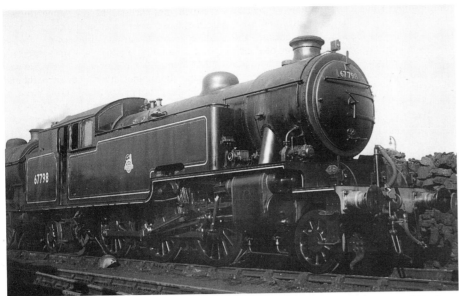

Had the L1 'concrete mixer' 2-6-4T's been replaced by anything other than Baby Deltics and North British type 2 diesels they would scarcely have been missed. As it was the replacements proved to be anything but superior and it was some time before the diesel-worked outer-suburban service achieved any sort of reliability. The L1's worked from all three ER termini and one of the Great Central batch, 67798, poses at Neasden in 1955.

the power outputs needed for GN trains, mainline and local alike. 2000hp had been provided for 8P duties when another 500hp - at least - was essential whilst the local trains such as the Cambridge Buffets needed an absolute minimum of 1200hp if time was to be kept. Instead we received a batch of North British 1000hp engines from Scotland plus a handful of similarly rated Baby Deltics from English Electric, neither of which was capable of timing a train if they could run at all.

For suburban work we were sent three classes of diesel-electrics: the 1000bhp North British, the 1100 bhp Baby Deltics and the 1100 bhp Sulzers built at Derby. The North British locomotives were not powerful enough for anything else than the inner-suburban service which they had taken over from the N2 0-6-2T's and were in fact so unsatisfactory that after a short while we got rid of them to Scotland to be nearer their manufacturers. A run on one of these engines on a outer suburban

train was like sitting on an L1 2-6-4T which was short of steam.

The Baby Deltics had a very troublesome start and eventually had to be thoroughly overhauled by English Electric after which (1964) they were outbased at Hitchin where, in the hands of a limited number of crews they performed fairly well but had nothing in reserve with regard to power. The Sulzer 1100 bhp engines were based at Hornsey and were mainly used on the widened lines mineral traffic between Ferme Park and the Southern. They also saw use on ECS and occasional inner-suburban work but lacked sufficient power to recover from any en-route delays.

We - British Railways - came in for a considerable amount of criticism over the poor performance of the new engines which was rather unfair since most of the trouble stemmed from faulty design work and unsatisfactory components; the result of inexperience on the part of the manufacturers. We should have

tested the water more carefully rather than putting our faith in a medium which was untested and untried.

So far as mainline work was concerned of the five 2000hp locomotives frequently only one would be available for work and this had to be turned out for the Sheffield Pullman which had first call for a diesel. A proposal to allocate an A4 as stand-by at Darnall was turned down whilst the Sheffield men who worked the Pullman had been given a guarantee that their working would be provided with a diesel. The result of this was that whenever a substitute had to be provided, a fresh set of men had to be found. Fortunately the Pullman had priority for a diesel engine and it was only very rarely that a steam engine had to take over.

The poor availability of the English Electric's did at least provide the opportunity for our Pacifics to perform a swan-song, both they and their drivers rising to the challenge and producing results that only a short time ago would have been considered unthinkable. Who at the beginning of the decade would have believed an A3 Pacific could steam pretty well continuously for thirteen hours and cover the 540-odd miles of a Newcastle return trip in between?

Such palliatives were not available to assist with the working of the suburban service which declined to an extraordinary level thanks to late deliveries of diesels from the manufacturers and the fact that when we did receive them they did not work. In the end we had to institute a crash programme of general repairs to the N2 0-6-2T's in order to keep things on the move.

The grim reading of the availability reports occasionally intruded into my personal reality as happened one morning when my train - now diesel-hauled - failed near New Barnet. The 'experts' poked and prodded in an attempt to coax the thing back into life whilst I set off for assistance in a more tangible shape which I found in the form of an Austerity 2-8-0 running north on its way light to Hitchin. The driver was a model of co-operation and without a moments hesitation he crossed over to the up mainline and coupled up to the failed train. I could not recall a time when an Austerity had worked into Kings Cross before - I was probably setting a precedent - nor had I any idea of what restrictions there were, if any. Neither had anyone the time to start looking them up - published clearances for uncommon engines off the beaten track are tortuous to say the least - so the best I could do was to tell the driver to enter the terminus under extreme caution adding that he was running tender first and that Austerities had a reputation for becoming derailed on tight curves. Fortunately the fates were with me that morning and we got to Kings Cross in one piece with all wheels on the track.

Gradually the position in respect of the suburban and local trains improved as we got rid of the dead-wood and took possession of the Brush Type 2's (Class 31) in large quantities. These engines had proved themselves on the Great Eastern which had dieselised rather earlier than the GN and proved to be about as reliable as one could reasonably expect a diesel to be.

The North British Type 2's were shunted into a siding at Peterborough - the Scottish Region refused to have them back until someone tipped off the press and caused a minor

One of the great surprises of the last few years of steam was the way the A3 Pacifics returned to prominence, partly because of the difference the Kylchap double blastpipe made but also because of the necessity to use them on diesel diagrams where they were required to run from London to Newcastle and back in the same day - a feat that would have been almost beyond belief a short time before. Double chimney A3 60108 'Gay Crusader' is prepared for its next working at New England on 9th July 1960.

scandal whilst the Baby Deltics stagnated at Stratford until English Electric could be persuaded to take them back for rebuilding.

I do not know how much standardisation the planners had expected when they first put pen to paper but by the time the dust had settled in the early 1960's we had as much variety in our motive power as we had had in steam days. Most of the local trains were worked by the Class 31 engines whilst Sulzer Class 24 Types 2's handled the widened lines goods traffic and assisted with local and ECS work. Class 20 Type 1's were allocated to Hatfield for local goods traffic whilst Hitchin hosted the rejuvenated Baby Deltics. On top of that we had a handful of miscellaneous Type 1's which handled ECS and goods work around Kings Cross whilst a number of local trains were worked by multiple units based on Western Sidings at Finsbury Park.

Steam remained in charge on the express front until 1962 when the NER started to operate its Class 40 and Class 45 locomotives into London; the changeover accelerating the following year with the arrival of the first Deltics; one of the few engines we had which proved to be almost as reliable as the steam locomotives which they were replacing.

I went down to Peterborough one morning to have a ride on one of the new engines only to be stopped short at Abbots Ripton by the news that a train on the up road was on fire at Woodwalton. We went forward at caution and I dropped off at the scene of the trouble to find the leading coach of the Norseman (10.15 Newcastle - Kings Cross) well and truly ablaze. The traincrew had acted with great presence of mind, the fireman having - rather courageously - uncoupled the burning coach from the rest of the train to allow it to be drawn forward so that the fire brigade could attend to it without having to worry about the rest of the train. After the fire had died down and the luggage - or what remained of it - had been transferred I had the coach shunted onto the slow line and then backed the engine, an A4, onto the train to continue forward to London. I mounted the footplate with the intention of riding back to London in order to see whether there were any signs from the engine of anything that might have started the fire. The three of us by now were as black as the ace of spades and thinking that nothing more could go wrong the gauge glass promptly burst. The remainder of the trip was an anticlimax, the engine behaved perfectly, refused to throw any fire whilst the ashpan appeared to be in good shape. At the end of the day I don't believe that any cause of the fire was ever established. My first trip on a Deltic had to wait however.

The swan song of the A4's came in 1961 when we had to run three special trains in connection with the Duke of Kent's wedding at York - readers can draw their own conclusions from the fact that we used Gresley Pacifics for the job rather than the new diesels. On the return trip some sort of problem arose - for which the railway was not to blame - and meant that one of the A4's had to pare about twenty minutes off the timings if a punctual arrival was to be achieved in London. The wedding and all that was connected with it had attracted considerable public attention and any lapse on our part would have given the press a field day. Conscious of this the crew of the Pacific coaxed their engine into three figures on the descent of Stoke - in spite of the 90 mph limit which had been imposed with the arrival of diesels -

and got into Kings Cross on time. Inspector Hart was riding on the locomotive and I can recall to this day the dead-pan exchange - the sort of thing that Victorian editions of Punch used to delight in - which took place between him and an unusually observant passenger.

Passenger: How fast were you going down Stoke bank?
Hart: 90
Passenger: And the rest...?

Unfortunately we had to rely on diesels for the everyday running of the division, a task that was made especially difficult during the 1962/3 winter which was the most severe since 1947 and saw a reversion to steam traction for many trains because the diesels were either unworkable or were unable to heat their trains. Unfortunately by this time there were not enough steam engines left to cover all the workings and I had to resort to ingenuity where Hitchin's Baby Deltics were concerned. On

these engines excessively low temperatures - such as those experienced in 1962 - caused the lubrication oil to become viscous almost to the point of solidity; a situation which often resulted in burst flexible pipes. My solution was to stable the engines in a row every night and couple the train heating pipes through which steam was passed from a withdrawn New England A2 Pacific. By this means the steam generators acted as radiators and, mirabile dictu, the scheme worked admirably.

All too quickly steam disappeared from the GN and with it a way of life. I, and most of my colleagues, managed to adapt to the new order but it has to be said with less enthusiasm than of yore. After all, had we not been promised a Utopian existence once steam had been superseded? It was a hollow promise and one that had not only damaged our traditional way of working but had brought the industry to such a low ebb that it was difficult to see it ever re-

One of the blessings of my job was the freedom to go for a ride on a steam engine; something that blew away the cobwebs of paperwork as well as keeping me in touch with the real world. Now and again I extended the priceless experience to others, the scene above being taken by Herr Peter Abt, of the Swiss Rack and Pinion family, as A3 Pacific 60111 'Enterprise' stormed through Welwyn North on the climb to Woolmer Green. The engine was in its final form, rock steady and without a sign of exhaust at the chimney in spite of the hard work being done.

An O2 2-8-0 prepares to come off shed at Grantham prior to working a High Dyke iron ore service in 1959. O3 locomotives had originally been used for the High Dyke trains and I successfully obstructed a move to replace them with Austerity 2-8-0's, managing instead to obtain an allocation of O2's. Grantham normally had an allocation of about twelve 2-8-0's for the iron ore traffic.

gaining the public respectability it had once enjoyed.

Our standard express passenger engine, apart from the Deltics, were the Brush Sulzer 2750hp locomotives - inexplicably referred to as Hawker-Siddleys on the GN - of which I had about 50. At first they behaved quite well and were powerful enough to substitute for a Deltic on the timings we were running at the time although it has to be said that the Deltics behaved themselves sufficiently well to make such substitutions uncommon and most of the Class 47 - as the Hawker-Siddley's became - work was on fitted goods - of which we still had quite a lot - parcels trains and a handful of lesser expresses. In addition they took over from the 2-8-0 and 2-10-0 steam engines, the heavy New England - Ferme Park mineral traffic. Thus in the course of a few days an engine could work such widely divergent services as the 13.00 Kings Cross - Newcastle express and

Heavy repairs and examinations at New England were carried out in the works section where engines had to be parted from their tenders in order to be accommodated on the traverser. V2 2-6-2 60948 waits for attention on the 16th June 1963. Most GN top link drivers would take a 'Green Arrow' in preference to most other engines - Pacifics included - whilst I thought them the most graceful of all the engines in my charge.

The business end of Kings Cross in 1958 with A4 60027 'Merlin' about to head for home with the 09.30 Elizabethan. In the rear a new English Electric 2000hp diesel is prepared in the passenger loco for the 10.00 Flying Scotsman.

the 09.25 Ferme Park - New England mineral and this was something that had never happened before.

The Deltics, on the other hand, were restricted solely to express passenger work and the only time they were permitted to work anything of a lesser nature was when we would put them onto a parcels train in order to get them to Doncaster works for a major examination. I recall one of my assistants overlooking this on one occasion in 1965 and utilising one of the class as one of the High Dyke pilots - probably the lowest order of work ever devised for an engine and usually a working for a Brush Type 2. I believe the fellow concerned still recalls the roasting he got for his sins.

The 47's could not stand up to such treatment and from 1965 started to become very troublesome, probably resulting in the lowest availability ever recorded for a class of locomotive. Of my 50-odd allocation it was rare to find more than 50% of them available for work and it was probably only due to the generous allocation at Clarence Yard together with considerable ingenuity on the part of the diesel controllers that the service from Kings Cross did not, at times, come to a grinding halt.

The problem in part may have been due to the very intensive working that we expected of engines on the Great Northern and it has to be said that neither the Great Eastern, who used the type on the Liverpool Street - Norwich workings from 1967, or the Great Western who

From close quarters the Gresley Pacifics lost some of their graceful curves and neither the external blower pipe, washout plugs or footstep on the outer footplate added to their appearance. The double chimney did nothing to improve matters although it made a wealth of difference to their performance, making the engines quite the equal of a class 8P. Shortly after being equipped with its double chimney in 1958 60073 'St Gatien' of Heaton waits at York with a southbound express.

The 3300hp Deltics had originally been intended to work from Euston on the LNW but, thanks to a change of mind, the prototype came over to the GN for trials in 1959 with the production engines appearing in 1961. To maintain a tradition all those allocated to the Great Northern were named after racehorses although D9001 is seen on a test run just after delivery and prior to receiving its name. Thankfully this was one class of diesel which came up to the claims of the manufacturer and were worthy successors to the A4's.

employed them interchangeably with their 'Western' class hydraulics, suffered anything like the same problems that we did although all were united in the belief that diesel availability, when compared with that of steam, left a great deal to be desired.

Something urgent had to be done, not simply for operational reasons pressing though they were, but for the image and credibility of the railway industry. More than once the press had picked on us - rather unfairly given that we no longer built our own locomotives - for trying to operate with classes of engines which were all but useless and the prospect of Fleet Street focusing malevolently upon one of our principal express types was something that did not bear thinking about.

The first to act was the British Railways Board who, in conjunction with the manufacturers, derated the class from 2750 to 2558 hp in the belief that the reduced power output would ease the stresses that were causing many of the problems. The extent to which this was

necessary - the expression 'knee-jerk reaction' had not been coined at the time but had it been, it might have applied - was never put to the test since we, the Eastern Region, implemented our own solution whilst expressing considerable concern at losing a good deal of horsepower from our second division locomotives.

Also at the back of my mind was the reserve that the engines would have in hand once the electric heating and air conditioning of passenger trains was supplied by the locomotive; something we were experimenting with at the time. It was initially considered that the train supply would be a considerable drain although, after some road tests with 9001 'St Paddy', it was later demonstrated that the diversion of power for heating, etc, had little effect on performance.

We, at the operating level of the Eastern, knew that the source of the trouble lay at the maintenance level and that it was in this area that reform was needed. An early error had been the assumption that the diesels would

work to long and complex cyclic diagrams without difficulty and, on this assumption, had their various examinations at stages in the workings. In actual fact the locomotives rarely stayed in a diagram for as long as twenty-four hours and this resulted in some engines being examined several times a week whilst others went for considerable periods without being checked at all.

At first I attempted to identify the engines that were overdue for major examinations and tried to run a one-man operation in getting them to Clarence Yard or Doncaster without upsetting traffic routines; a scheme that was defeated by the number of engines concerned and the fact that many of them failed in action before they could be examined. In the end the solution came from embracing all Eastern Region (even in 1968 we were still very LNER orientated) diesel locomotives and giving each a code which indicated the day and time that each was to be in its home depot for examination. Thus, for example, if engine 1508 had a code of F23 it had to be on shed by 23.00 Friday come what may. The discipline associated with the programme was rigid and it was decreed that no engine was to work, under any circumstances, after the time indicated by its maintenance code and in fact once the deadline had been passed the locomotive was considered as being non-existent so far as traffic needs were concerned, even if it meant the cancellation of a train.

The success of the scheme lay in its simplicity. Each engine was permitted so many days work between examinations - two days for a Deltic, three for a Type 4, four for Types 3 and 2, and so on - and the time element of the code would reflect the time that an engine started work after having had an examination. A Deltic, therefore, coming out of examination on Monday and working the 11.35 Kings Cross - Leeds would be given the code W11 indicating that it was required for its next examination at 11.00 the following Wednesday. A similar procedure was followed for major examinations which were performed at Crewe for Sulzer engines and Doncaster for English Electric locomotives.

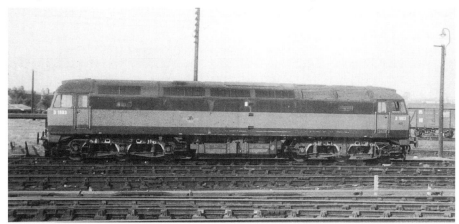

Even after the passage of some years it is difficult to think dispassionately of the Brush-Sulzer Type 4's which Kings Cross was supposed to rely so heavily upon. Over 54 of the class were allocated to Clarence Yard (Finsbury Park) yet it was rare to have more than half available for work and the New England 9F 2-10-0's had to be kept in service until 1965 in order to provide reliable power for the New England - Colwick mineral trains. Had it not been for the Deltics and the fact we had many more type 4's than were actually needed, the passenger service would have gone to the dogs. D1883 of Immingham stands at Grantham between Scunthorpe - High Dyke workings in 1966. The shed had been closed three years earlier and the only locomotive resources that remained were a couple of sidings for stabling the odd diesel.

The English Electric 2000 hp Type 4's were quickly ousted from east coast main line workings by the Deltics and Sulzer Type 4's although the class made daily appearances until 1968 from Kings Cross on the 14.20 semi-fast to York and the 23.20 Edinburgh sleeper which was booked non-stop to Newcastle. York, Gateshead and Haymarket retained a considerable number of these engines and from time to time they made their way to the Kings Cross division. D249 waits in the sidings at Grantham in 1965 after being taken off an east coast express.

Although the greater part of the scheme was implemented without undue difficulty, some of the Controllers - those at Liverpool Street in particular - refused at first to have anything to do with it unless they received an increase in salary (which they eventually got) whilst open war almost broke out when it was proposed to locate a technically trained maintenance controller in each of the district controls to work alongside the traditional running controllers. Who thought up the idea I cannot remember although it was probably the Board who could generally be relied upon to come up with extreme varieties of reductio ad absurdum when they thought no-one was taking any notice of them.

The idea was to have a technically trained man in the control who could speak to drivers of failed engines in order to suggest to them how they might restart their locomotives. It was the sort of notion that an Institute of Transport student would have in his first year and reject in his second since apart from the fact that drivers were not technically educated and were therefore not allowed to attempt repairs, the idea of a driver failing at, say, Saltersford and walking all the way back to Grantham South signalbox to have a learned discussion over the telephone on a subject he would probably be totally unfamiliar with was almost as laughable as was the prospect of the same driver then attacking his engine with skills and tools that he did not possess. For all their professionalism in certain directions the extent of most driver's mechanical knowledge went as far as opening and shutting the cab door and the last thing I wanted was the prospect of a driver blocking the mainline for God knows how long whilst he attempted to repair a broken crankcase with a screwdriver. In addition to this it should be added that in cases of failure a drivers principal responsibility was to protect the line(s) ahead of his train.

To add insult to injury the maintenance controllers were installed at a higher salary than the running controllers and were perceived as having jumped the promotional queue. In the end the running controllers were given parity of pay and the two thereafter cohabited in an attitude of mutual distrust.

Assessing the efficacy of the controlled maintenance scheme is made rather difficult by the fact that the moment the thing was introduced, all our goods traffic disappeared leaving much less of an intensive workload for the engines that had been falling to bits through overwork. The failure rate of locomotives, and the Sulzer Type 4's in particular, decreased although whether this was the result of disciplined examination procedures or simply the fact they had less work to do, it is impossible to determine.

Once the 1965 national freight train plan had been implemented the character of the Great Northern changed abruptly. Up to that time we had been a freight railway - in spite of a public perception to the contrary - and for years the system had been clogged up with innumerable, and very lengthy, mineral trains which worked continuously between Colwick and New England and, after remarshalling, from New England to Ferme Park. To indicate the scale of the freight business during the 1950's New England shed - the largest on the GN - had an allocation of about 200 engines, only 11 of which were for passenger work. Of the remainder 44 were used for mixed traffic and fast goods duties leaving about 150 locomotives for mineral, pick-up and shunting services. Indeed it was impossible to stand on any GN station for any length of time without seeing an Austerity or 9F trundle by with 70-odd wagons in tow whilst the approaches to the goods line bottle-necks at Arlesey and Sandy would be jammed solid, engine to brake van, with mineral trains waiting for a margin to move. The energies and resources expended on the express passenger business was but a small fraction of that devoted to goods and mineral working.

Overnight this activity vanished and the result was a castrated railway. The slow lines north of Hitchin sprouted weeds whilst those

Although the 1750hp English Electric Type 3's were well distributed throughout the Eastern Region, it was only on the Great Eastern that they could be found in significant numbers on passenger workings. Their appearances at Kings Cross were confined to two daily services leaving at 16.12 and 18.45, both running to Cleethorpes with Immingham-based engines. They were reliable locomotives and gave little cause for concern. One of the Immingham batch pulls out of Kings Cross with the 18.45 East Lincs express in 1965.

beyond Peterborough turned yellow through lack of use. The activity at New England ceased as though someone had turned a tap whilst the miles of marshalling yards were reduced to a handful of sidings which rapidly started to disappear under a sea of weeds.

In the London area the up yard at Ferme Park was closed - something that would have been considered inconceivable only a couple of years previous - whilst a small section of the down side remained operational for combining together the Temple Mills and Kings Cross sections of the very few fitted goods that remained. The south lines traffic which had seen goods trains running through Kings Cross station at frequent intervals also ceased and the connections to the Southern closed very soon afterwards.

To balance the loss of fast freight trains we had been led to believe that they would be replaced with something altogether more modern and optimists held the view that the future lay in the freightliner concept with container trains replacing the conventional vanfit. This was not the first attempt I had seen on the GN to update the fast freight and a considerable investment had been made early in the 1960's with the roadrailer experiment using road trailers which could be made up into a train. The inaugural service set off from London in a blaze of publicity but became derailed at Huntingdon and, for reasons no-one seemed to understand, was promptly forgotten. The much-vaunted Condor service between London and Glasgow on the neighbouring Midland was another short-lived scheme which cost a great deal of money, attracted a considerable amount of (BR generated) publicity and then seemed to fade into obscurity.

The freightliner lasted rather longer although it started badly on the Great Northern

The camera manages to catch D9015 starting one of its engines prior to leaving Kings Cross with the 19.30 to Aberdeen in 1966. The engine farthest from the driver had to be started first with the starting button for each engine being held down for a minimum of thirty seconds. The engine would then emit a series of low growling sounds until the engine exploded into life, emitting a large oily cloud of exhaust. On the three days preceding Good Friday in 1965 and 1966 the 19.30 Aberdonian was diagrammed to be double-headed by two Deltics as far as York. Unfortunately for those who turned up to witness the spectacle the working did not materialise except for one occasion in 1966 when two Deltics worked the train in tandem - probably the only instance of programmed double-heading by the class.

with the first departure leaving York Way, Kings Cross, an hour and a half late because of brake difficulties. We did what little we could do help it pick up time; the driver was a goer (as they used to say at Kings Cross) and, sensing this, Graham Parker, the district controller put the down Aberdonian in the slow road for it - probably the only time an East Coast Express has ever been deliberately side-tracked for a goods train - and allowed it to pick up a few minutes before it passed out of the district at Stoke. (In spite of its humilia-

tion the lordly Aberdonian still managed to get to Grantham on time, not that it saved Controller Parker from a few uncomfortable minutes on the carpet a day or two later when the he and the Line Superintendent found they had differing views on the subject of initiative). The early freightliners, incidentally, were vacuum braked and until 1968 included a brakevan, usually a passenger full-brake.

On the passenger side of the business matters were almost as depressing in spite of the fact that express trains ran more frequently

In 1966 we started what appeared to be a renaissance of the LNER by inaugurating a high speed service to Leeds and Harrogate, running non-stop between London and Wakefield. Although the service was far faster than anything we had had since the war, it spite of Deltic haulage and a load of only eight mark 1 coaches, the train was only four minutes faster to Leeds that the pre-war West Riding Limited had been. We could, had it been needed, have knocked at least ten minutes of the schedule whilst the 2750hp Sulzers had no difficulty in timing the service. D9020 'Nimbus' wheels the 15.55 Kings Cross - Harrogate through Retford shortly after the train's inauguration.

With characteristic plumes of exhaust a Deltic gets the 14.00 Kings Cross - Edinburgh 'Heart of Midlothian' on the move from York in 1967. Within a couple of hours of reaching Edinburgh the engine would be on its way back to London with an overnight express; a degree of utilisation that these particular engines seemed to thrive upon.

from Kings Cross than had ever been the case in the lines' history. As a general rule we had an Edinburgh departure on the even hour, a Newcastle train in between with Leeds services at twenty minutes past each hour; those on the even hour calling at all stations between Huntingdon and Doncaster. In addition to these there were a handful of miscellaneous services to York and Hull plus the parliamentary trains to Peterborough which called at all stations north of Hitchin.

Whilst the trains were both fast and frequent and looked impressive in the timetable, to railwaymen they lacked any sort of operational challenge since one looked very much like another and they were so light that they hardly merited being called a train. In steam days an express worthy of the name had consisted of fifteen or sixteen coaches going to a myriad of destinations whilst the Deltics hardly ever pulled a train with more than about ten coaches. One hope that still flickered was the possibility of reviving a high speed service with an individual character which would raise both raise morale and give the system a sense of prestige. Unfortunately the Railways Board had fixed its sights on the dull spectre of standardisation: all trains running to more or less the same timings although some adrenaline had started to flow in the late fifties with the introduction of the Talisman service which we not only ran well for its own sake but also because it 'competed' with the LMR Caledonian. Neither service came up to the mark of the pre-war streamliners but the difference that the trains made to morale had to be experienced to be believed. The Talisman continued into diesel days (which is more than can be said for

the Caledonian) but was no different from the other Edinburgh workings.

In 1965 we were told that the standardisation of passenger timings was to be diluted with a high speed service to Leeds and the to say the news came as a fillip would be an understatement. A couple of tests were run between London and Doncaster behind 9001 - for some

reason St Paddy was almost always chosen for trial trips - to see what reserves the Deltics had and to ascertain how they would perform whilst electrically heating a train. This was something new to us all since at that time steam heating was universal and it came as a surprise to the pessimistic theorists from Derby and Doncaster to find that in practice the en-

Multiple-units worked the inner-suburban services from Kings Cross to Welwyn and Hertford with occasional trips to Peterborough and Cambridge. They were based at Western Sidings, Finsbury Park, working quietly and unobstrusively with no-one suspecting their potential for danger. Fortunately the results were far less serious than they might have been.

gine sacrificed only a couple of hundred horsepower and not the large amounts of power that had been forecast.

The Leeds fliers started running in 1966 and what a disappointment they proved to be. Matched to the 3,300hp of the Deltic locomotives were a mere eight coaches (later increased to nine) on a timing which had been equalled by an A3 Pacific a generation earlier. Little wonder we lost traffic to the roads and airlines.

In addition to doing what I could from behind a desk to keep our diesels moving, I also had the responsibility for superintending matters such as main line accidents and derailments, sombre matters perhaps but elements of life which did at least get me out of the office.

Although there were several spectacular mishaps (or pitch-ins as we called them) which I had to sort out none was quite as messy as the crash at Abbots Ripton which blocked the east coast for several days in 1962. A brand-new Deltic diesel - probably en route from Doncaster works - was working south on an up fitted goods and ran into the rear of another freight on the slow line at Woodwalton in very foggy weather. The debris obstructed the adjacent up main line and was immediately run into by a V2 2-6-2 on a third fitted freight whilst a fourth, worked by an A3 Pacific and approaching from the south, completed the pile-up.

The pile of damaged wagons once the dust had settled was mountainous and took the best part of two days to clear. The Deltic was the last item to be rerailed and was rather a tricky business as the track was badly damaged underneath the locomotive and had to be relaid in situ whilst the 99 tons of Diesel was lifted sufficiently high enough for the platelayers to work underneath. Using two 45-ton cranes, which required very careful setting up, I managed to bring it up clear until it could be settled on the new track before returning it to Doncaster.

On another occasion a fitted freight hauled by a Class 47 ran through the end of the up

Not all the new diesels were a flop and although the GN suburban dieselisation got off to a bad start, the delivery of Brush type 2 A1A-A1A locomotives ushered in a degree of reliability that had been lacking in earlier types. From 1959 these engines handled most of the outer suburban services to Hitchin and Cambridge until replaced by electrification.

loop at Sandy, coming to rest with thirty-seven wagons piled up behind it. Both the Peterborough and Kings Cross cranes were summoned to the scene with the New England crane working from the north end of the derailment and the London crane at the south. The problem was that the New England crane had nowhere to dump the wagons lifted out of the wreck because the proximity of the bridge and abutment walls of the LNWR branch. To get round the difficulty the Cambridge crane had to be sent for and located on the single line of the Bedford branch, which had to be closed for the duration, damaged wagons being relayed from the Peterborough to the Cambridge crane, the latter placing the debris in an LNWR siding.

Some finesse had to be exercised in moving the locomotive, which was on its side, when we eventually came to it. The class 47 superstructure was not especially robust and I had to send to Peterborough for the New England carpenter in order for him to shore up the cab-

sides in order to prevent them from being crushed when the engine was lifted. In fairness to him - I have to confess that his name escapes me - he did a first class job and with his help I was able to rerail the locomotive with the minimum of damage.

Sandy was not all bad news. One of the wagons contained a load of fish which had to be disposed of immediately by being sold to the break-down crew for a nominal sum. I went home with a beautiful plaice which cost me the princely sum of 6d.

A few years later, 1969, I was back at Sandy to deal with an incident that could, but for extreme good fortune, have taken its place in the annals of major railway disasters.

Sandy, as most enthusiasts know, was located in the centre of the racing stretch between Stevenage and Offord, a long falling section where any time lost in the London area was usually made up; trains frequently travelling at speeds of 100 mph or more.

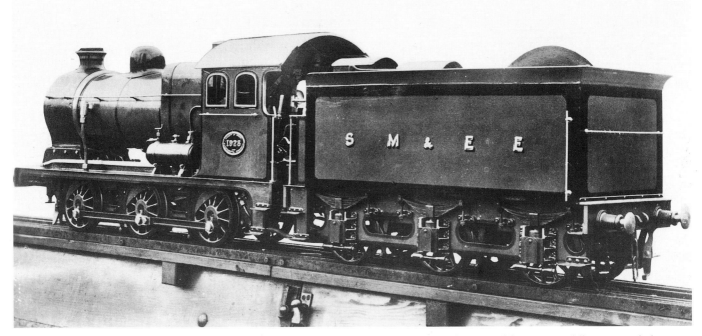

As life on BR became less challenging my thoughts returned to my roots - the steam engine - and my involvement with live-steam modelling in my early days as a railwayman. One of my first essays in driving had been with the 0-6-0 belonging to the Society of Model and Experimental Engineers. The engine had been painted in Great Eastern blue - with paint from the GER stores - and one side of the tender retains the original paint to this day. I resumed my driving career - after rather a long break in service (sic) - with this particular locomotive in 1990.

The fascination of live steam modelling lay in recreating a detailed working representation of the original and getting it to work with neither size nor complexity being an obstacle. In a demonstration of extremes one my colleagues produced a working model of an Atchison, Topeka & Santa Fe 2-8-8-2 compound. The model produced a drawbar pull of no less than 44lbs whilst the low pressure cylinders worked on hot water.

On this occasion, during the long hot summer experienced that year, the 17.37 Yorkshire Pullman from Kings Cross to Leeds, became derailed at 95 mph just south of Sandy station, the engine, a Deltic, remaining on the road but becoming uncoupled from the rest of the train which, although completely derailed, remained upright and in line - a momentous testimonial to the effectiveness of the buckeye couplings which the GNR had pioneered. Incredibly the only casualty was an elderly lady who suffered a slight injury to her ankle as she was assisted from her derailed coach.

As a matter of instinct I regarded it as a priority to clear the line as quickly as possible and ordered three cranes to the scene. The route was opened to traffic, after a night of intensive work, the following morning which I considered pretty good going until I returned to my office to face insinuations of extravagance in employing a third crane!

The cause of the mishap turned out to be the long continuous welded track which had buckled in the heat of the exceptionally hot summer of that year.

In addition to clearing wreckage away in order to allow the normal service to resume, I also had to determine the cause of any accident and this, on occasions, called for considerable detective work.

One such which put a strain on the grey cells for a time happened at Hatfield when a derailed wagon in a train smashed into the footbridge at the south end of the station, knocking down its support and bringing down the electricity and gas supplies that crossed the track by using the bridge. The station was plunged into darkness, the only relief to the gloom being the occasional flashed of electricity from the severed cables.

Coping with the damaged wagons of the train was not too difficult whilst the utility supplies were soon rectified by the civil engineers department who were called out to deal with the bridge. My job, after getting the running lines clear, was to find out what it was that had gone wrong.

This model of a Kirtly Goods 0-6-0 represented the ultimate challenge to the engineer. It had started life as a static model but later had been fitted with a coal fired boiler. The valve gear was beautifully accurate whilst the boiler was fed by injector.

The vehicle which had collided with the bridge was badly smashed up and it was initially thought that it was the sole cause of the accident although I still had to pinpoint the event that caused it to run amok in the first place. Mistrusting first impressions I turned my attention to the wagon which had been immediate ahead of it in the train and noted that it had been loaded with a container, the door of which was open. Reasonably certain that the open door had not been caused by the crash I took a look at the contents of the container and found them to be compacted charity

collecting boxes in packs about the size of an ordinary house brick.

I wondered whether it was possible that the container door had become open during transit - or perhaps not closed at all when the train started its journey - and that one or more of these packs had fallen out under the wheels of the following vehicle and caused it to derail. We instigated a search of the track upon which the train had run and sure enough we discovered one of the packs at a right-hand curve just before the point of derailment giving just the right set of circumstances to lift

One great advantage of building live steam models was that one became a CME without any restrictions. All that was required to produce an eight-coupled, four-cylinder compound was the skill. There were no civil engineers to get in the way.

<u>Allocation</u>

<u>AIR MINISTRY TYPE JOINTS</u>

Leaking Air Ministry type joints must not be re-tightened if the bell mouth of the pipe is not showing above the flange.

When the bell mouth of the copper pipe is below the flange the joint must be completely dismantled and the copper pipe annealed, and bell mouth reformed. Upon re-assembly the copper pipe should protrude through the flange approximately $\frac{1}{8}$".

District Motive Power Superintendent

Bill

The owners of 60003 would have done well to have seen this Standing Order!

Above: Standing Order 124 drawing attention to the procedure for dealing with joints on A4 Pacifics. The author has annotated the order for the attention of one of his assistants.

CLARENCE YARD CLASS 47 CYCLIC WORKING (1964)				
Day	Arr	Point	Dep	Train
1		Kings Cross	19.34	Parliamentary
	21.40	Peterborough		
2		New England	02.10	Mineral
	06.24	Ferme Park		
		Kings Cross Gds	16.00	Fitted
	22.00	York	01.09	Parcels
3	03.50	Newcastle	light	
		York	12.40	Fitted
	23.50	Ferme Park		
4		Kings Cross	01.15	Express
	05.08	York	07.45	Express
	10.54	Kings Cross	13.09	Passenger
	14.40	Cambridge	15.05	Passenger
	16.30	Kings Cross	18.12	Express
	21.54	York	23.50	Fitted
5	05.55	Kings Cross Gds		
		Kings Cross	15.00	Express
	19.48	Newcastle	22.20	Express
6	04.50	Kings Cross	light	
		New England	10.10	Mineral
	13.20	Ferme Park	14.20	Mineral
	17.35	New England	18.55	Goods
	20.09	Whitemoor		
		March	21.00	Parcels
	23.53	Doncaster	01.55	Goods
7	04.55	New England	07.30	Goods
	13.15	York	21.05	Fitted
	02.40	Kings Cross Gds		
8		Kings Cross	04.00	Express
	08.41	Leeds	10.50	Express
	13.43	Kings Cross	16.43	Parliamentary
	19.20	Grantham	22.32	Parcels
	01.25	Kings Cross Gds		

The Class 47 diesel-electrics were - in theory - the most versatile engines ever to run on British metals and it was unfortunate that they were not robust enough to stand up to the requirements of the GN mainline. The table to the left shows an eight-day cycle (excluding Saturdays and Sundays) for one of the Clarence Yard (Finsbury Park) locomotives, the idea being that on day one of the diagram it would leave Kings Cross with an evening stopping train for Peterborough and work routinely through all the duties to reappear at Kings Cross at 01.25 about a week later. In practise the cycle never - ever - worked and engines had to be replaced daily because of failures of one sort or another.

The diagramming was intensive in the extreme and the engine was booked to cover extreme distances in addition to a wide variety of trains. The most northerly point reached by Clarence Yard type 4's was Newcastle - they were only booked to travel north of the border on special workings although in fact appearances at Edinburgh (and other parts of Scotland) were by no means uncommon since the North Eastern often had to use them on their own workings due to failures of other type 4's - and this particular example worked to Tyneside with an afternoon 'second division' express from London, returning south with the sleeping car service which ran via Sunderland and Eaglescliffe.

The Great Eastern at that time had no large diesels, except for the English Electric 2000hp engines allocated to the Norwich - Liverpool

Street workings, and to assist the Clarence Yard diagrams included an evening parcels train from March to Doncaster via the joint line, a route that saw a heavy volume of mineral traffic but few trains of a fast nature.

Although New England men worked most of the Ferme Park mineral services, by 1964 the shed had lost its allocation of engines (except for a handful of 9F's retained for the Colwick services) and each morning a type 4 had to be sent light from Kings Cross passenger loco to assist with the workings. Thus an engine which a few hours earlier had been thundering up the east coast with an overnight express from Newcastle, suddenly had to acclimatise itself to the haulage of heavy coal traffic - as great an extreme of contrasts as could be imagined.

Apart from the difficulties of routine maintenance, I have little doubt that the problems encountered with the GN class 47's arose from the range of duties that were expected of them. Depots such as Langwith (Shirebrook) and Knottingley whose engines worked the same type of trains, day in day out, experienced nothing like the troubles I had at Kings Cross and it would probably have been a good idea to have segregated the Kings Cross engines into two sub-classes: one being retained for express passenger and fast goods work and the other for mineral services. Unfortunately by the time any solutions presented themselves the goods and mineral traffic had either disappeared or been transferred to the Great Eastern.

Judging from the look on the author's face on arrival at Grantham, A3 4-6-2 60111 'Enterprise' had done a good job and the crew are thanked for a making a good effort. One of the authors' assistants reveals that although A.J.Somers was not a outward disciplinarian - outbursts of temper were unusual - it was as well to know how far one could go before overstepping the line and it was not until well after his retirement that the author learned of the pseudonym bestowed upon him by his subordinates. His myopic stare and amiable smile - when pleased - earned him the nickname 'Blink Bonny'...........there were very few people who received the accolade of being named after a Gresley Pacific.

the wheel off the track and derail the wagon so that it was sufficiently misaligned to hit the bridge.

Hatfield, like Sandy, tended to be something of a trouble spot and on another occasion at about the same time I was called out to attend an incident in which a Temple Mills - Welwyn Garden City goods had failed to stop at Hatfield's down slow home signal and had crashed into the abutment of the road bridge just beyond the north end of the station, killing both members of the train crew.

Expecting the train to stop the signalman had correctly set the road for the dead-end siding which ended at the bridge but I was deprived of any footplate evidence as to why the engine - a class 31 - maintained its speed and failed to stop.

As I saw it there were four likely causes: The train being overloaded, defective locomotive brakes, excessive speed and/or inattention by the traincrew.

The engine - and its brakes in particular - received a thorough examination after it had been extricated but was found to be in good order whilst the train load was discovered to be slightly over the stipulated load but not so much to have caused any significant loss of control. To test this I arranged for a trial to be run with an engine of the same class hauling an identical tonnage but was able to stop within a few yards of the home signal. Defective brakes and an overweight train could therefore we ruled out of the equation which left a choice between the third and fourth options, both of which reflected on the traincrew. It

was not a happy conclusion nor one I drew without first considering any other alternative possibilities, partly because it is a wretched business having to point the finger at blame at two people who were not in a position to offer a defence but I am afraid that at the end of the day the cause of the crash had to be attributed to poor locomotive handling.

One thing I never expected to be involved in was an accident caused deliberately and maliciously by a railwayman yet such a thing did come within my orbit of experience on the Great Northern.

One night in the early summer of 1967 the 22.30 Deltic-hauled overnight express from Kings Cross to Edinburgh was inexplicably derailed at Connington - about half way between Huntingdon and Peterborough - the rear five coaches of the train for no apparent reason overturning and falling down an embankment with five passengers being killed in the wreckage.

Initially there was an absolute dearth of clues as to why the accident should have happened and the only starting point that suggested itself was the facing point over which the train had been passing when the derailment occurred.

A facing point is simply a junction in the track which allows a train to be switched from one direction to another but which is electrically interlocked with the signals in such a way that it is impossible to signal a train for one route and then change the points for another. In addition all facing points have to be fitted with heavy and secure locking bars to prevent

any mechanical failure from allowing the points to change direction whilst a train is passing over them.

I examined the facing points and whilst initially sceptical - because their general safety had been proved beyond doubt in years of use - I discovered a tiny bruise on the end of the movable toe of the point together with further signs that the derailment had actually taken place on the point which indicated that somehow it had reversed under the train, causing the rear section to change direction at high speed.

The locking and signalling apparatus was thoroughly examined and found to be in good order and for a time all the investigators, including those from the Ministry of Transport were baffled. Matters were not helped by one senior railway officer who - and he should have known better - appeared on television holding up a piece of buckeye coupling and declaring it to be the cause of the accident. In fact it had broken as a result of the incident as opposed to being the cause of it although tests on the buckeye bolt demonstrated that some considerable sideways force had been transmitted to the coupling which drew us to the conclusion that the rear section of the train had indeed taken the wrong line whilst passing over the facing point.

It then remained to be discovered how the point had come to be reversed when it ought to have been locked in position and after a great deal of investigative work involving the Transport Police it transpired that the signalman - who left the railway shortly after the crash -

There were few cheers at Kings Cross when the Pacifics started to be withdrawn. Engines that had been part of the scenery for years were going for scrap whilst their replacements were still very uncertain. The most famous of all - Flying Scotsman - was purchased privately in 1963 and is seen leaving Kings Cross for the last time under BR ownership. The sadness of the occasion was been accompanied by the grinding of teeth at the exhaust emitted by 60103 as it started away. In earlier days an Inspector had been based at Kings Cross to ensure - usually by vocal means - that nothing more than a light haze could be seen coming from the engine. It was, some thought, more the sort of performance one might have seen at St Pancras....

had discovered a way of neutralising the electrical locking system and had reversed the points under the speeding train 'simply to see what would happen'.

After leaving the railway the signalman enlisted in the army but was rejected, after a short time in uniform, as being emotionally unstable. He was later arrested, tried and convicted and served a period of time in prison.

When not engaged in clearing up the debris of derailments our cranes were often used for engineering jobs such as the replacement of bridges; work that for the staff involved was highly paid and jealously guarded by the gang in whose breakdown area the work was to be undertaken.

The Kings Cross district crane was located at Finsbury Park, a 75-tonner of a type which had an unenviable reputation for stability. Several others of the type had overturned and because of this record the Kings Cross civil engineer was very unhappy about using the Finsbury Park machine for a bridge that needed replacing over the Tottenham & Hampstead. Initially arrangements were made for the Cambridge and New England 45-ton cranes to assist with the job but this created such an outcry from the Finsbury Park staff - who protested that their crane was suitable for the job and in no way connected to the amount of overtime that they might forfeit - that they and their crane were eventually permitted to assist provided that I was present to supervise - for the entire 24 hours that the job was booked to take.

Expecting the worst I watched every single movement that was made throughout the twenty-four hour period and at the conclusion of the job I had to admit that not only had the Finsbury Park crane worked extremely well but that its presence had shortened the possession by some hours.

Whether or not my presence had made a difference, modesty prevents me from putting forward an opinion but the 75-tonner was used on a similar job - at which I was not present - when just about everything that could go wrong did.

Someone once said that an occasional shock is good for the system but I am pretty sure that whoever said it had never been wakened by telephone at one o'clock on a Sunday morning to be told that a 75-ton crane had fallen on its side.

I got to the site at Holloway to find that the foreman of the crane had attempted to lift an entire bridge without first properly securing the crane to compensate for the tremendous weight that the jib was going to take. Even so, all might have gone well had it not been for the fact that the foreman took the weight of the bridge into account but not - due to a failure of communication with the contractor - the amount of ballast that happened to be on the bridge. Somehow - with the help of the Stratford crane - I managed to get the crane righted and the job completed. I even managed to get the blame put upon the contractor but I was very wary about using 75-ton cranes on engi-

neering jobs thereafter and gave instructions to ensure that when they had to be used they were securely propped.

With little to do with regard to locomotive work now that most of our traffic had evaporated, my final years at Kings Cross were, to a large extent, involved with footplate staff during a time of great alteration and the relentless pursuit of economies. One of the unproductive costs which greatly irritated me was that associated with road learning, the means by which a driver familiarises himself with the routes over which he is declared competent to drive trains.

The traditional method, employed for as long as anyone could remember, had involved a driver accompanying a train over the route he was learning for as long as he, the driver, thought necessary. (Sometimes the system produced extremes as in the case of drivers transferring to the Southern Region who would be 'lost' for months whilst they were route-learning). There was very little control over what the man did or how long it took before he was prepared to sign for a particular route and much of the time was almost wholly unproductive.

Whilst I was mulling around for some sort of solution - and any proposal would have to be 'sold' to the union representatives who could be ultra-conservative (small c) when it suited them - my attention was drawn to the methods used in the Sheffield Division for the new Tinsley Yard which was about to open for traf-

Another fine mess..... Hatfield in 1965 and I wipe my brow whilst pondering the quickest way to clear the line.

fic. The track layout there was completely new and so there was no experience from which to draw. Someone therefore had the brilliant idea of taking colour slides of the yard and its signals and using them for road learning in the classroom - a completely novel idea which was a great success. It would be nice to claim that I came up with an idea that was similarly original but I concluded that my best bet was to 'borrow' the idea and have slides taken of all signals, etc., in the Kings Cross district and to instigate a system of classroom teaching in order to reduce the costs traditionally incurred in road learning.

Somewhat to my surprise the scheme worked wonderfully. The equipment was purchased, slides were taken, a room allocated and an Inspector given the task of running the venture. The only fly in the ointment came from the Traffic Manager who suggested that it would be better to dispense with the slides and use a cine camera instead. I had to point out to him that if we did this then every time a signal was repositioned - as they regularly were - a new film would have to be made and not only should we need an MGM-sized budget but the

economies which were the object of the exercise would disappear overnight.

Although it was pleasing to have made a success of a rather hum-drum matter, office-orientated problems did not really appeal to me since I saw myself as a nuts-and-bolts railwayman rather than a glorified clerk and it was with some relief that a number of difficulties with our multiple-units rescued me from the boredom of HQ administration and drew me back to the real world.

One of the units had hit the buffers in Kings Cross and caused a number of injuries amongst the passengers who, as usual, were standing up ready to alight as the collision occurred. I examined the unit where it had come to rest and questioned the driver who claimed that he had made a perfectly normal brake application but that the brake had failed to act; a familiar excuse and not one that normally held much water.

In his statement he claimed that he had reduced speed gradually so as to approach the buffers very cautiously in order to stop his train smoothly with a very gentle final application. If his story was to be believed the brakes had

worked perfectly in bringing the train down to about three mph but had failed in the last few yards.

Something in the drivers' demeanour indicated that there was more to his report than a simple excuse for carelessness and I had a series of more than usually detailed tests made at Finsbury Park depot to see if the fault could be simulated.

Much to my surprise and everyone else's astonishment we discovered that when a light application was made at low speed - as had been the case when the collision took place - the brakes did not always respond, a finding which led to the stripping of the unit where it was revealed that the brake cylinder were fitted with a Great Western type of sliding band which could not guarantee to operate properly under certain conditions.

At first there was some mystification as to how a Cravens DMU - which had never worked on the GW - came to be fitted with Western brake cylinders. I discovered in the course of my enquiries that when multiple-units had first been proposed it was decided to equip them with GW brake cylinders as standard.

Prior to the growth and expansion of London Transport there were quite a number of mainline services which penetrated into Central London although the post-1914 era saw the end of almost all of them. Moorgate services to and from the GN and Midland survived long after the remainder had gone, the Great Northern trains being worked by N2 0-6-2T's and those of the Midland by Fowler 3MT 2-6-2T's. The passenger service was limited to the peak hours only after 1939 although a considerable number of daily freight trains - Midland and GN - used the route until 1966. N2 0-6-2T 69499 runs into Faringdon with a Moorgate service circa 1955.

It later transpired that these bands should have been replaced by a safer roller ring type but that not all the units in the class had been dealt with. (Whether or not GW drivers were instructed to be heavy-handed with the brake, I don't know, but I was surprised that it took an incident on the Great Northern for the defect to be discovered).

A less alarming, although troublesome, problem landed in my lap in 1967 when I received a batch of Rolls-Royce units from the Great Eastern - the Stratford district had just completed its last piece of electrification - which promptly fell down with seized engines and torque converters. The Great Eastern had put up with the trouble for years by rather blithely putting the cause down to 'cold running' - whatever that was - and cheerfully spending a fortune on repairs.

LP would have had a blood bath had he been alive at the time and it was his training legacy that prompted me to peer more closely at the seizures to discover that the root of the trouble lay in inadequate radiator cleaning which lead to high coolant temperatures which in turn caused the engines to seize up. For want of a little blowing out of radiator grills the Great Eastern could have saved enough in engine repairs to have electrified its suburban system several times over.

By the mid-seventies with more than forty years service under my belt and with high speed diesels and suburban electrics on the horizon I

started to wonder whether the time for British Railways and me to part company had arrived.

My first love in life had been the steam engine whilst my second was the tempo of activity within the railway industry and both had disappeared completely since the mid-1960's. The first thirty years of my career had been a rough and tumble existence where my skills and talents had been used to their limits whilst latterly I might have found as much excitement working in a bank. It was all rather depressing and in idle moments - of which there were a few - my thoughts often returned to my early days on the LNER when I had joined the Model Railway Club in London to perpetrate in miniature what I was paid to do by the Railway.

My interest lay in model steam locomotives rather than the electrically operated small scale layouts which were beginning to appear at the time - and which interested the majority of members - and prompted me to join the Society of Model and Experimental Engineers whose live steam system was a regular feature at the annual exhibition at the Central hall, Westminster.

My status as a 'real' railwayman cut very little ice at first and I had to serve my time by loading children onto the trolleys which passed as carriages on the 100ft length of track that the society owned.

In 1935 my efforts as an unpaid twelve-inch-to-the-foot porter achieved some sort of recognition when I was invited to accompany

the society to Paris for the centenary of the PLM system, travelling via Newhaven/Dieppe over what must have been some of the noisiest permanent way in Christendom with roaring rails most of the way from Dieppe to Paris..

Used to the spacious accommodation at Westminster, we were rather nonplussed to find that the French had considerably underestimated the length of our track and it took a considerable bending of the entente cordial to get them to permit us to extend it through a convenient corridor in order to provide the sort of running distance we were used to. With our request for more *lebensraum* satisfied our hosts were surprised to see that our principal model was coal fired and this alone contributed to large crowds queuing up to view the *locomotive a vapeur Anglais* which was scaled down even to the coal in its tender.

In our turn we were surprised to find that the only French working model - a three and a half inch Est 4-8-2 - was paraffin fired and a very poor steamer. Our attempts to get the thing to steam were not altogether successful and I recall filling the hall with oily smoke from the paraffin burner - in defiance of a large 'Defense de Fumer' sign - as my colleagues and I tried ineffectually to get the thing to run. The 4-8-2 wasn't the only thing to cause a fog and during the exhibition the well-known enthusiast Baron Vuillet - whose name could be found in most pre-war copies of the Railway Magazine - made an appearance to postulate the signalling system that the SNCF were working on at the time. The only feature of the discussion that I can recall was that an absolute stop - I don't know what other sort he had in mind - was given by two red signals and our track superintendent did nothing to cement relations by covering up one of the red lenses and saying "Peut-etre casse" which made no more sense to the Baron than it did to me but I must have laughed at the right moment since I found myself promoted, in the field, to being an official exhibition driver.

Our engine was pretty well the handiwork of our track superintendent, W.B.Hart, and was an 0-6-0 modelled largely on Great Eastern lines and retained for exhibition duties, most of which consisted of running up and down a relatively short length of track with a respectable load of children behind the drawbar. It was both powerful and reliable unlike the Etat 4-6-2 which started us on our way home but ran into trouble en route with its rocking grate. Bill Hart leant over to me and said, conspiratorially "Get the society's engine out, Somers…"

Thus began a long career of driving miniature and model steam locomotives, a pastime which not only honed my enthusiasm for my full-time work but brought me into contact with some of the giants of the locomotive world such as Sir Nigel Gresley and W.A. Stanier; the latter being a very regular visitor to our exhibitions. I also rubbed shoulders with well known amateurs such as C.J.Allen, J.N. Maskelyne and F.C. Hambleton.

A particularly distinguished visitor to the exhibitions was J.C.Crebbin, one of the pioneers of small gauge coal fired locomotives who could occasionally be found at the controls of one of his own engines, a 2-8-8-2 Mallet compound: an essay in engineering that would have been remarkable at full size let alone three and a half inch gauge. Unfortunately his driving methods were not the equal of his engineering skills and he had an unfortunate habit of lifting both hands in the air after closing the regulator and before applying the truck brakes. Normally he was successful in coming to a stop but on one instance he was caught out - forgetting that the Mallet being a compound kept on steaming for some time after the regulator had been closed - and ploughed through the stops at the end of the line with the front half of the 2-8-8-2 hanging perilously over the end of the trestle.

One of the star performers of those days was a 5" gauge model of a Kirtley 0-6-0; remarkable because it had originally been a glass case static model which a Dr Robinson had decided to rebuild with a working boiler. The valve gear on the original had been so accurately made that not only did it work perfectly but allowed the engine to run in midgear in either direction. Other unusual features of the locomotive included a regulator which worked from left to right and valves which fell off their faces when steam was shut off, leading to a sharp blow up the blast pipe when the regulator was opened. The valves, I recall, seated themselves with a distinct clap. I also remember that this engine was the first model in which the boiler was fed by a proper injector alone; other engines of the day relying on axle or motion driven pumps.

Another excellent engine was a 5" model London Tilbury & Southend 4-6-4 tank, an impressive locomotive but rather under-

The 1100hp 'Baby' Deltics failed to show the promise of their larger stablemates. One of the first types of diesel to be allocated to the GN, their availability was so poor that they had to be withdrawn en masse and rebuilt, not returning to traffic until 1964 by which time it should have been realised that 1100hp was insufficient for the needs of the line. The class was allocated to Hitchin loco and worked the less demanding outer suburban services to and from Kings Cross. One of their turns for a time included the 15.35 Cambridge Buffet Car express and it was always touch and go as to whether the engine could keep time. The slightest check and all hope of a punctual arrival was lost. The rebuilding, however, transformed their availability and from 1964 it was unusual not to find the entire allocation at work.

Thankfully there were times during the dull days of modernisation when old skills were called upon and my last steam test was performed on GNR 0-6-0 1247 which had been purchased privately and preserved in running order.

cylindered. To get the best out of it the boiler pressure had to be close to blowing off point - 100 psi - at which pressure the injector become extremely touchy causing more reliance than was desirable on the force pump.

These recollections and others claimed much of my attention during my final years with BR and did nothing to relieve the feeling of under-use from which I was suffering on the 'new' railway from which all sense of challenge had disappeared. I longed to get back to my true genre, that of fashioning com-

plex and interesting pieces of machinery from lumps of metal and to preoccupy myself with the thousand and one problems of getting them to work efficiently. Whether the engine was used to haul a dozen children at an exhibition or fifteen corridor coaches down the east coast main line did not really matter - the satisfaction was derived from the challenge of getting boiling water to move a machine and the scale of the thing was beside the point. I had to move on or stagnate in a flood of memories.

BACK TO BASICS

With dieselisation, modernisation and rationalisation things of the past, I return to my element and set about the rebuilding of Prince in the Boston Lodge shops of the Festiniog Railway. The picture was taken in 1978 and, nearly twenty years on, I can still be seen peering into the nether regions of steam engines in and around Portmadoc.

Sitting in my office at Kings Cross with little to do other than twiddle my thumbs as retirement approached I decided that there were still areas of the country where steam traction was dominant and that perhaps my salvation lay in that direction. I ruled out the various standard gauge preservation organisations since they were seasonal in their nature and - at the time - consisted of no more than a handful of engines. (This is not to deny to them their value but how much better would it have been had the various factions united in the 1960s to concentrate their efforts on restoring a single piece of main-line - Leicester to Rugby, for example - rather than ending up with the miscellany of small lines that has come to pass).

My father had retired to Knebworth where I lived - at home - until the LNER moved me away from London, returning to the town upon my return to the southern end of the GN. Coincidentally most of the Great Northern HQ activities had been located there during the war, not moving back to London until 1959. If there was any especial reason for my family selecting Knebworth it arose from LNER driver, Bill

Sparshatt, pointing the place out to me from the footplate, shouting "If the sun shines anywhere, it shines at Knebworth". True or not, I passed the information on to my father who took it seriously enough to settle down in the village for the rest of his days.

Sunny or not, Knebworth had nothing to offer me in retirement and so I decided that Mohammet would have to move to the mountain (literally) and I purchased a cottage in Penrhyndeudraeth, the grounds of which was bisected by the Festiniog Railway.

Of all the steam railways in operation at the time, it was the Festiniog which had a particular attraction for me. It had a relatively long main line, was steam operated (most of the time) to a proper timetable and possessed a large and well appointed work shop for construction and maintenance purposes. It was, in short, the very miniature of a proper system.

Retiring from BR in 1976, I dragged my uncomplaining wife and moveables from the urbanity of the home counties to the wilderness of the Welsh mountains and, as soon as

the dust had settled, set off for Boston Lodge to see if there was anything in progress to which I could make a useful contribution.

'Bob' Harris, who at the time was in charge of the erecting shop walked me over the place and came to a stop in front of Prince's frames, telling me that the volunteers who had been working on the engine for many years had not received the support to which they thought they were entitled and as a result had become somewhat disheartened. He asked me if I would care to join the team and, of course, I assented without a seconds hesitation.

I have always been something of a solitary individual and it came as a surprise to find that no sooner had I rolled up my sleeves and got to work that a number of other volunteers who had earlier shied away from the project, decided to lend their weight; something which allowed sufficient progress to be made to persuade the company to transfer a number of full-time employees to work on aspects of the job which were beyond our capabilities if the engine was to be finished within a reasonable time scale.

Boston Lodge and no sign of any modernisation schemes. The author gives some advice as work on Prince progresses.

It was a tenet of the LNER that a Railway Officer should be able to turn his hand to anything and clearly it was a philosophy taken to heart by the Festiniog.
Having got the engines steaming properly I find myself building a boundary wall a few miles outside Blaenau Festiniog.

In its final years on the old FR and as first put back into traffic by its new owners, Prince suffered problems with the transfer of traction stresses from the cylinders to the rear drag box although in 1962 Alan Garraway improved matters with a partial rebuilding which included channel irons from the cylinders to the rear of the cab to absorb the traction load. These channel sections I rearranged so that, fastened to a heavy plate bolted right across the cylinders and front of the frames, they formed a rigid assembly from the front to the rear of the locomotive.

As originally mounted the boiler was allowed to expand forwards instead of the usual way, backwards, thus slightly shifting the chimney in relation to the blastpipe which affected the engine's steaming. An alteration at the rear allowed the boiler to expand backwards in the normal manner and thus prevent misalignment of the blastpipe and chimney.

Placing the heavy plate across the cylinders and frame eliminated the tendency of the cylinders to work loose and the result of these alterations of design and construction is the very robust engine that can be seen at work on the system today.

The real reward was not the enthusiastic team which was now working on Prince, nor the fact that the engine was coming back to life. My happiness revolved around the fact that I had been restored to my natural element with the last fifteen years seeming like a bad dream. By disposition and training my place in the order of things was based upon my skill in turning pieces of iron and metal into working locomotives and here I was doing exactly that.

We - the team rebuilding Prince - were not without our critics and there were many who either thought we were wasting our time or that the engine would never be powerful enough to be of use to the system. Suffice it to say that we proved them all wrong and Prince - as it can be seen to this day - can handle up to six coaches with competence which is no small load given the mountainous nature of the route.

After finishing the project and seeing the engine back into traffic I turned my hand to some civil engineering work - a railway is nothing if not versatile - and with Geoff Hall - one of the Prince team - spent a year and a half reconstructing the dry stone boundary wall between Tan-y-Grisiau and Blaenau Festiniog.

This proved to be my last major input into railway operations - advancing years were catching up with me - but it allowed me to boast that I had been a railwayman - continuously - for over 60 years and, modernisation apart, I had enjoyed every second of it. Railwaymen, any more than old soldiers, do not die and for many months yet the careful enquirer may find me pottering rheumatically away on light jobs in the darker corners of the carriage shop at Boston Lodge.

A long way from Stratford but perhaps my skills have not diminished with time and bring a welcome echo in the Snowdon mountains. Prince tackles a respectable load on the Festiniog Railways' deviation route in June 1983.